RETHINKING KARMA

THINK SANGHA

"Buddhist" Intellectual Practice Tools for Integrating Spirituality and Social Change Work

Think Sangha is a socially engaged Buddhist think tank affiliated with the Buddhist Peace Fellowship (BPF) in the United States and the International Network of Engaged Buddhists (INEB). We use a Buddhist sangha model to explore pressing social issues and concerns. The group's methodology is one based in friendship and Buddhist practice as much as theory and thought. The Think Sangha's core activities are networking with other thinker-activists, producing Buddhist critiques of social structures and alternative social models, and providing materials and resource persons for trainings, conferences, and research on social issues and grassroots activis. For more articles and information, visit the Think Sangha web page at: https://ogigaya.wordpress.com/think-sangha/, or contact us at:

Jonathan Watts, Coordinator
Ogigayatsu 4-7-1, Kamakura
Kanagawa 248-0011
JAPAN
e-mail: ogigaya@gmail.com

RETHINKING KARMA

THE DHARMA OF SOCIAL JUSTICE

JONATHAN S. WATTS
Editor

INTERNATIONAL NETWORK OF ENGAGED BUDDHISTS (INEB)

Published in 2009 by Silkworm Books
Reprinted in 2014 (2nd edition) & 2020 (3rd edition) by
International Network of Engaged Buddhists (INEB)
666 Charoen Nakorn Road, Banglumpulang, Klong San
Bangkok 10600 Siam (Thailand)
secretariat@inebnetwork.org
http://www.inebnetwork.org

National Library of Thailand Cataloging in Publication Data
Watts, Jonathan S.
Rethinking Karma.- Bangkok: International Network of Engaged Buddhists (INEB),
2014.
272 p.
1. Karma. I. Title.
294.3122
ISBN: 978-616-374-191-2

Cover illustration by Namsom Supanan
Typeset by Silk Type in Gentium 10 pt.

Printed in Thailand by Parbpim Printing House, Bangkok

10 9 8 7 6 5 4 3 2 1

CONTENTS

Editor's Note vii

Pali Canon and Text Abbreviations xi

PROLOGUE

Karma in Buddhism: A Message from Suan Mokkh 3
BUDDHADASA BHIKKHU

INTRODUCTION

Karma for Everyone: Social Justice and the Problem of Re-ethicizing
Karma in Theravada Buddhist Societies 13
JONATHAN S. WATTS

THE DHARMA OF KARMA:
REDISCOVERING CIVILIZATIONAL ETHICS

Karma: The Creative Life Force of Human Beings. 39
NALIN SWARIS

An Awakened Vision: Dr. B. R. Ambedkar's Struggle to Re-ethicize
Indian Society 67
MANGESH DAHIWALE

The "Positive Disintegration" of Buddhism: Reformation and
Deformation in the Sri Lankan Sangha 91
JONATHAN S. WATTS

Goodness and Generosity Perverted: The Karma of Capitalist
Buddhism in Thailand 133
SANTIKARO AND PRA PAISAN VISALO

THE KARMA OF STRUGGLE:
KARMIC FATALISM AND SOCIAL INJUSTICE

Burmese Buddhism's Impact on Social Change: The Fatalism of
Saṁsāra and Monastic Resistance 157
MIN ZIN

Liberation as Struggle: Overcoming Karmic Fatalism in Shan State,
Burma 177
KHUENSAI JAIYEN

The Meaning and Practice of the Buddhist Precepts as a Political
Action Framework 189
UPASEKA YASO

Buddhism and Domestic Violence: Using the Four Noble Truths to
Deconstruct and Liberate Women's Karma 199
OUYPORN KHUANKAEW

CONCLUSION
The Karma of the Rings: A Myth for Modern Buddhism?. 227
DAVID LOY

EPILOGUE
Giving Dāna that Doesn't Cost Any Money and Leads to Nirvana . . 245
BUDDHADASA BHIKKHU

Author Profiles 249
Index 253

EDITOR'S NOTE

RETHINKING KARMA: THE DHARMA OF SOCIAL JUSTICE

In February 2003 at the Third International Think Sangha meeting in Chiang Mai, Thailand, a group of grassroots Buddhist activists focused on the issues of karma and social justice. In response to experiences of extreme social suffering in many parts of Southeast Asia, especially the conflict areas of Sri Lanka and Burma, questions about forgiveness, acceptance, and justice were discussed at length. What is a Buddhist response to political oppression, to economic exploitation? Does Buddhism encourage passivity and victimization? Can violent perpetrators be brought to justice without anger and retributive punishment? What does Buddhism say—or imply—about collective karma and social justice?

A common Buddhist reaction is that retributive justice is not necessary since the law of karma exacts a precise form of justice in the suffering that violent people eventually bring upon themselves, perhaps later in a future lifetime. Such a typical explanation suggests a whole host of issues and problems raised by the ways that traditional Buddhist societies have confronted (or not confronted) injustice. The subtle manner in which the Buddha distinguished his teaching of karma from the Brahmanical and Jain understandings has become blurred in Buddhist societies, giving way to: (1) a rigid karmic determinism that produces an attitude of fatalism towards injustice; that is, those who experience suffering deserve it based on bad actions in a previous lifetime; and (2) an accompanied ritualization of karmic action that views the overcoming of personal suffering not as a confrontation with social injustice but as making traditional offerings to the monastic order in order to gain karmic merit for future rebirth in more favorable circumstances.

This lack of engagement with social injustice has created a moral myopia within traditional Buddhist societies towards the fundamental forms of structural and cultural violence underpinning the more visible acts of violence and oppression. The common understanding of karma often serves to perpetuate structural and cultural violence, such as sexism, classism, and political oppression. In addition to these social issues, which contemporary Buddhism must address, some teachings within the Buddhist tradition need to be critically reexamined in light of the Buddha's fundamental practice of nonviolence (*ahiṃsā*):

- What is the true meaning of karma (literally "action") in the Buddhist tradition? Is it ritualistic action to gain merit, the just deserts or results (*vipāka*) of an unforgiving cosmic force, or the quality of intention (*cetanā*) behind present actions?
- What is the true meaning of the ideal of equanimity (*upekkhā*)? Is it resignation and passivity in the face of violence, or a sense of detachment towards the results of trying to make our lives and the lives of others better?
- What is the true meaning of the ideals of generosity (*dāna*) and doing good (*puñña*)? Are these confined to calculated acts of giving by lay followers to the monastic order by which to gain favorable rebirth, or is there a much broader realm of intentional moral action in which Buddhists should engage?

Today such a critical reevaluation of the Buddhist tradition is especially important for the countries of southern Theravada Buddhism (Sri Lanka, Bangladesh, Burma, Thailand, Cambodia, Laos, and parts of India, Malaysia, Indonesia, and Vietnam).

The contributors to this volume are, for the most part, not academics but thinker-activists who have been deeply involved in these issues at the grassroots level and who speak from their own experience in trying to solve them. From their perspectives, these issues have come to light as seminal ones for deeper contemplation and greater sharing, not only within the Buddhist community at large but among all those who seek to bridge the gaps between our idealization of human harmony, our tendencies toward violent confrontation, and the need for greater social justice.

Most of this manuscript was published as a double issue of *The World Fellowship of Buddhists Review* in October 2004 (vol. 41, no. 4) and March 2005 (vol. 42, no. 1). For this present volume, the authors have updated all their manuscripts, and two new essays have been added: the prologue by Buddhadasa Bhikkhu, who has served as an ongoing inspiration to many of the authors, and the essay on gender by Ouyporn Khuankaew who served as the host of the meeting in 2003 which gave birth to this project. As the editor of this volume, I would like to thank Dr. Tavivat Puntarigvivat, the former Editor-In-Chief of *The World Fellowship of Buddhists Review*, for his interest and efforts in seeing this project first come to print. I would also like to thank Sulak Sivaraksa of the International Network of Engaged Buddhists (INEB) for introducing us to the fine people at Silkworm Books; Trasvin Jittidecharak, the director of Silkworm Books, for showing interest in and accepting the manuscript; and Susan Offner, an old friend who has acted as our copyeditor for the final manuscript.

Jonathan S. Watts
Kamakura, Japan
November 25, 2008

PALI CANON AND TEXT ABBREVIATIONS

A.	*Aṅguttara Nikāya*
D.	*Dīgha Nikāya*
D.A.	*Dīgha Nikāya Aṭṭhakathā*
Dh.	*Dhammapada*
Dh.A.	*Dhammapada Aṭṭhakathā*
Iti.	*Itivuttaka*
J.	*Jātaka*
M.	*Majjhima Nikāya*
S.	*Saṃyutta Nikāya*
Sn.	*Sutta Nipāta*
Vis.	Buddhaghosa's *Visuddhimagga*

PROLOGUE

KARMA IN BUDDHISM:
A MESSAGE FROM SUAN MOKKH

BUDDHADASA BHIKKHU

As Buddhists, we must understand karma—action and the result of action—as it is explained in Buddhism. We should not follow blindly the karma teachings of other religions; otherwise, we will spin around pitifully according to karma without being able to get beyond its power or realize its end.

Why do we need to know the essence of karma? Because our lives are inseparable from it and happen according to it. To be more precise, we can say that life is actually a stream of karma. Wanting to do something causes one to perform actions and receive the results of those actions; then, desires to do other actions arise again and again incessantly. Therefore, life is merely patterns of karma. If we rightly understand karma, we can live our lives at peace, without any problems or suffering.

TWO PRIMARY KARMA DOCTRINES

One doctrine of karma has been taught since before the Buddha's time and is still taught outside Buddhism; the other is the Buddhist principle of karma. The first doctrine presents only half of the story. In that doctrine, one cannot conquer karma and remains always under its domination; one actually desires to be under its power and asks for its help without ever trying to fight for one's own liberation. One thus performs karma as if accumulating assets for more

This article was prepared by Achan Buddhadasa as part of a series of pamphlets to be distributed at a major exhibition on his life and work organized by Achan Ranchuan Indarakhamhaeng and other students at Chulalongkorn University in Bangkok. This translation is by Santikaro.

satisfactory rebirth. One never thinks of ending karma. One expects to rely on it instead of trying to end it. In Buddhism, we can understand karma more fully so that we can conquer it and be liberated from it, that is, not carry the burden of karma any more. We neither sit waiting for things to happen, nor leave our fate in the hands of gods, nor follow superstitions like purifying our karma in sacred rivers.

To be beyond karma seems incredible to most people; they may consider it a deception or a huckster's trick. Nonetheless, it really is possible if we take the Buddha as our true and noble friend. This will help us in practicing the complete set of Ten Rightnesses (*sammatā*): the Noble Eightfold Path plus right insight knowledge and right liberation in accordance with the law of specific conditionality (*idappaccayatā*). In such practice, there is no foolish feeling that leads to desire for the various results of karma (actions). A doctrine master from Southern India and contemporary of the Buddha heard that the Buddha taught the cessation of karma. He then sent his disciples to ask the Buddha questions and to ask for his instructions. This well-known story is told in the *Solasapañhā* (Sixteen Questions), the last chapter of the *Sutta Nipāta* (Sn. 976–1149). Traditionally, many people have memorized the Buddha's answers to these questions and taken them for guidance in their study and practice.

Nowadays, wrong teachings concerning karma are publicized in books and articles by various Indian and Western writers with titles such as "Karma and Rebirth." Although they are presented in the name of Buddhism, they are actually about karma and rebirth as understood in Hinduism. So the right teaching of Buddhism is misrepresented. This should be recognized and corrected so that the Buddhist karma principle can be preserved in its undistorted essence. The Buddha accepted as correct—that is, as not a wrong understanding of karma—the half-formed teaching concerning good and evil deeds and their results that was presented before his time and outside his teaching. However, he added to it a final aspect, namely, the end of karma, which is the essential Buddhist principle that completes the teaching on karma. This cessation of karma goes by two names. It can be called "the third kind of karma," because there are good deeds, evil deeds, and the karma leading to the end of both good and evil deeds. Sometimes four kinds of karma are distinguished: good deeds, evil deeds, mixed deeds, and the karma that is the end of all karma. When enumerated in this fourfold way, the additional karma taught in Buddhism becomes the fourth kind of karma. However, if we consider mixed karma as made up of good actions and evil actions, there are basically three kinds of karma, again with the karma that ends all karma as the third kind. This threefold formulation is easy, convenient, and concise. If this third kind of karma is left out, the teaching misses the essence of karma in the true Buddhist sense.

KARMA AND REBIRTH

Rebirth occurs every time one does a deed, and that rebirth occurs spontaneously at the moment of action. We need not wait for rebirth to happen after death, according to the usual worldly understanding. When one thinks and acts, the mind changes spontaneously through the power of desire (*taṇhā*) and clinging (*upādāna*), which immediately lead to becoming (*bhava*) and birth (*jāti*) in accordance with the law of dependent origination (*paticcasamuppāda*). There is no need to wait for physical death in order for rebirth to occur. This truth should be realized as the true teaching of Buddhism, as a core principle of the original, pristine Buddhism that states there is no self (*attā*) to be reborn. How the concept of rebirth after death crept into Buddhism is difficult to explain, and we need not concern ourselves with it here. Simply preventing rebirth within the stream of dependent origination is enough for us to be free. Stopping egoistic rebirth is truly in accordance with Buddhism, and such action will be the kind of karma that can be taken as refuge. When a good deed is done, goodness spontaneously arises; when an evil deed is done, evilness spontaneously arises. There is no need to wait for any further results. If there will be any birth after death, that rebirth only occurs through the karma one has done in this very life and the results of which have already occurred here. We need not worry about rebirth such that it obstructs our practice.

RECEIVING THE FRUITS OF KARMA

We should see the truth that the mind that performs a deed is karma itself and the subsequent mind is the result (*vipāka*) of that karma. Other results that follow it are only uncertain byproducts, since they may or may not occur, or do not keep up with our expectations due to other interfering factors. That the results of actions occur to the minds performing them is most certainly in line with the Buddhist principle that there is no self or soul to be reborn, as stated by the Buddha on numerous occasions. To hold the view that a soul or somebody is reborn deviates from the truth of not-self (*anattā*). Whenever a good or evil deed is done, goodness or evilness spontaneously arises accordingly without having to wait for later results. Nonetheless, most people expect certain results according to their wishes; then, they are disappointed when other factors interfere. Such intervening circumstances may lead one to hold a wrong view that good actions bring bad results and bad actions bring good results. We should be careful of this wrong view and should develop right understanding concerning the fruits of karma.

Our understanding of how the results of karma are received or experienced must always be self-apparent (*sandiṭṭhiko*), immediate (*akāliko*), and inviting of inquiry (*ehipassiko*), and should never contradict the truth that the five aggregates (*khandha*) of human life are not-self. Mind is merely a phenomenon pushed this way and that by conditions, stimulated to do things by environmental factors. The resulting reactions are unescapable and are regarded as good or evil according to one's feelings of satisfaction or dissatisfaction. Either kind pushes us into suffering, thus we should aim at ending karma and getting beyond it. Then, we will have realized, awakened, and fully blossomed, which is genuine Buddhahood.

There is a moralistic teaching of karma that retains an illusion of self that owns this and that. This version contradicts the principle of not-self stressed by the Buddha. We should correctly understand this perspective; otherwise, we will not benefit from practicing karma teachings, since we will not be able to go beyond karma. Endlessly remaining under the power of karma is not the karma teaching of Buddhism. Instead, wholeheartedly practice the karma that ends all karma. This will prevent us from unwittingly going astray.

ACTIVITY AND RESPONSE

The actions or movements of sentient beings that are done with volition (*cetanā*), particularly that of craving and arising through defilements (*kilesa*), are called karma. An activity that is not caused by defilement, for example, one with an *arahant*'s intention, is not called "karma"; it is called *kiriyā* (activity). The result of *kiriyā* is called *patikiriyā* (reaction), the natural consequence of the activity, while the result of karma is called *vipāka* (fruit of action). These results occur justly in accordance with the law of nature. Ordinary people have ordinary volitions as the causes of their actions, which are consequently karma. Good volition leads to good action; evil volition leads to evil action. Through moral and cultural training, everybody is taught to do good deeds that do not cause trouble to others and bring good results to everyone. Therefore, karma concerns the law of nature and can be investigated scientifically.

TYPES OF KARMA

There are many types of karma depending on the characteristics of the deeds and their doers. Some act with selfishness concerning the selves they desire to be. Some perform actions that lead to the ending of the self-illusion and the realization of nirvana. Some people are pleased with worldly prosperity, others with heavenly prosperity, and some with the realization of nirvana— aims that seem to be in perpetual contradiction. Some like to show off their good deeds, while others perform their good deeds secretly. Some proclaim their meritorious deeds with fanfare, while others do not need such fanfare. Some do their deeds with excessive ritual, while others do theirs without any ceremony at all. Some do theirs out of magical or superstitious fear, while others do theirs properly as Buddhist practice. Obviously, there are many types of karma. Nevertheless, they all can be classified into two categories: those with self and for the sake of self, and those that aim for the ending of self-clinging and selfishness. Some do deeds in a business-like manner, expecting excessive profits. Others wish for the end of the vicious circle of life and death. See for yourselves! Ordinary people do good deeds merely for the sake of inordinate profits.

KARMA AND NOT-SELF

The question of karma and not-self is confusing and difficult to understand for various reasons. A monk once asked the Buddha, "How does karma done by not-self give results for self?" This question arose because of the teaching on not-self that points out how the "actor" is merely a mind-body process void of self. After an action (karma) is done by a selfless mind-body, how could it have any results for a "self" who is the "doer" who intentionally did that deed? The new concept of not-self contradicts the old concept of self. There is a self-consciousness that claims to be not-self and does things in the name of not-self, but the sense of self still exists to receive the results of the deeds. Hence, this monk's question. If we see it rightly, we will understand that when the mind-body is not-self, the results of its actions will happen to a selfless mind-body, also. However, if that mind-body is full of a sense of self, the results of its actions will always happen to this apparent self. If karma is not-self, its result will be not-self, and what occurs in accordance with karma will be not-self. The things, whether human or animal, that we conventionally speak of as "actors" or "doers of karma" will also be not-self. The facts of karma and not-self are never separate and never oppose each other.

KARMA AND NIRVANA

The ending of karma is the same thing as nirvana, in other words, is synonymous with nirvana. From where, then, do the teachers come who teach people that death is the end of karma? When someone dies, people murmur, "Oh well, his karma is finished." Moreover, they often say that one dies according to one's merits and karma, without realizing that what is happening to them as they speak is also according to their good and bad karma, until they really reach the end of karma, namely, nirvana.

Nirvana is freedom from karma and its results. Further, nirvana is freedom from the vicious cyclic existence (*saṁsāra*) that keeps spinning according to karma. Nirvana, therefore, is lovely and loveable, not frightening in the least. Even so, people prefer being trapped within the vicious cycles of birth and death according to their karma, particularly the karma they desire as a result of their defilements, although they never really get what they wish. People with big egos usually fear and hate the end of karma, because egoism seeks karma-results that seem pleasing to it.

KARMA IS BURDEN (*UPADHI*)

When one performs karma, life happens according to karma, that is, one is bound by karma no matter whether it is good or evil karma. Good karma makes one laugh and bad karma makes one cry, but both weary us almost to death. Even so, people still like to laugh, since they misunderstand that good karma is great virtue. When karma does not bind our lives, it is as if there are no chains on our legs, whether iron chains or diamond-studded golden chains. Life becomes a burden when it is weighed down by karma and we have to carry and support it. The end of karma makes our lives light and free, but only a few people appreciate this as it is obscured by the veils of *attā* (self).

CONCLUSION

As Buddhists, let's try to do only the karma that is the end of karma. When we see that karma has occupied and ruled our lives, we will strive to practice, improve ourselves, and fight in every possible way to triumph over both good and evil karma so that neither of them will oppress our minds. Let's develop minds that are clean, clear, and calm because they are no longer disturbed by karma and its results. Nowadays, most people understand karma as something bad and undesirable. This is correct because both good and evil karma are despicable in that they cause the vicious cycles of birth and death to go on without cessation.

Karma in Buddhism is that karma (action) which leads to the end of all karma so that life is above and beyond karma. Far from despicable, it is something to be understood and fully integrated into our lives. "Living beyond karma" is something to be realized and attained.

Mokkhabalārāma, Chaiya, Thailand
April 7, 1988

INTRODUCTION

KARMA FOR EVERYONE:
SOCIAL JUSTICE AND THE PROBLEM OF RE-ETHICIZING KARMA IN THERAVADA BUDDHIST SOCIETIES

JONATHAN S. WATTS

INTRODUCTION

Deciphering the flow of karma in any given situation is certainly not an easy thing to do. For example, is the present situation in Iraq the karmic fate of the Iraqi people? Did they do something bad in the past for which they are now being punished? Are the American struggles there a karmic result of past actions in places like Vietnam? Indeed, the Buddha warned that the precise trajectory of karma is one of four things that are unfathomable (*acinteyya*). "The [precise working out of the] results of karma is an unconjecturable (*acinteyya*), that is not to be conjectured about, that would bring madness and vexation to anyone who conjectured about it" (*Aṅguttara Nikāya* 2005, A.iv.77). However, karma is still a topic he recommended for contemplation:

> There are five facts, bhikkhus, which ought to be often contemplated upon by man and woman, layfolk and monk ... [The fifth is] "I am the owner of my actions (karma), heir of my actions, actions are the womb from which I spring, actions are my kin, actions are my refuge" ... For what good reason should man or woman, layfolk or monk, often contemplate [this]? ... In one who often contemplates on the responsibility of their actions, such evil conduct will either entirely vanish or will be weakened. (*Aṅguttara Nikāya* 1975, 11–14, A.v.57)

The above two passages make an important distinction about how to engage with the issue of karma. The former refers to an unresolvable guessing game about what has happened in the past and what will exist in the future. The latter recommends an exercise in awareness designed to affect the present. It is a reflection of personal responsibility, a kind of intentional ethical action.

This distinction between karma as the mysterious trajectory of fate from the past into the future and karma as intentional ethical action remains a very problematic issue for Buddhists. These different understandings of karma imply very different views about how we are to live with each other and in turn how we are to shape our communities and societies. The debate over the nature of karma is an extremely old one, but one that remains very relevant for those societies influenced by Indian culture and, of course, for Buddhist societies, including those expanding rapidly in the West. Since the debate about karma is basically an ethical one about how we are to live with each other, it also has meaning for other societies struggling with similar ethical and social issues. In short, if Buddhists can craft a progressive personal and social ethic that encourages peaceful societies, this may offer a valuable resource for similar endeavors in non-Buddhist societies. In my estimation, the ultimate vision is for Buddhism to be able to work with other religions and value systems to craft a *civilization ethics* based on a dharma of tolerance, plurality, nonviolence, and justice.

WHAT HAS GONE WRONG? KARMIC SUFFERING AND INJUSTICE

The various chapters in this volume present a very concrete view of how karma is understood in the contemporary Buddhist world, especially in Theravada Buddhist societies, and how these understandings have had significant cultural and social ramifications. The dominant and popular understanding of karma presented in these chapters is: karma is the result of one's actions from previous lives (somewhat like the idea of destiny or fate). Through the law of dependent origination (*paṭicca samuppāda*), our bad or good actions from a previous life create the conditions for a bad or good existence in this life, which consequently influence the path we take towards rebirth in the next life. In this popular understanding, karma acts as a remote and transcendental force. The only ones who can realistically alter its course *in this life* are monks who can fully practice the way of the Buddha and realize enlightenment by extinguishing all karmic forces. For lay followers, especially women, the ability to practice like a monk is severely limited, and so the lay sangha tends to focus on mostly ritualistic practices by which to gain merit (*puñña*) towards a beneficial rebirth. The ideal rebirth is as a monk who can then attain liberation or nirvana directly. The principal practice for gaining merit is making offerings (*dāna*) in support of the monks' material sustenance. Other important, but less emphasized practices, are maintaining the five lay precepts (*sīla*) and practicing meditation (*bhāvanā*).

Another important aspect of this popular understanding of karma is its highly deterministic nature. This is famously expressed in the Buddha's words, "As the seed, so the fruit. Whoever does good, receives good. Whoever does bad, receives bad" (*Saṁyutta Nikāya* 2000, 328, S.i.227). This passage is understood to mean that whatever action one has done in the past will, without doubt, have consequences in the future. Coupled with the popular belief in rebirth, this deterministic understanding has several important social consequences. First, the causes of one's present suffering lie in the distant past actions of a previous life, and due to the inescapable law of karma, their consequences must be endured. In this way, equanimity (*upekkhā*) as the strength and patience to endure suffering has become an important social value.

This situation is presented in both of the chapters from Burma, where Burmans and ethnic minorities alike are taught that their suffering is due more to the transcendental power of *saṁsāra* than to the immanent power of an oppressive military junta. According to this understanding, the solution lies in cultivating *upekkhā* towards *saṁsāra* rather than engaging in intentional ethical action to reform the political system. In another chapter, we also see how the teaching of *upekkhā* is used in Thailand and other parts of Southeast Asia and South Asia to encourage women to endure violent husbands. In these examples, suffering is seen as a largely personal matter rather than a social one related to various structural and cultural factors, especially exploitation by others. This personalization of social injustice is explored further in our chapters from India, where social inequalities are legitimized as the sacred roles of caste based on inherited karma, and from Thailand, where ostentatious merit-making activities legitimize and sanctify the social status of the rich.

In short, a simplistic understanding of karma that says your past actions have completely created your present reality supports a retributive rather than a restorative form of social justice. There can be no negotiation with the complete and inescapable law of karma, and so the economic-, political-, or gender-based suffering that various people experience is their punishment or karmic fate in the grander scheme of *saṁsāra*. This suffering may be painful and undesirable, but it is inherently just since it is based in the natural law of dependent origination (*paṭicca samuppāda*).

This way of understanding karma supports cultural violence. It legitimates an entire religious culture that effectively tells people to be passive and subservient, not only to religious authority but to other forms of social authority. This in turn legitimates structural violence; for example, economic disparity—the gap between rich and poor—is depicted as a result of differences in personal karmic fate. This ultimately leads to the conditions for direct violence when governments are seen as legitimate in violently oppressing those who reject their marginalized situation. This volume will not only explore in detail how this cycle of cultural, structural, and direct violence works in various societies, but our writers, with their grassroots perspectives, will also introduce us to creative ways to transform this cycle into one that empowers individuals and restores harmonious community.

THE DEVELOPMENT OF THE TEACHING OF KARMA

If we can agree that the Buddha taught about how to end suffering and that his teaching on karma must have been a part of his central concern to end suffering, then his teaching on karma must differ in certain key aspects from the popular one outlined above. So what are the key elements in the Buddha's teaching of karma? The first step in answering this question is to broaden our view and recognize karma as a pan-Indian concept, an integral part of the worldview of most Indian spiritualities, especially Brahmanism/Hinduism and Jainism. In Theravada Buddhist societies, which are the particular focus in this issue, the influence of this larger Indian tradition is significant. It is from not appreciating the differences among these traditions concerning the teaching of karma that Buddhists have become confused about the essential aspects of the Buddha's teaching on this matter.

The original meaning of the word *karma* or *karman* in the earliest Vedic texts is "act, action, performance, business" (Krishan 1997, 4). In the early Vedic period dating before 800 BC, the term never had the sense of our present understanding as the moral law of rewards for good and bad action. This early notion of karma as "action" refers specifically to forms of *ritual* action meant to secure a favorable birth in heaven. *Iṣṭāpūrta*, literally "the fulfillment of that which is desired" (Mahony 1987a, 262), is an important related term that means filling up heaven with merit (*puñña*) from ritual action (*karma*) to be enjoyed after death (Krishan 1997, 5). So from the beginning we can see that merit making is closely connected with the idea of karma.

The development of the teaching of karma as ritual action to gain heaven paralleled the emergence of a priestly class (*brāhmaṇas* or Brahmins) who gained wealth, influence, and power from their exclusive sanction to perform such rituals. There were a number of ritual practices in this tradition, the most significant being life cycle rites (*saṃskāra*), ancestor rites (*śraddhā*), and sacrificial rites (*yajña*), especially the well-known fire sacrifice (*agni*). These latter, sacrificial rites became an especially pernicious method by which Brahmin priests mythologized and legitimized a developing class stratification (Swaris 2008, 106). A powerful priestly class and elaborate ritual action, however, were not an original feature of the earliest Vedic religion before 1100 BC, but emerged in the second period of Vedic development with the *Brāhmaṇa* texts (1100–800 BC) (Hiltebeitel 1987, 340). The rise of Brahmanism and the division of society into multiple classes or castes came about with the shift of the Vedic Aryan peoples entering northern India from nomadic, pastoral tribes to sedentary, agricultural societies. It was also a particular feature of the societies in the northwest region of Kuru Pancala, as opposed to the less stratified societies of the northeast region of the Majjhimadesa, from where the Buddha came (Swaris, 2008, 85).

The key point about this early Vedic view is that karma was ritualistic and not ethical in character. One's fate in the afterlife was contingent on karmic actions pertaining to the proper execution of Brahmanic ritual, not on ethical behavior towards other persons. For example, to end up in hell after death meant that one had not properly observed Vedic rituals and taboos, not that one had been a mean or violent person (Obeyesekere 2002, 100). This is not to say that the people of these early Vedic communities were not moral and ethical, but rather that they had not "universalized" their ethical culture. Although such Vedic ritual could be done on behalf of the community, such as a ruler performing a ritual for the prosperity of the domain, the right or power to engage in such ritual action was not inclusive or universal. In Brahmanism, neither women nor members of lower castes could engage in such merit-making ritual action, thereby making them dependent on high-caste males who were in turn dependent on Brahmin priests. When a culture is fully ethicized, the good life in the present or in the afterlife is based on ethical action, that is, the quality of the way we interact with and treat others. Ethical action, as opposed to ritual action, is something not only available to everyone but inherent in the social nature of human beings. Thus, a culture that is not fully ethicized will deny this ethical agency to certain others, usually women, people of low class, and/or foreigners (Obeyesekere 2002, 174).

It is not until the beginning of the third Vedic period of the *Upaniṣads* (800–500 BC) that karma assumes its more common meaning as the moral law of rewards for good and bad action. While the Brahmin priest seems to represent one type of specialization from the shamans of the earliest Vedic nomadic tribes, the forest ascetic or *samaṇa* appears to have been the other important type branching off from this early shamanic culture. *Samaṇa* literally means "striver" and denoted those who withdrew from society to realize self-liberation (Swaris 2008, 111). The solitary and introspective culture of the *samaṇa* shifted the idea of sacrifice (*yajña*) from a priestly rite— usually involving animal slaughter—recreating the *outward* conditions of cosmic harmony, to an ascetic practice (*tapas*) bringing one's *inner* being into harmony with the outer world. In this mode of thought, karma is no longer linked with merit as a positive means to create a permanent celestial self or soul (*ātman*) as in Brahmanism. Rather, karma is seen in a negative light as the undesirable residue or effect created by action motivated by desire. The Upanishadic tradition understood that karma as "work" or "endeavor" and the merit (*puñña*) gained by such work would eventually perish; from a Buddhist standpoint they are both impermanent (*anicca*). This meant that any merit created by proper ritual action and resulting in heaven would eventually run out, thrusting the individual back into the world of turmoil and struggle through rebirth.

It is at this stage that we can see the emergence of the pan-Indian notions of the cycle of death and rebirth (*saṃsāra*), of karma as the actions that determine the course of *saṃsāra*, and of extinguishing all karma as a means towards liberation from *saṃsāra*. In this way, the Upanishadic tradition marks the *partial* ethicization of the Vedic tradition, because one's fate in this life and the next depended on the quality of personal action and not on the quality of ritual action. This shift was a significant challenge to the Brahmin monopolization of salvation through the idea of karma as ritual action. The Upanishadic yogin was empowered to experience his own personal liberation through his own efforts. In this way, the development of wisdom (*jñāna*) became more important than sacrifice (*yajña*).

To repeat, however, this ethicization was only partial and not universal in character. This point can be seen in the very meaning of the word *upaniṣad*, often defined as "mystical" or "secret" (Hiltebeitel 1987, 341; Obeyesekere 2002, 112). The literal meaning of *upaniṣad* is "to sit nearby" and referred to a seeker of salvation entering into an order of esoteric learning and secret knowledge, often transmitted in a one-to-one manner from a teacher or guru, to whom he sat close by (Mahony 1987b, 148). The sacredness and secrecy of this knowledge meant it was not for all to hear, and so we find in the *Upaniṣads* various references to taboos against women and members of low castes receiving this knowledge. Thus, although altering one's karma and gaining liberation from *saṃsāra* could be experienced personally and directly through ascetic practice, this practice was not universal and open to all persons. Furthermore, the experience of liberation itself was personal and not collective. The limited ethical scope of the Upanishadic thinkers is in part due to the way karma was understood as an almost material substance, a residue that had to be cleansed from the body and soul. Thus, for the yogi, karma was altered, and ultimately exorcised, through meditation and austere practices.

The Jains, who also came more directly out of the *samaṇa* tradition of asceticism, understood karma in an even more materialistic way. The passions, or defilements (*kilesa*) in Buddhist terminology, endow the soul with the capacity to absorb karma. In this way, even unintentional actions, such as killing small insects while walking along the road, create bad karma and keep the soul bound to the cycle of transmigration and suffering. However, the Jains generally developed more ethical conclusions from this understanding of karma. First, they were the strongest force in articulating and developing the now pan-Indian culture of non-harming (*ahiṃsā*) and vegetarianism that led to the end of animal sacrifice (*yajña*). Furthermore, they attempted to articulate their ascetic tradition in a popular form and create lay communities. This marks another step in ethicization, because it brought the secret truths of the *samaṇa* and Upanishadic traditions into the public world, which meant everyone could benefit.

Ultimately, the conflict between the old Brahmanic ritualism and the new Upanishadic asceticism was resolved by harmonizing their diverse elements. For example, in the Brahmanic practice of ancestor rites (*śraddhā*), the idea of karma as a material substance could be employed so that karma and merit could be transmitted from one person to another, especially through family bloodlines. Theistic devotionalism (*bhakti*) is perhaps the best example of the harmonization of these conflicting ideas about karma. It was on the rise at the time of the Buddha (563–483 BC), developing most strongly after the fall of the Buddhist Mauryan dynasty in 185 BC and reaching its peak with the final maturation of the *Bhagavadgītā* text around AD 400. Theism has its origins in the early Vedas, for example, in the *Ṛg Veda*, Purusha is the primordial being who creates the universe (Hiltebeitel 1987, 342). The *Upaniṣads* also often advocate a form of theism, even if it is a formless one such as para-Brahman. Karma as ritual action in Brahmanism depended on having the material resources of a high-caste person, while ascetic action in the Upanishadic and *samaṇa* traditions required arduous training. In theistic devotionalism, however, the way of *bhakti yoga* offered a more popular method available to everyone through "the loving surrender to God's will" and fulfillment of one's social role or duty. This third trend could be seen as a further ethicization of the tradition in that it opened up salvation to the common person and, at its best, encouraged a more collective salvation through selfless social action.

In these developments, we can begin to see the seeds for the misinterpretation of karma by Buddhists. The problem of caste in India is traceable first to the mythification of the class stratification that was emerging in the shift of some Aryan tribes into sedentary, agricultural societies; for example, the *Aitareya Brāhmaṇa* states, "Like a Vaishya ... tributary to another, to be eaten by another, to be oppressed at will. Like a Shudra, the servant of another, to be removed at will, to be slain at will" (7.29, in Swaris 2008, 106). Caste ideology further gained currency, despite the Buddha's efforts, in the Majjhimadesa region among the new monarchies as a means to subjugate conquered peoples, especially forest tribes that had resisted sedentary agriculture and who are thought to have become the first untouchables (Swaris 2008, 240). Finally, this system was codified in the partial universalization of Brahmanism into theistic devotionalism, specifically with the *Dharmasūtras* (300 BC–AD 400), which include the *Code of Manu* (*Manu Smṛti*), and the *Bhagavadgītā*. In these texts, castes are said to originate from the body of Purusha and salvation is gained by fulfilling one's caste role or duty (Mahony 1987a, 265). Karma is not understood as either ritual action as in Brahmanism or ascetic action as in the *Upaniṣads*, but rather selfless action in fulfilling one's caste duty as an act of devotion or love (*bhakti*) towards God.

Krishan sums up these concepts of karma as providing "a most rational explanation of the inequalities of life, of affluence and poverty, of happiness and suffering in the lives of individuals ... In consequence, the economic and social inequalities and inequities which individuals suffer are not the results of selfish individuals or classes who exploit weaker sections of individuals.

They are the products of each man's own karma in previous births" (Krishan 1997, 459). In Thailand, the situation in which the wealthy legitimize their authority through their ability to buy salvation in gaudy merit-making rituals clearly derives from the Brahmanistic understanding of karma. On the other hand, the materialistic understanding of karma in the *Upaniṣads* and especially in Jainism, according to which only esoteric knowledge and extreme asceticism can liberate one from past karma, makes salvation for the common person a distant prospect only realizable through numerous rebirths. This implies that suffering in this life must be faced with equanimity (*upekkhā*), which generally means passive resignation in Burma and Thailand. The Buddha saw these pitfalls, however, and directly addressed both understandings:

> When one falls back on what was done in the past as being essential (*pubbekaṭavāda*), monks, there is no desire, no effort [at the thought], "This should be done. This shouldn't be done." When one can't pin down as a truth or reality what should and shouldn't be done, one dwells bewildered and unprotected . . . When one falls back on creation by a supreme being as being essential (*issarakaraṇavāda*), monks, there is no desire, no effort [at the thought], "This should be done. This shouldn't be done." When one can't pin down as a truth or reality what should and shouldn't be done, one dwells bewildered and unprotected. (*Aṅguttara Nikāya* 2005, A.iii.64)

The movement toward a more universalized and ethicized understanding of karma also signals a movement towards a more compassionate, restorative understanding of social justice. Although the Vedic tradition moved away from an exclusivist and less ethical Brahmanistic understanding of karma, that movement was incomplete, because the nature of karma as the moral law of rewards for action remained simplistic and deterministic. In theistic devotionalism, moral duty and ethical behavior are based on the divine word of Vedic texts and the power of a supreme being. In this way, moral law is absolute, unchangeable, and nonnegotiable. This creates a more absolute sense of moral transgression sharply contrasting sin and righteousness.

When sin becomes more absolute, it must be dealt with more severely. Justice is understood as the retributive power of an all-powerful being's will.

However, an understanding of karma that replaces the power of a creator being with the power of karma as a natural law does not necessarily avoid this pitfall. When karma is understood too simplistically as the result of all previous actions, it also becomes absolute, unchangeable, and nonnegotiable. The punishment handed down by a creator God is replaced by the punishment produced through the machine like efficiency of an implacable law. The result, as seen above in the Buddha's words, is a great passivity towards these undeniable forces, and as we will see in this volume, it leaves many "unprotected" against social forces that co-opt these cosmic powers.

A BUDDHIST VIEW OF KARMA

The Basic Etymology and Construction of Buddhist Karma

Buddhism shares with the other Indian religious systems the basic understanding of karma as "work" or "action." The Vedic concept of karma is qualified as ritual action. The qualifier in the Buddhist understanding of karma is volition or intention (*cetanā*), so that karma is more precisely understood as "action based on intention" or "deeds willfully done" as seen through these words of the Buddha: "Monks! intention (*cetanā*), I say, is karma. Having willed, we create karma, through body, speech, and mind" (*Aṅguttara Nikāya* 2005, A.iii.415). In this way, it is understood that "actions that are without intention are not considered karma" (Payutto 1993, 6). This immediately distinguishes Buddhist karma from the Upanishadic and Jain understandings of karma as largely a material force. Buddhism emphasizes karma as fundamentally non-material, mental. As we saw above, the Buddha repudiated past karmic determinism (*pubbekaṭavāda*) and theistic determinism (*issarakaraṇavāda*), because they lead to passive resignation and discourage taking action that can be of direct benefit. However, because of this emphasis on the quality of the mind, the Jains considered Buddhists as embracing the view that human action is inconsequential (*akriyāvāda*) (Macy 1991, 171–72).

Indeed, an extreme interpretation of karma as *cetanā* can lead to a focus on the mere purification of thought and away from positive action. Such a position can be seen in certain interpretations of Buddhism in which monastics should completely withdraw from any kind of social involvement and focus entirely on the purification of their minds through reclusive meditation. When the Buddhist tradition is interpreted this way, it moves towards the ascetic ideal of the *Upaniṣads*, likewise becoming less inclusive, less engaged, and less ethical. However, the Buddha said, "Having willed, we create karma, through body, speech, and mind;" that is, not just through mind. This emphasis on intention should actually be seen as a means to engender skillful, positive activity to resolve karmic constructions, which occur most often in the context of relationships with others. If karma is truly a law governing moral and ethical behavior, then it becomes increasingly difficult to speak about it in terms of solitary asceticism, because individuals cannot be moral objects unto themselves. The ground of morality is always established in a community of social relationships (Obeyesekere 2002,113).

This point becomes clearer by examining another key concept in the Buddhist understanding of karma, *saṅkhāra*, which has been translated in various ways but should be understood here in terms of dependent origination (*paṭicca samuppāda*) as "volitional formations" (Payutto 1993, 8), "mental concocting" (Buddhadasa 1998, 28), or "constructs" (Swaris 2008, 179). In *paṭicca samuppāda*, the consciousness (*viññāṇa*) that develops from the power of ignorance (*avijjā*) and *saṅkhāra* (concocting, constructing) will be labeled as positive, negative, or neutral feeling (*vedanā*) without the power of mindfulness (*sati*) to stop it. This feeling gives rise to desire (*taṇhā*) and craving (*upādāna*), which give rise or birth (*jāti*) to a sense of self and ego (*attā*). Through the continuing power of ignorance (*avijjā*) and *saṅkhāra*, one continues to engage in this process of co-dependent ego construction that is never able to find sustained satisfaction.

In this process, consciousness (*viññāṇa*) is not found to arise from a transcendental source like a Self (*ātman*) or Subject (*nāma*). Rather, consciousness is a dependently originated concoction or construct (*saṅkhāra*) that arises from the coming together of sense forms (*rūpa*) and sense bases or media (*nāma*). By understanding that consciousness, the mind or "subject" (*nāma*), and the object (*rūpa*) co-dependently arise, the Buddha deconstructs and lays bare the fallacy of mind/body duality that leads to a fetishization of the mind as a transcendental force of causation, like God, Ātman, or Scientific Law.

In this formulation of *paṭicca samuppāda*, the Buddha lays the basis for his whole radical ethical and social message, also articulated as the three marks: "All *saṅkhāra* are impermanent (*anicca*); all *saṅkhāra* are suffering (*dukkha*); and all realities (*dhamma*) are without substance (*anattā*)" (Dh.277–79). In such a deconstruction, the transcendental claims to truth and authority that Brahmins had used to sanctify an unjust social order and that Upanishadic recluses had used to posit a private and elitist form of salvation are seen for what they are: speculations at best, pernicious lies at worst. The Buddha's conclusion to this insight was not further speculation in another metaphysic but rather a deep ethic, as seen in his declaration after gaining enlightenment: "House builder you have been found out. You shall build no house again. Your rafters lie shattered. Your rooftop lies in ruins. Consciousness is deconstructed. Desire (*taṇhā*) is destroyed" (Swaris 2008, 177, Dh.153–154). The ignorant consciousness that drives us to control and manipulate others is deconstructed and laid bare. Desire and craving are thus rooted out, liberating and empowering the individual to work and live for the benefit of all beings.

Unfortunately, mainstream Theravada Buddhism, and in fact most of the entire Buddhist tradition, slid back into such transcendental and ontological understandings by interpreting *paṭicca samuppāda* as a process spanning three lifetimes—an interpretation developed in the later *Abhidhamma* texts and specifically in Buddhaghosa's *Visuddhimagga*. This interpretation says that *saṅkhāra* produced from a previous lifetime will condition consciousness in this lifetime that leads to the karmic result (*kamma-vipāka*) of rebirth (*jāti*) in the next life (Buddhadasa 1992).[1] *Saṅkhāra* expresses itself in the next life as the

---

1. In this work, Buddhadasa strongly criticizes this popular understanding of *paṭicca samuppāda*, derived principally from Buddhaghosa's *Visuddhimagga*, which he describes as a form of Brahmanism.

meritorious (*puññabhi-saṅkhāra*) or non-meritorious formations (*apuññabhi-saṅkhāra*) that condition the way life is experienced (Payutto 1994, 28).

In the understanding of *paṭicca samuppāda* that focuses only on this lifetime and is found in the *Sutta* discourses of the Buddha, *jāti* is not the rebirth of the self in another body. Rather, it is the rebirth of an ego over and over again in this life whenever *saṅkhāra* conditions an ignorant consciousness, thus leading to ignorant desire as craving (*taṇhā*) and attachment (*upādāna*). Like Upanishadic thought, the Abhidhammic multiple-lifetime understanding sees *saṅkhāra* in a more material or essential way as the unchanging factors of mind (*nāma*) that condition future rebirth. On the other hand, the single lifetime understanding views *saṅkhāra* in a more conditioned way as the constructs that frame consciousness and the way the world is perceived.

In either understanding, *saṅkhāra* is understood as a form of karma, that is, the force that plans and organizes the movements of the mind and that through repetition results in character traits, physical features, and repercussions from external forces (Payutto 1993, 7–8). However, the understanding of *paṭicca samuppāda* that focuses on this lifetime is closer to the Buddha's emphasis on karma as intention, because it makes this whole process observable and changeable in the present life condition. Swaris sums up this point eloquently:

> If "birth" [*jāti*] here is understood as physical birth then human suffering becomes an ontological condition and can be ended only with physical death or eventual nirvana understood as the extinction of being, not craving [*taṇhā*]. This surely makes the Buddha's claim that suffering can be ended in this very life meaningless. (Swaris, 208, 242)

When Buddhists miss these key distinctions in the foundation of the Buddha's enlightenment experience, that is, his experience of the unfolding of *paṭicca samuppāda*, they miss the entire ethical and transformative (both personal and social) thrust of his teachings. For when the Buddha deconstructed consciousness and found no creator God (Brahma) or ultimate Self (Ātman) behind it, he deconstructed the whole mythic power of the Brahmin priests and the violent system of class and patriarchy founded on their and the ruling classes' desire (*taṇhā*) for wealth and temporal power. In more than one discourse, such as the *Madhupiṇḍika Sutta* (M.i.108) and the *Mahānidāna Sutta* (D.ii.55), the Buddha explains the process of *paṭicca samuppāda* beginning with the concocting of ignorant consciousness and develops it into an explanation of how quarrels, violence, and warfare result. In these discourses, the ethical and social intent of the Buddha's realization is clear. Nirvana is not a transcendental, ontological void, but rather the sustaining of mindfulness (*sati*) that empowers one to quench egoistic desire for the purpose of intentional, ethical action (karma) on the behalf of all.

Contextualizing the Law of Karma

In the *Abhidhamma* literature, the law of karma (*kammaniyāma*) is placed alongside four other kinds of natural law concerning environment and weather (*utuniyāma*), heredity (*bījaniyāma*), mind and sense (*cittaniyāma*), and the natural interdependence of all things (*dhammaniyāma*). The law of karma is the law that governs human behavior. In this way, the highly respected Thai scholar monk Ven. P. A. Payutto emphasizes that we must not reduce these laws into the single law of karma and that "not all events are the workings of karma" (Payutto 1993, 4–5). Payutto further emphasizes that a major problem is the confusion of the law of karma with societal customs and laws, which vary from society to society. What may be impure or evil in one society (for example, eating pork) may not be in another. In this way, karma may or may not work in line with social customs. The common misapplication of it, which we have seen above, is that if one desires to go against social norms (such as eating pork or abandoning a violent husband), one may be threatened with some sort of punishment—in the Buddhist case, the threat of accumulating bad karma. The contextualization of karmic law as one of many laws also steers us away from a deterministic understanding of karma and a retributive sense of justice that reduces suffering to the result of karmic sin. Instead, it moves us towards a deeper investigation of the wide variety of causes behind suffering and the ways to remedy them.

Another oversimplification is equating karma with its results (*vipāka*), or to put it another way, equating the constructs (*saṅkhāra*) of a person's mind with the unfolding of their life. This confusion is connected to the conflation of karma and social custom. According to Payutto, karma can lead to *vipāka* on a number of levels, such as (1) accumulated mental tendencies and the quality of mind; (2) physical character, mannerisms, and behavior; (3) worldly conditions and the events of life; and (4) larger social conditions. The law of karma is dominant on the first two levels, and then begins to interact with social customs on the third and fourth levels.

When people misapply the karmic formula of "good actions bring good results, bad actions bring bad results," they usually do so on the third and fourth levels. Thus, if a person is born as a poor woman, she must have bad karma resulting from bad actions in a past lifetime, and so must endure the suffering of sexism and classism (the third and fourth levels) regardless of whether she has a kind and gentle character (first and second levels). On the other hand, if a person is born rich and male, he is seen to be enjoying the good karma of good actions done in a past life and will receive social honors and respect regardless of the quality of his mind and behavior. Buddhadasa Bhikkhu often clarified this confusion by saying that karma does not mean fortune or the results; it just means action (Buddhadasa 1988, 18). In combating the prevalence of this confusion in terms of rebirth, Payutto goes so far as to say, "As for the unfolding of the present life, the results of previous karma stop at birth, and a new beginning is made" (Payutto 1992, 76).

The conflation of karma with *vipāka*, which leads to a deterministic understanding of karma, is incompatible with the Buddhist understanding of causality. The fundamental teachings of not-self (*anattā*) and emptiness (*suññatā*) reject both (1) the ideas of a creator God or an original source like a Self or Soul (*attā/ātman*) and (2) a purely material universe. In the former case, if there is an all-powerful creator God or immutable original source, power moves in a one-way flow from the Godhead or original source. Power never moves back towards it, making this source unchangeable and unconditionable. In the latter case, causality (the movement of energy or power) is too simplistic, moving in a linear one-to-one correspondence between physical forces and denying any causal role for the mind (Macy 1991, 29–30).

Since Buddhist causality is interpenetrative, with things interacting and conditioning each other, power is understood in a much more dynamic and complex way and cannot be reduced to an unconditionable source or a rigid determinism. Mind and matter, self and other, are intimately interconnected through the non-dual, not-self, and empty nature of reality. This means that power surges through all sectors of the intricate web of physical and mental relationships. When the world is seen in this way, the flow of large and complex systems becomes more varied and less predictable, progressively losing any sense of linear causality (Macy 1991, 168). This is why the Buddha spoke of determining the results of karma as unfathomable (*acinteyya*) and refused "either to identify the agent of action with the experiencer of the result, or to separate him from it" (Macy 1991, 163). In the same discourse in which we saw the Buddha reject theistic determinism and past karmic determinism, we see him elaborate this point of non-determinancy.

> Monks, for anyone who says, "In whatever way a person makes karma, that is how it is experienced," there is no living of the holy life, there is no opportunity for the right ending of suffering. But for anyone who says, "When karma based on a certain kind of feeling is made, results arise in conformity with that feeling," there is the living of the holy life, there is the opportunity for the right ending of suffering. There is the case where a trifling evil deed done by a certain individual takes him to hell. There is the case where the very same sort of trifling deed done by another individual is experienced in the here and now, and for the most part barely appears for a moment. (*Aṅguttara Nikāya* 2005, A.iii.99)

In the non-dual world of not-self and emptiness, the *structure* of our experience (*saṅkhāra*) is not different from the *function* of our intentional actions (*karma*); they are two faces of one way of being. Karma is not the fate into which we are born or our inevitable destiny. It is rather our identity and continuity in the present, our resource and our fate (Macy 1991, 165). As the

Buddha said, "I am the owner of my actions, heir of my actions, actions are the womb from which I spring, actions are my kin, actions are my protection" (*Aṅguttara Nikāya* 1975, 12, A.v.57).

This is why the understanding of *paṭicca samuppāda* over three lifetimes moves us away from the true intent of the Buddha's teaching. It creates an excessive space between action and result that distinguishes sharply between doing good and receiving benefit, when doing good is actually benefit in itself. As the Buddha noted, "Wisdom is purified by morality, and morality is purified by wisdom... and the combination of morality and wisdom is called the highest thing in the world" (*Dīgha Nikāya* 1995, D.i.124). In the understanding of *paṭicca samuppāda* within this lifetime, it is clearer that *saṅkhāra*—as the malleable nature of consciousness—is impermanent and not-self. The results of previous intentional actions expressed in *saṅkhāra* are alterable through present intention. As the inevitable consequences of a previous life, *saṅkhāra* are mysterious and distant. As present mental tendencies, they become an object of change through mindfulness and intentional moral action. In this way, the Buddha constantly exhorted the development of energy and vigor (*viriya*) up to his last words, "All *saṅkhāra* are of the nature to decay (*anicca*), strive on untiringly!" (*Dīgha Nikāya* 1995, D.ii.156).

This leads to the conclusion that since karma involves intentional action of a moral nature, it requires ethical behavior in dealing with others. On a personal level, by acting morally we not only create good karmic results (*kamma-vipāka*) in the quality of our mind and behavior (levels 1 and 2) but also engender positive conditions around us that help to create a positive society (levels 3 and 4). In this way, the model of an ascetic who shuns society in pursuit of liberation can never represent the epitome of human religious culture. This epitome is rather found in the interdependent struggle of all beings to attain liberation, and so entails a compassionate ethic that cannot passively accept the exploitation of others. If karma is not passive fatalism to past actions or creator gods, then it is also not acquiescence to unjust social customs or authority figures. Karma as intentional action is ethical and should always follow the five cardinal precepts (*pañcasīla*) based on non-harming and nonviolence. Payutto sees the practical results of this kind of understanding of karma as a series of empowerments that (1) encourage self reliance, diligence, and a sense of responsibility, and (2) endow all people with natural and equal rights based on their mental qualities and behavior, rather than on class, gender, or race (Payutto 1993, 99–100).

The Retreat of Ethicization

We have seen that the Buddha made a number of key changes in the understanding of karma that helped to fully universalize and ethicize it. His emphasis on intention (*cetanā*) empowers the individual to create action (*karma*) in the present, instead of being controlled by a priestly class that dictates ritual action, being paralyzed by the weight and power of past karma, or being cowered by the absolute power of a creator deity. The Buddha's emphasis on not-self (*anattā*) undercuts tendencies towards unskillful theistic devotionalism, while his emphasis on the unfathomable (*acinteyya*) nature of karma undercuts tendencies towards reducing karma to an all encompassing explanation for personal and social suffering. Finally, his formulation of morality (*sīla*) into a number of different ethical systems for different types of communities shows the inescapable ethical core of the path towards liberation; for example, the guidelines for a moral king (*dhammarāja*) in the *Cakkavatti Sutta* (D.iii.58–79), for the householder in the *Siṅgālovāda Sutta* (D.iii.180–193), and for republican congresses in the *Mahāparinibbāna Sutta* (D.ii.74), which provided the model for the monastic *vinaya*.

This concern for interpersonal relationships in Buddhism is what marks the full ethicization and universalization of the Vedic and *samaṇa* cultures of India (Obeyesekere 2002, 113). Brahmanism with its emphasis on ancestral rites (*śraddhā*) focused on relationships in the life of the householder, yet remained constrained by its sexism, classism, and the domination of the priestly class. The Buddha often harangued Brahmin priests for the emptiness of their Vedic rituals, while he rationalized and ethicized Brahmanistic ritual concepts. For example, in the *Kūṭadanta Sutta* (D.i.144–47), the Buddha teaches a wealthy Brahmin that the best form of sacrifice (*yajña*) is not a ritual one involving slaves and animal slaughter, but rather an ethical way of living that provides for people in one's community, supports the monastic Sangha, and practices morality, meditation, and insight to gain enlightenment.

In this way, it would seem that the Buddha would have agreed with the Upanishadic view that ritual action to make merit towards a better rebirth is an inferior form of practice unable to lead one to final enlightenment. While the Buddha certainly gravitated more towards the Upanishadic and *samaṇa* focus on a renunciate lifestyle, he rejected its exclusiveness and lack of concern for general society. Perhaps the best expression of the Buddha's universal ethical concern is found in his opening the monastic Sangha to all seekers, conspicuously women and those of lower caste. Buddhism, and to a certain extent Jainism, differed from most of the ascetic communities of the time by being concerned for the welfare of householders and by creating a system of reciprocity between the lay and monastic. This was a middle path that harmonized the two communities into a collective whole.

This system of reciprocity is based on giving (*dāna*) in which lay people provide monastics with material requisites and monastics offer instructions on the teachings and practice. While this system represents the height of Buddhist ethicization, it also contains pitfalls. Over time it has become formalized and overly ritualistic, reverting into a form of Brahmanism. As such, *dāna* often loses its wider ethical meaning as helping anyone in need and becomes a kind of Brahmanistic karma, that is, ritual action designed to gain merit towards a better rebirth. The practice of making merit (*puñña*) in Buddhism remains a very problematic issue. The Buddha recognized the role of merit making, often referring to the monastic Sangha as "fields of merit" (*puññakkheta*); for example, "Such an assembly [of monastics] is . . . an incomparable field of merit for the world . . . that a small gift given to it becomes great and a great gift greater" (*Ānāpānasati Sutta, Majjhima Nikāya* 1995, M.iii.80). As we will see in a number of chapters in this issue, the contemporary practice of merit making strikes at the center of the ethicization process in Buddhism. The practice of reciprocal *dāna* was an attempt to bring the worlds of lay and monastic together into a harmonious, ethical community focused on the good life and liberation from suffering. It harkened back to the days of the earliest Aryan communities when *dāna* was as an act of economic justice through the voluntary redistribution of wealth among tribe members. This was before the development of sedentary agriculture, when nomadic pastoralism prevented the hoarding of surplus goods and the less stratified clan structure discouraged the creation of outcastes.

Over time, the unique insights of the Buddha have been difficult to sustain, and as we have seen, a number of key concepts and teachings have become blurred, most centrally the understanding of nirvana. Although there are numerous examples of lay people attaining nirvana during the time of the Buddha, the fact that the Buddha himself was a monastic led to the sensibility that nirvana is best attained through the deep and highly personal experiences of assiduous ascetic practice.[2] Swaris, in his brilliant analysis of this issue, comments that "conceptualization and reification leads to a fetishization of nirvana. The deluded disciple then goes on to relate himself or herself to nirvana in much the same way that members of other schools relate either to personal gods or philosophical constructs" (Swaris 2008, 185). The understanding of nirvana stopped being the deconstruction of ignorant consciousness and reverted back to Upanishadic notions of the ecstatic oblivion of having one's consciousness absorbed and dissolved back into the Godhead or eternal Self, Ātman. This is an ontological crossing over from one realm to another, ultimately only attainable through physical death,[3] as opposed to the Buddha's crossing over from bondage to liberation, immanently attainable in this body and this life (Swaris 2008, 123). This conceptualization and reification of nirvana is a mistake that the Buddha himself directly warned his disciples to avoid:

> There is the case, monks, where an uninstructed run-of-the-mill person (*puthu-jjana*)—who has no regard for noble ones, is not well-versed or disciplined

---

2. Buddhadasa, a dedicated forest monk himself, writes in an essay entitled "Insight by the Nature Method" of the fallacies of reclusive meditation as the only means to nirvana (Buddhadasa 1993, 81). See note 1 in my other essay in this volume on Sri Lanka.

3. This is another key issue that Buddhadasa liked to discuss in detail, such as in the essay, "*Nibbāna* for Everyone," in which he cites one of the synonyms for nirvana as "the end of concocting [*saṅkhāra*]." He further comments that "*Nibbāna* has nothing in the least to do with death . . . It is the coolness that remains when the defilements have ended" (Buddhadasa, 1996).

in their Dhamma; who has no regard for people of integrity, is not well-versed or disciplined in their Dhamma—perceives earth as earth . . . He perceives nirvana as nirvana. Perceiving nirvana as nirvana, he conceives about nirvana, he conceives in nirvana, he conceives apart from nirvana, he conceives nirvana as "mine," he delights in nirvana. Why is that? Because he has not fully understood it, I tell you. (*Mūlapariyāya Sutta*, M.i.4)

With this shift, nirvana became remote and impractical even for the common monastic, and Buddhism began to take on the worst aspects of the Vedic notions of karma. For the lay person, nirvana could only be attained through ritual action to build merit (*puñña*) towards a better rebirth. In this way, the role of the monastic Sangha became fetishized as an "incomparable field of merit" to which the giving material requisites became the highest form of generosity (*dāna*). As the chapter from Burma shows, lay practice has often become focused on this kind of ritual action that is more "an investment in *samsāra*" than working toward nirvana. For the monastics, nirvana could only be attained through a cloistered life dedicated to intensive meditation practice. In the chapter on Sri Lanka, we will see how monastic practice and vocation split into those who became overly integrated into society through ritual and scholastic activities and those who shut themselves off from society for intensive meditation and ascetic practice. As we see in the all the chapters, these trends mark a closing down of the universal and ethical character of Buddhism.

CONCLUSION

The discourses of the Buddha found in the Pali suttas offer a great resource for deepening our understanding of karma. However, these discourses are not without their problematic aspects, as the discussion of merit making shows. Another difficulty we find in the discourses is the Buddha's focus on the individual level of action. It is typical to find him speaking of how the individual can act ethically towards others in order to prevent harm to them and bring benefit to oneself. In those cases where one is the recipient of harmful action, the Buddha's teaching is almost always focused on how to maintain and develop wholesome mental states, for example *upekkhā*. The situation that is not well addressed in the Buddha's discourses, nor anywhere in Buddhist teachings, is how to take the next step of stopping the harmful actions of others and of society. For example, concerning the caste discrimination of Brahmins, the Buddha often addressed Brahmins directly on this issue, but rarely if ever do we find him instructing those of low caste about how to deal with a direct experience of severe discrimination.

This remains an important missing link in the construction of a Buddhist social justice, especially in these post modern times when it is more often social structures rather than individuals that oppress people. Where is the karmic justice for those who purify action, word, and thought yet still suffer from structural violence? As Buddhists, must we once again rely on miserable promises of a better rebirth? This chapter has tried to show how individuals can use Buddhist teachings to promote positive intentional action towards improving their lives (karma on levels 1&2). However, essential work still needs to be done to create positive intentional *communal* action in order to disable harmful social conditions and create beneficial *kamma-vipāka* for society as a whole. The chapters that follow are, I believe, a step in that direction.

References

Aṅguttara Nikāya: The Discourse Collection in Numerical Order. 1975. Translated by Nyanaponika Thera. Kandy, Sri Lanka : Buddhist Publication Society.

Aṅguttara Nikāya: The Further-Factored Discourses. 2005. Translated by Thanissaro Bhikkhu. From http://www.accesstoinsight.org/tipitaka/an/index.html.

Buddhadasa Bhikkhu. 1988. *Buddhism in All Aspects.* Translated by Santikaro. Unpublished manuscript, reedited and reprinted as *It All Depends* (2015, Wisdom Publications, Boston, Masschussetts)

Buddhadasa Bhikkhu. 1992. *Paṭicca Samuppāda: Practical Dependent Origination.* Translated by Steve Schmidt. Surat Thani, Thailand: Dhammadana Foundation.

Buddhadasa Bhikkhu. 1993. *Handbook for Mankind.* Translated by Rod Bucknell. Surat Thani, Thailand: Dhammadana Foundation.

Buddhadasa Bhikkhu. 1996. "*Nibbāna* for Everyone." Translated by Santikaro. http://www.suanmokkh.org/archive/arts/message/nibbevry.html.

The Connected Discourses of the Buddha: A New Translation of the Saṁyutta Nikāya. 2000. Translated by Bhikkhu Bodhi. Boston: Wisdom Publications.

Hiltebeitel, Alf. 1987. "Hinduism." In *The Encyclopedia of Religion*, edited by Mircea Eliade. New York: MacMillan Publishing.

Krishan, Yuvraj. 1997. *The Doctrine of Karma: Its Origin and Development in Brahmanical, Buddhist and Jain traditions.* Delhi: Motilal Banarsidass Publishers.

The Long Discourses of the Buddha: A Translation of the Dīgha Nikāya. 1995. Translated by Maurice Walshe. Boston: Wisdom Publications.

Macy, Joanna. 1991. *Mutual Causality in Buddhism and General Systems Theory.* Albany, NY: State University of New York Press.

Mahony, William K. 1987a. "Karman: Hindu and Jain Concepts." In *The Encyclopedia of Religion*, edited by Mircea Eliade. New York: MacMillan Publishing.

Mahony, William K. 1987b. "Upaniṣads." In *The Encyclopedia of Religion*, edited by Mircea Eliade. New York: MacMillan Publishing.

The Middle Length Discourses of the Buddha: A New Translation of the Majjhima Nikāya. 1995. Translated by Bhikkhu Nanamoli and Bhikkhu Bodhi. Boston: Wisdom Publications.

Obeyesekere, Gananath. 2002. *Imagining Karma: Ethical Transformation in Amerindian, Buddhist, and Greek Rebirth.* Berkeley, CA: University of California Press.

Payutto, P. A. 1992. *Buddhist Economics: A Middle Way for the Market Place.* Translated by Bruce Evans. Bangkok: Buddhadhamma Foundation.

Payutto, P. A. 1993. *Good, Evil and Beyond: Karma in the Buddha's Teaching.* Translated by Bruce Evans. Bangkok: Buddhadhamma Foundation.

Payutto, P. A. 1994. *Dependent Origination: The Buddhist Law of Conditionality.* Translated by Bruce Evans. Bangkok: Buddhadhamma Foundation.

Swaris, Nalin. 2008. *The Buddha's Way to Human Liberation: A Socio-Historical Approach.* Nugegoda, Sri Lanka: Sarasavi Publishers.

THE DHARMA OF KARMA
Rediscovering Civilizational Ethics

KARMA:
THE CREATIVE LIFE FORCE OF HUMAN BEINGS

NALIN SWARIS

The problem of suffering has exercised the minds of sages from the beginnings of civilization. For those who actually endure unspeakable suffering without any hope that it will ever end, their miseries may seem like some divine curse or an evil fate. Similarly, those who are born into conditions of wealth and privilege may believe that they have been blessed by the gods or the fates. This crude evaluation of "good" and "evil" has been typical of most religious beliefs. But the agonized cry rising up from suffering masses down the centuries has been, "Why do the ways of the wicked prosper?" Dominant ideologies seek to provide pseudo explanations to assuage the protests of the oppressed against their condition by assuring them that wrongs will be righted and justice vindicated in another world or a future life after death. Georges Balandier clarifies the ideological function of such explanations. "They *explain* the existing order in historical terms and *justify* it by presenting it as a system based on right. Those myths that confirm the dominant position of a group are obviously most significant; they help to maintain a superior situation" (Balandier 1972, 118, emphasis his).

Orthodox Buddhist ethics explains social differences through a trinity of doctrines: (1) successive individual rebirths, (2) cycles of *saṁsāra*, (3) one's evil or morally imperfect deeds (karma). These beliefs were in circulation in the Buddha's day. There are many places in the Theravada canon where the Buddha himself is quoted as having expounded karma as a law of retribution.

This article is an abridged version of chapter 11 in Nalin Swaris's book, *The Buddha's Way to Human Liberation, A Socio-Historical Approach*, published in 2009 by Sarasavi Publishers, Nugegoda, Sri Lanka.

However, there is also sufficient evidence in the same canonical scriptures to conclude that the Buddha and the first Buddhists rejected such a view. The Buddha proclaimed that the separate self with a unique soul was a delusion and a fabrication of craving. The dreadful prospect of the same individual going through endless cycles of rebirth was ended with the realization that there is no one to endure it.

"Karma" is a word that in ordinary everyday language to this day simply means labor, work, deed, or practice. Its ordinary meaning was and is self-evident to people who actually do manual labor to earn a living. In Sri Lanka, workers are called *kamkaruvo*. This designation is similar to the term *kammakara* used for wage laborers in the Pali scriptures. Poor, exploited Sri Lankan Buddhists who believe their lot is due to bad karma refer to themselves as *karmakkarayo*—miserable people cursed by karma.

Very early in the history of Buddhism, the theory of karma as an iron law of immanent justice was incorporated into Buddhist orthodoxy. The ordinary word for "work" (karma) was hypostatized into "karma," a system of impersonal justice that dispenses rewards to good deeds and punishments to evil deeds. Karma rules in the *interregnum* between births and deaths. It is based on crude and primitive notions that associate "good" with "good life" and high social status, and "evil" with poverty, misery, and low social status. In karmic justice, good deeds are rewarded by birth as a male, enjoyment of power and privilege, comeliness, health, and worldly pleasures. Evil deeds are punished by birth as a female, ugliness, physical deformities, poverty, servitude, and low social status (low caste). In India and Sri Lanka, birth into high or low caste is attributed to a person's good or evil deeds in a previous birth. The only way the wretched of the earth can change their woeful lot is to accept their plight and perform their lowly tasks without a murmur as expiation for their sins committed in a previous life. Meanwhile, they are to hope that at the next toss on the roulette table of *saṁsāra*, they will be born into a more propitious social situation. All women who are born into this culture, not just Buddhist women, must docilely fulfill their domestic duties, praying that they will be reborn as men, and then work their way up the *saṁsāric* ladder until they become predestined to join the order of monks, which is the surest guarantee of realizing nirvana—total liberation from *saṁsāra*.

The irony of this system of justice is that the social grid of inequality and of "high" and "low" has to remain unchanged to make sure that the good will be rewarded and the evil punished. The theory precludes the possibility of changing a patently unjust social system. Buddhism, as taught and practiced today, is a religion for the private salvation of individuals. Caste is very much a part of the social fabric of Sri Lankan Buddhism. Even the one, undifferentiated monastic Sangha founded by the Buddha is divided into monastic sects divided along caste lines in Sri Lanka.

COLLECTIVE KARMA

J. G. Jennings argues that the theory of karmic rebirths is not compatible with the Buddha's teaching on *anattā* (not-self), and he suggests that what is rebirthed is craving that sustains ego or "self" consciousness. "If the epithet *ponobhavika* ['leading to rebirth'] be applied to *taṇhā* (craving), and translated as 'tending to arise again and again, repeating itself, recurring' (that is causing the rebirth of itself, not of the individual), it is fully in accord with the doctrine of altruistic responsibility" (Jennings 1947, xxxvii). This application of *ponobhavika* to craving (*taṇhā*) as a proclivity to repeat or rebirth itself is consistent with the Buddha's declaration that ego consciousness ceases with the destruction of craving. Centuries later Sigmund Freud and Jacques Lacan confirmed that the ego is a function of desire. Striving to realize selflessness is, writes Jennings, "[An] ethical ideal of complete altruism of such beauty that it would be worth presenting in a concrete form even if that form were not strictly historical. Of its historical truth, however, in the life of Gotama Buddha, there appears to be sufficient proof" (Jennings 1947, xxii).

If the notion of the individual self is a fiction and there is no transcendental self, how should one understand effective human agency? Jennings suggests that we should understand the Buddha's teaching on karma as a *theory of collective karma* (Jennings 1947, xxxvii). According to him, the individualistic theory of karma is the work of "after-men" trying to reconcile *anattā* with the dominant value system.

> This reconciliation savors more of his metaphysical successors than of Gotama himself who declared he did not deal in metaphysical questions but with the Eightfold Path of Conduct. Gotama calls for self-dependence and eager activity in the present, not however on behalf of the self, since such grasping, whether for immediate or ultimate reward, is the source of all sorrow, therefore necessarily on behalf of others. (Jennings 1947, xxxvii, xlvi)

Jennings regards the reconciliation of *anattā* with individual rebirth to be a key element in the Hinduization of Buddhism:

> In the Hindu view the same individual acts and suffers in different lives; the usual modern Buddhist view is the same; but the strict original Buddhist view is altruistic, the actor being one, and the ultimate sufferer or beneficiary another, individual. Allowing that the reconciliation is later, it may be assumed that Buddha, teaching the doctrines of no-permanent soul, moral responsibility, and altruism, taught a doctrine of altruistic responsibility or collective karma, according to which every action, word, and thought of the individual, transient though he may be, brings forth inevitable consequences to be suffered or enjoyed by others in endless succeeding generations. (Jennings 1947, xxxvii)

Jennings' proposal that karma be understood as the collective karma of human beings opens up a theoretically refreshing perspective to look at karma or human agency as the distinctive potential of the "species nature" of human beings as such, irrespective of gender, race, class, or historical period. The theoretical concept "species nature," therefore, needs to be clarified.

HUMAN AGENCY AS SPECIES POTENTIAL

To explain what is meant by the "species nature" of humans, one must turn to Karl Marx, who introduced the concept. This recourse to Marx may seem like an attempt to read into the Buddha's teaching on the interpretation of karma, a meaning that has no basis in the canonical scriptures. Before prejudging the issue, readers are invited to first follow the theoretical clarification given below and see if it is relevant to a contemporary understanding of the Buddha's extraordinary perception of the specific character of human agency.

In contrast to the teleological or predetermined movement of history, Marx insisted that humans make their own history under the specific conditions they have inherited. There are no "iron laws" of history working independently of humans who think, plan, and act. The totality of human activity may not always achieve the intended goal. The uniqueness of human beings, writes Marx in *The German Ideology*, may be variously defined, theologically or philosophically. "[But,] they themselves begin to distinguish themselves from animals as soon as they begin to produce their means of subsistence" (Marx 1975). Humans are unique because of their actions in the world. All other living beings are circumscribed by their environment. Their lives are naturally adapted to suit their environment, whereas humans have historically adapted the resources of their environment to suit their own needs. They are culture-producing animals. There is no such thing as "pure nature" once humans become architects of their own environment. Marx clarifies the difference between animals as follows:

> A spider conducts operations that resemble those of a weaver and a bee puts to shame many an architect. But what distinguishes the worst of architects from the best of bees is this: the architect raises his structure in imagination before he erects it in reality. At the end of every labor process, we get a result that already existed in the imagination of the laborers at its commencement. (*Capital I.174*, Marx 1977)

Spiders have not changed the webs they weave or bees the hives they build. Every generation mutely repeats what was done by the previous generation, whereas humans have changed their life conditions through a long process of cultural evolution. It is this ability to produce effects in the world that vests human action with a moral quality. This ability, Marx points out, is not due to an abstract human essence. "The human essence is no abstraction inherent in each single individual. It is in reality the totality of the social relations" (*Theses on Fuerbach VI*, Marx 1975).

The totality of social relationships is in fact a social division of the species nature or capacity of human beings. In other words, it is a diversification or a branching out of the same species potential. With the social division of work, humans begin to produce for and to serve each other's needs. It is through social cooperation that the primitive human group survived, and it is through social cooperation that humans have historically enhanced their life conditions. "The fact that the need of one can be satisfied by the product of another, and vice versa, proves that each of them reaches beyond his own particular need, as a human being, and relates to one another as a human being; that their common species being (*gattungswesen*) is acknowledged by all" (Marx 1973).

I produce the need of an "other," because I know that my own nature needs it in the first place. This does not happen in the animal world. Marx elaborates, "It does not happen elsewhere that elephants produce for tigers, or animals for other animals" (Marx 1973). Animals are diversified into different species. From generation to generation, they act according to the instincts of their natures. A beehive may seem to be bustling with collective activity, but the bees perform the same task for the same purpose, to build hives in order to produce honey. Century upon century has passed but bees have not changed the architecture of their hives. "A hive of bees comprises at bottom only one bee, and they all produce the same thing" (Marx 1973). All the bees perform the same task to produce the same thing, honey. They do not have a social division of work and do not produce different things.

It is important here to understand the sociological term "social division of labor." At a determinate stage of development, humans created a social division of labor. That is to say, the species potential of humans developed socially, similar to the branching out of a tree. People began to produce different goods for one another enhancing the potential of the entire group. Some specialized in food production, others in producing goods for agriculturists—metal tools, furniture, pots, etc. Different products that were socially exchanged were produced by different groups, and so individuals came to be identified by their occupations.

The division of work among humans that began as an expression of social cooperation became exploitative and a source of suffering when one group, a minority, began to live off the work, that is to say, the expended life energies of other human beings. Social exchanges became negative and unequal. Eventually status differentiation of "high" and "low" occupations emerged with the development of horizontal caste/class divisions. Ideologies were elaborated to determine that occupational differences were an articulation of the separate natures of groups and not as the expression of the same human species potential. Dominant groups were then able to exploit the dominated groups, in the same way an ox or an elephant was exploited for production, by preventing any change of occupation or of social mobility, saying it was (and still is) against nature. In this way, the ruling classes have often reduced the laboring masses to the level of dumb beasts; for example, Brahmins have referred to Shudras as "two-footed cattle."

The Buddha was once asked if he subscribed to any of the various views current in his day to explain the cause of suffering in the world, namely:

1. *adhiccasamuppanna*—happiness and suffering are chance happenings; the strictly materialist position
2. *paramkatam*—they are due to an external cause, for example, divine pre-destination, fate, etc.
3. *sayamkatam*—they are self-caused; in contemporary terms, the view of liberal individualism
4. *sayamkatam-paramkatam*—they are due to a concurrence of one's own action and an external cause. This would correspond to the conventional explanations of karmic law or the Christian theological explanation of the concurrence of divine grace and free will to perform supernaturally meritorious deeds.

The Buddha stated that none of these explanations were his own. He said what he taught was that "happiness and suffering conditionally co-arise (*paticca samuppanna sukha-dukkha*)" (*Saṁyutta Nikāya*, S.ii.19–22). Note that the Buddha does not use the past participle "caused" (*kratham*) in his formulation. Human agency takes place *within* the law of conditioned co-arising and instances it. By situating karma within the law of dependent origination (*paticca samuppāda*), the Buddha ends the false dilemma created by the opposition of freedom and necessity. Freedom can be realized through insight into this necessity, not by hubristically defying it. Human agency does not take place in a cosmic void or social vacuum. It takes place under specific conditions (*idappaccayatā*). We shall see below how the Buddha applied this principle to explain the origins of the various occupational groups of his day. Social practices are conditions and are themselves conditioned by other social practices.

THE *VĀSEṬṬHA SUTTA*

The *Vāseṭṭha Sutta* is a discourse handed down in the *Sutta Nipāta* as a response to a question put to the Buddha by two young Brahmin students of theology, Bharadvaja and Vasettha. They asked the Buddha whether there was any truth in the doctrine they had been taught that an individual is a *brāhmaṇa* by birth and another a non-*brāhmaṇa* by birth. The Buddha replied, "I will explain to you in gradual and very truth, the differentiation by kind of birth (*jāti*) of living things, for there is species differentiation (*jātivibhaṅgaṁ pāṇānaṁ*) according to 'other-other' species (*aññamaññā hi jātiyo*)" (Sn3.9:600).

A Morphological Classification of Living Beings

The Buddha begins with a general morphological classification of the various forms of life in the world according to habitat and behavior:

> There is variety of plant life from grasses to trees.
> There is a variety of animals that live in the earth and dust, like worms and ants.

There is a variety of four-footed beasts.
There is a variety of long-backed creatures, like reptiles.
There is a variety of fishes.
There is a variety of winged animals, who fly through the air. (601–606)

After each of these classifications, the Buddha observes that among these life forms there are distinct species-constituting marks (*liṅgaṃ jātimayaṃ*). These species-constituting marks signify other-other species (*liṅgaṃ jātimayaṃ tesaṃ aññamaññā hi jātiyo*). There are several noteworthy features in this system of classification. First, life forms or *rūpas* are generically classified according to the modality of their life-activities and habitats: moving in water, air, on the earth, or rooted to one place (plant life), and common observable external features: all birds have beaks, feathers, claws, etc., fish have scales and gills, etc. However, within each genus, significant differences could be noted in the common marks. On the basis of these different marks, one could distinguish different subspecies among plants, reptiles, insects, fish, birds, and quadrupeds. Unlike Aristotle, the Buddha does not conclude that distinguishable behavior patterns and external features are signs of hidden essences or substantial forms. Neither does he hierarchize life forms according to a Great Ladder of Being. The discourse is not propelled by a human will to power over the universe by which Man [*sic*] is placed at the apex of a pyramid of being. The Buddha undercuts the possibility of constructing such hierarchies. He totally rejected the Brahmin theory of innate nature (*svabhāva dharma*).

Human Beings: One Undifferentiated Species

After dispassionately examining the diversity of life forms and recognizing species differences among them, the Buddha turns to the human form or *rūpa*.

> *Yathā etāsu jātīsu liṅgaṃ jātimayaṃ puthu,*
> *Evaṃ natti manussesu liṅgaṃ jātamayaṃ puthu*
> Whereas in these species there are distinct species-making marks,

In humans there is no separate (or distinguishable) species-making marks. (607)

To substantiate this general conclusion, the Buddha proceeds to a detailed examination of the external features or "marks" of the naked human form. There is no mark (*liṅga*) that could be singled out as a sign or signifier of substantial differences among human beings that could be attributed to their own distinctive natures.

> Not in the hairs, nor in the head
> Nor in the ears, nor in the eyes
> Nor in the mouth, nor in the nose
> Nor in the lips, nor in the brows
> Nor in the shoulders or the neck
> Nor in the belly or the back
> Not in the buttocks or the breast
> Nor in the anus or genitals
> Nor in the hands, nor in the feet
> Nor in the fingers, nor the nails
> Nor in the knees, nor in the thighs
> Nor in their color or in voice;
> Here there are no distinctive *jāti* marks
> As with other kinds of *jātis*. (607)

This item–by–item listing of the parts of the human form, without calling it male or female, is a *tour de force* of de-signification. The mind is focused and concentrated on the perceived form without letting it be biased by pre-"conceptions." The naked human form is clinically examined without prudishness. There are no "marks" to indicate any species difference. There is only a differentiated organism.

On the basis of this empirical-clinical examination of the human form, the Buddha formulates a general principle:

liṅgaṃ jātimayaṃ neva yathā aññāsu jātisu
paccattaṃ ca sarīresu manussesvetaṃ na vijjati
vokārañca manussesu samaññāya pavuccati

Here, there are no species-constituting marks as among other species.
Looked at individually, this does not apply to the human body.
Differences among humans are designations of speech.
Differences spoken of among human beings are purely conventional. (610–611)

The Buddha acknowledges that there are indeed perceptible physical differences among human beings, but none of the physical differences are indications of belonging to different species or sub-species. No single feature of the human form—the genitals, pigmentation, the timbre of the voice, the shape of nose, the color or texture of the hair—is singled out as a "mark" (*liṅga*), or sign of ontological sexual and racial differences in the human (*manussa*) species (*jāti*). Among humans there is only one species, the human species. Differences within the human species, the Buddha insists, are constructed by naming or denomination. These are not "intrinsic" differences, but conventionally spoken of differences.

Men and women share a perceptibly similar form. Differences in the genital organs are not seen as signs of biologically different natures. Similarly, people belonging to various ethnic (cultural-linguistic) groups share an undeniably similar external form and common physiology. The best proof of this, the Buddha pointed out in another exchange with Brahmin scholars, is that men and women belonging to different classes and ethnic groups, though separated into different species or *jātis*, do have intercourse with each other and produce human offspring, not some hybrid creature. Whereas, when a mare is mated with a donkey, the offspring is a mule, as the Buddha pointed out (*Assalāyana Sutta*, M.ii.153). It is social convention that prohibits persons of one social group or religion from marrying one another, as if they belong to different species. The Buddha undermined all ideologies that attempt to create eternal differences based on religion or pseudo biological arguments.

Human conflicts arise when historically and culturally arising differences are regarded as eternal and unchangeable.

When discussing the marks that constitute *jāti* difference among other living forms, the Buddha used the term *aññamaññā*—*añña* means the opposite, the contrary, the different. The term *aññamaññā hi jātiyo* is used by the Buddha to distinguish between different species—they are "other-others." The word *samañña* on the other hand, is compounded from *san* (*con*) "with," + *añña*. It denotes "with the other" (*PED* 1925, 13). In other words, the Buddha uses this term for the human *rūpas* to indicate shared common features. The differences among humans are differences among likes (*samañña*), not differences between un-likes (*anañña*). The Buddha does single out perceived differences to name (*nāma*), classify, and hierarchize beings sharing a common form (*rūpa*). All humans belong to the one and same *jāti*. There is no divine intent or evolutionary biological dynamic that has stratified the human species in terms of "high" and "low." As R. Chalmers observed, "Herein Gotama was in accord with the conclusion of modern biologists, that *anthropidae* are represented by the single genus and species, man" (Chalmers 1894, 396).

The affirmation by the Buddha of the biological unity of the human race is not a platitude—an equalization in some celestial kingdom after death. This unqualified insistence of the equality of all human beings—irrespective of perceived gender, class, and ethnic differences—was part of a social campaign against the hierarchization of society and against man's inhumanity to man. As the Sri Lankan Buddhist scholar O. H. de A. L. Wijesekere points out:

> The Buddha was the first thinker of India, not to say of the whole world, to give up the theological approach and adopt a rational attitude in such matters . . . .
> If one believes that he revolutionized the theological and metaphysical standpoint of Brahmanist religion and philosophy, it would be absurd to hold that the Buddha failed to condemn their sociological implications. (Wijesekere 1951, 4)

Human Differentiation as Differentiated Practices

Having established the biological unity of the human race, the Buddha proceeds to answer the inevitable question: If all human beings are members of the same species (*jāti*), how is it that humans seem to be dispersed from birth to death into different classes and occupational groups? The question continues to be asked to this day, and the Buddha's answer is as relevant today as when it was first given twenty-five hundred years ago. In the Buddha's day, the social division of labor—a historical development—had taken on the appearance of a natural phenomenon, because it was reproduced from generation to generation. People had come to believe, and Brahmin ideology reinforced this delusion, that some individuals are predestined by their natures to labor, to serve, and to provide pleasure; other individuals pre-ordained to conquer, subjugate, and exploit. The Buddha unraveled this mystery of social life to the two young Brahmins who prided themselves on being *brāhmaṇa*—the most excellent of beings by birth.

Know well that whoever among humans makes a living by farming is a farmer, not a *brāhmaṇa*.

Know well that whoever among humans makes a living by crafts is a craftsman, not a *brāhmaṇa*.

Know well that whoever among humans makes a living by trading is a trader, not a *brāhmaṇa*.

Know well that whoever among humans makes a living by serving is a servant, not a *brāhmaṇa*.

Know well that whoever among humans makes a living by stealing is a thief not a *brāhmaṇa*.

Know well that whoever among humans makes a living by weapons is a soldier, not a *brāhmaṇa*.

Know well that whoever among humans makes a living by priestly craft is a ritualist, not a *brāhmaṇa*. (612–618)

The Buddha did not exclude the "blue bloods" of the period from this general law: "He who governs the city and realm is a *raja*, not a *brāhmaṇa*" (619). The Brahmins had constituted themselves as the normative speaking subjects on the order of things and humans. The Buddha exposes the strategy behind this will to power. The Brahmins had established themselves as a substantially different species (*jāti*) of human beings by way of negation—they are *not* another *jāti* like *khattiyā*, *vessā*, and *suddā*. They presented themselves as unique creatures born out of the mouth of Brahma. They had appropriated the term *brāhmaṇa* as a designation for themselves as the ritually pure and most excellent of status groups. As the Buddha clarifies, the Brahmins did this through verbal jugglery—a *brāhmaṇa* is not a *khattiyā*, *vessā*, and *suddā*—not an "other." They then argued that there was an intrinsic identity between the linguistically differentiated *brāhmaṇa* and the concept "excellent." They claimed that as skilled philologists (595) they alone knew the correct relationship between a sound and its signification. This was, they proudly asserted, a natural endowment of birth, not an acquired skill. They were the mouth-born sons of Brahma, the ultimate source of all signification in heaven and on earth. The Buddha exposed the spurious character of the Brahmin claim. The meanings attached to words are social conventions. There is no intrinsic, divinely determined, necessary relationship between a word as sound-signifier and its meaning. Moreover, "whoever makes a living by priestly craft is called a ritualist, not a *brāhmaṇa*." The Buddha then added, "I do not call anyone a *brāhmaṇa* because of his birth from a particular mother, even if he may be addressed as 'Sir' and may be wealthy" (620).

This last statement would have touched the raw nerve of Brahmin pride. The Brahmins traced their origin to a heavenly father. The Buddha sticks close to more certifiable facts. A person's paternity could be dubious, but never the maternity. The Buddha drives home his point unrelentingly. Even if the Brahmins founded their claim on the surer ground of being born of a Brahmin mother, he still saw no reason why this should be a basis for pride and for demanding respect and subservience. In a radical reversal of values, the Buddha redeploys the term *brāhmaṇa* as a designation for those who lead morally unimpeachable lives.

Who has cut off all fetters and is no more by anguish shaken. Who has overcome all ties, detached. He is the one I call a *brāhmaṇa*. Who has cut each strap and thong, the reins and bridle as well. Whose shaft is lifted, the awakened one. He is the one I call a *brāhmaṇa* . . . . Who does not flare up with anger, dutiful, virtuous, and humble . . . . Who has laid aside the rod against all beings frail or bold. Who does not kill or have killed [*sic*] . . . . Who leaves behind all human bonds and bonds of heaven . . . . Whose destination is unknown to gods, to spirits, and to humans. An *arahant* with taints destroyed. He is the one I call a *brāhmaṇa*. (621–644)

The Buddha sweeps aside all claims to holiness based on ritual activities or esoteric knowledge. What matters is not what a person *thinks* or says he/she is, or is believed to be, by gullible people. What is important is the moral quality of a person's life. The rites performed by a priest are just as much routinized practices as the activities of a "herder," a "soldier," or a "trader." It is just another way of earning a living! Anyone who lives by stealing is a robber, no matter by what name society may think fit to call him—"priest," "king," or "merchant." If social convention does not prevent it, any person, male or female, could learn, for example, the bag of tricks and practice priestcraft. The Buddha did not spare his own renouncer disciples. The shaven head and yellow robes may signify "mendicant" (*bhikkhu/bhikkhuni*), but this does not necessarily imply that he/she is a person of excellent moral character. "There are many ill-natured, unrestrained imposters who wear yellow robes" (Dh. 307), he once noted.

The Buddha explains that the social division of labor is the result of a division of practices (*kamma vibhaṅga*) within the same species. It is not due to a diversity of natures (*jāti vibhaṅga*).[1] This truth is mystified to make people ignorant of their own creative potential. The fixation of activity into ever recurring sets of relationships within a more or less unchanging system made society appear as an alien force existing outside human beings. Ideologists used this ignorance of the true beginnings of things to tell people

---

1. For an "historical" explanation of the genesis of social differentiation and hierarchy, see the *Aggaññña Sutta* (D.iii.27).

that their lowly social condition is the product of their inherent natures or a punishment by a law of natural justice—karma. The Brahmin theory of social order reversed the historical order of events and presented social practices as the exteriorization of ideas conceived by the divine mind of Brahma. The concepts of *brāhmaṇa*, *khattiyā*, *vessā*, and *suddā* were made anterior to the life practices of these social classes. A preexisting essence is made to determine existence. However, it is by abstracting from repeated practices that the "concept" of a priest, aristocrat, peasant, or slave is conceived.

Brahmin lawgivers, like Manu, used their social power to impose a fixed hierarchized order on society. The Buddha disturbs the holy innocence that surrounds this "law." A social identity is not a ready-made idea or an inner essence that enters the mother's womb at the moment of conception: "I do not call anyone by any name, because he/she is born from the womb of a particular mother" (*Sutta Nipāta* 1881, 113, 620). A person is called a servant (*dāsa-dāsi*) because the circumstances of life have forced him/her to practice subservience to another. A person is called a master, because he/she is able to exercise power over an "other." The practices of two individuals relate them to each other in a servant-master relationship. A servant is *not* a master, and a master is *not* a servant due to their respective practices and roles, not because two mutually negating concepts have entered their beings and fixed their inner essences or natures. The Buddha ended this section of the *Vāseṭṭha Sutta* by summing up his disclosure of the basis of social differences. A preexisting conceptual order did not produce the social division of labor. The conceptual order is an abstraction from or an inverted reflection of practices repeated from generation to generation, creating the illusion that these occupational specializations have been determined by birth. Dividing members belonging to one species (*jāti*) and calling them individuals of different *jātis* or natures is a perverse misrepresentation of actual origins. The different names given to various occupations are purely social conventions. These names do not in any way signify differences in nature. "For name and clan (*namagottam*) are assigned as mere designations in the world. Assigned here and there and originate in conventions" (648).

Names are conventional designations for modes of activity, not different natures. People act out social roles by following conventionally laid down rules of procedure, like forms of dress, uniforms, and modes of address. These are ways in which we "dress up" people and invest their roles and ranks with meaning and power or powerlessness. Behind the veil of appearances, everyone is the same. Male, female, prince, priest, and pauper alike are subject to the same law of impermanence—change, decay, and dissolution. The overriding law of impermanence (*anicca*), which no one can escape, equalizes all. Thus all talk of unique and unchanging natures is without substance (*anattā*). Things are changeable, because no thing is permanent.

A Flow of Interdependent Practices

In the final section of the *Vāseṭṭha Sutta*, the Buddha moves from the examination of particular practices to formulate a general theory about the character of human action in the world. The so-called fixed biological order of intrinsic differences turns out to be, on closer examination, a mental abstraction from the relatively stable social practices of individuals sharing the same species nature:

> For those who do not know this fact [the naming process],
> Wrong views have long underlain their hearts.
> Not knowing, they declare to us:
> "One is a Brahmin by birth (*jāti*)."
> [But] One is not a Brahmin by birth,
> Nor by birth is one a non-Brahmin.
> By action (*kamma*) is one a Brahmin.
> By action is one a non-Brahmin.
> For men are farmers by their acts,
> And by their acts are craftsmen too.
> And men are merchants by their acts,
> And by their acts are servants too.

And men are priests by their acts,
And by their acts are rulers too. (649–652)

The last two verses of this section sum up this grand and panoramic view of human agency in a precise and succinct formula:

Evametaṃ yathābhūtaṃ
kammaṃ passanti
paṇḍitā paṭiccasamuppādadasā kammavipākakovidā.

These indeed are thus become action,
Which the wise clearly see
As conditionally co-arisen results of action. (653)

The Buddha does not say that things are what they are, "thus being" (*yathā-attha*). That would have implied a hidden "essence," an inherent nature, "being as such," or "underlying meaning." It would also have implied that all beings have an innate, predetermined goal in life, since the word *attha* (Skt. *artha*) has a dual connotation of "meaning" as well as "goal." To avoid any such misconceptions, the Buddha states without ambiguity "thus-become-action" (*yathābhūtaṃ kammaṃ*). The death knell of ontologics is sounded with the declaration "the result of actions" (*kammavipākakovidā*). Egocentric individuals imagine that the world revolves around themselves. The Buddha shakes people awake from this delusion. The world (society) is reproduced by repeated practices. The term "karma" is used with reference to everyday practices and not to a hidden "law of karma":

Kammanā vattati loko
Kammanā vattati pajā
Kammanibandhanā sattā
Rathassāṇīva yāyato

Action makes the world[2] go round.
Action makes this generation turn.
Beings are bound by action
Like the chariot wheel by the linchpin. (654)

On another occasion the Buddha hammered home the centrality and the all-encompassing character of human practice by emphatic repetition.

Kammasakkā māṇava, sattā kammadāyādā kammayoni kammabandhu kammapaṭisaraṇā. Kammaṃ satte vibhajati yadidaṃ hīnappaṇītatāyāti.

Beings are action-accompanied,
action-heritaged,
action-born,
action-bonded.
Action is their refuge.
Action divides beings into high and low.
  (*Majjhima Nikāya* 1954–56, M.iii.203)

It is easy enough to see in this passage a reference to the hidden "law of karma," but the use of the plural "beings" underscores the fact that karma is first and foremost the collective action of beings sharing the same species potential. The social division of labor and the stratification of people into "high" and "low" is neither a divine design nor a manifestation of the intrinsic nature of beings. There is no mechanical cyclicity that holds human destiny in its grip. Human beings reproduce relationships (social structures and institutions) by repeating social practices under specific conditions. Social practices alone continue to produce and reproduce people as masculine/feminine, priest, monk, aristocrat, peasant, landless laborer, trader,

---

2. "World" has to be understood in the Buddha's own terms. The world of humans is *their world*, their construct. It is not the "cosmos" of ontological philosophies—a physical reality existing independent of human perception and practice.

professional soldier, etc. It is not the rituals of the priests (saṃskāras) or the action of a heavenly or earthly cosmocrat (Brahma or a wheel-turning monarch), but the everyday practices of ordinary men and women who produce (birth) and reproduce (rebirth) social order. Masters and slaves, priests and devotees, and kings and subjects are not separate individuals. Their identities are mutually conditioned/conditioning relationships, and they reproduce each other by their respective practices. Neither by birth nor divine blessing is one a king, and neither by birth nor divine curse is one a slave. Human perfection or human degeneration is ultimately a human responsibility. The key to the Buddha's revolutionary ethical practice is his penetrating insight into the "nature" of "things."

yathābhūtaṃ kammaṃ
paṭiccasamuppādadasā kammavipākakovidā.

Thus-become action, conditionally co-arisen, results of action.

Ideologists had blinded the people by presenting their oppressive conditions as the product of cosmic or meta-cosmic necessity, whereas the Buddha pointed out that these were humanly produced conditions. As such, the miserable "heritage of action" can be changed by changing the conditions that engendered it. Every human is a wheel turner. His/her actions can produce either a world of woe or a world of happiness. The Buddha unfolds the vision of a new possibility.

Sharing, kind words, and benevolence,
And treating all alike as each deserves,
These bonds of sympathy are in the world,
Just as the linchpin of a moving chariot.
(*Aṅguttara Nikāya* 1932–36, A.ii.32)

All the skills the Buddha mentions in this verse are social skills. This is not a vision seen from the narrow perspective of the separate ego and its preoccupation with personal reward and punishment. The Buddha is speaking of the historical possibility of living in peace and harmony in a reconciled world. To do this, humans have to reverse the motions of the wheel of *saṁsāra* by turning the wheel of dharma together.

KARMA: CONSTRUCTING-CONSTRUCTED

The Buddha insisted that he was a teacher of action (*kammavādin*), a teacher of effective action (*kiriyavādin*), and a teacher of energetic action (*viriyavādin*). We could, following Nanajivako Thera, understand karma in early Buddhist usage as "a designation for the whole range of problems concerning the organic connectedness of vital processes whose ripening results in creative activity" (Nanajivako 1990, 122). Karma is a creative vital process or *saṅkhāra*. The word *saṅkhāra* is derived from *sam-s*, plus the root / *kr*. Its indeclinable Sanskrit participle, *samskritya*, corresponds to the Pali *saṅkhata*. *Sam-s-kr* has the meaning of "to put together, forming well, join together, compose;" thus *saṅkhāra* refers to "putting together, forming well, making perfect, accomplishment, embellishment." *Kāra* is derived from the same root as the word *kamma* and signifies "to do, make, perform, accomplish, cause, effect, prepare, undertake" (*SED* 1899/1960, 301). The root / *kr* has the same connotation as the Latin *creare*. *Kata* (past participle) is "what has been done," "accomplished" (*SED* 1899/1960, 1120–1121). *Saṅkhāra*, as the Buddha uses the term, is the coordination of synergies in practical activity. Even thinking alone, for the Buddha, is karma—practical action. Physiological, verbal, and mental activities are "constructurations" (*kāyasaṅkhāra, vacīsaṅkhāra, manosaṅkhāra*). The Buddha classifies, not speech, but discursive thought (*vicāra*) and logical reasoning (*vitakka*) as verbal activity. This is because even before one speaks or even thinks in solitude, one thinks and reasons with the help of words. Therefore, thought has a social quality, because as the Buddha pointed out, language is a social convention.

Saṅkhata, the past participle of *saṅkhāra*, refers to the product: what has been "co-done"—as in the Latin *con-creatum*—in other words what has been "con-structured" by practical, sensuous action. The senses actively construct the forms seen, heard, smelt, tasted, and cognized. Therefore, what humans perceive and conceptualize are not the simple imprints of nature. What we call "nature" is a human construct, a human world (*loka*). Humans are also capable of exteriorizing their ideas through speech and actions. Rice growing in a paddy field is qualitatively different from its kind growing in the wild. The former is a cultural product and expresses a changed relationship between human beings and nature and between themselves. Humans, however, do not create out of nothing. They combine their capacities and the resources available to them in their environment to produce effects that fulfill their needs. In the *Mahāsudassana Sutta* (D.ii.169), the Buddha describes not only "natural" phenomena like elephants and horses, but also artifacts like cities, royal treasures, palaces, and carriages as *sankhatas*. All human products, from the most elementary forms of language and the simple tools of labor to imaginative and symbolic representations of "the world of gods and humans," texts sacred and profane, works of art, irrigation works, and temples and palaces are *sankhatas* or crystallizations of human energy and the forces of nature. Human ingenuity brings these together and rearticulates them in a creatively new fashion. Categories like karma and *sankhāra-sankhata*, understood within the underlying principle of *paṭicca samuppāda*, are indispensable for the formulating a revolutionary theory about the specific character of human action in the world.

HERITAGE OF ACTION

In one of the verses quoted above, the Buddha spoke of the "heritage of action," "origin in action," and of humans "bound together" through action. In English language commentaries, the Pali word *kamma* is often retained while explaining rebirth. Pali verses quoted and explained in the vernacular give "*kamma*" an esoteric character. *Kamma* and the heritage of *kamma* are always understood and explained as the *kamma* [*sic*] or the karmic heritage of separate individuals carried through from birth to birth. But if *kamma* is understood as the generic capacity of human beings, the formulation "heritage of action" takes on a profound significance. "Heritage of action" underscores the fact that humans are not born into a social vacuum. They inherit a world, that is to say, physical and social conditions brought into being by the generations that preceded them. They themselves will leave behind what they inherited either unchanged or significantly changed for the next generation. Humans can change conditions produced by others. This is not an abstruse theory. The world around us gives overwhelming proof of its practical truth. This is the breakthrough insight of *paṭicca samuppāda*.

Human beings have historically "gone forth" (*pabbajjā*) from limiting conditions, cultural as well as environmental, in which they have found themselves. Instead of being totally determined by pre-given conditions they have reshaped these life conditions through innovative action. Right Understanding is the precondition for Right Action. Humans, unlike animals, have species capacity to correctly understand and create new life conditions by "putting together, to form, to make"—in thought, imagination, and exteriorized works—which makes the world in which they live their own "accomplishment" and "embellishment," or their *sam s kritya*.[3]

The term *saṅkhāra-saṅkhata* must therefore be understood not just as mental formations but also as cultural practices and cultural products. Culture understood here not in the elitist sense of the "fine" arts or as "high culture," but in the fundamental sense of what all human beings produce in and through nature. The peasant is as much a cultural being as the intellectual and the artist. In fact, the accomplishments of the latter are very much dependent on the farmer's agri-"culture." *Saṅkhāra-saṅkhata* cuts through the conventional and takes for granted division between "nature" and "culture;" between "human nature" and "external nature;" and between "nature" and "super-nature." The Buddha sees these as "constructions" (*saṅkhāras*).

One cannot speak of a "natural law" or the "law of karma" as if they exist independently of the people who perceive recurring patterns of

---

3. The word in usage for "culture" in Sinhala is *sanskrutiya*. Etymologically it has the same meaning as *sam s kritya*.

relationship between events—not things—and practically intervene to regulate them. Humans have conceived "nature" in a variety of ways according to the level of their mastery of external forces: as "gods," as exteriorizations of a divine mind, as a rational logos, or as the workings of objective "scientific" laws. In each case, an imaginative construct of the mind is projected onto nature. The naturalization or supernaturalization of culture has been an ideological strategy of dominant groups to reproduce their privileges from generation to generation as if these were as recursive as the cycles of nature. This naturalization of culture (naturalistic sociology), Zygmunt Baumann points out, denies the possibility of social change in the historical order.

> [It] is fed by the predicative experience of the life-process as essentially unfree, and of freedom as a fear-generating state and it aptly supplies opposite cognitive and emotional outlets to both intuitions . . . . It assists the individual in his spontaneous efforts of disposing of the excessive, and therefore anxiety-ridden, freedom of choice, by either positing this freedom as illusion or advising him that such freedom is supported by reason which has been delimited and defined beforehand by society, whose power of judgement he cannot challenge. (in Giddens 1979, 196)

The Buddha understood the momentous responsibility humans carry for the world and for themselves because of the effects of their actions, which are independent of their subjective intentions. They can overcome themselves, live like herd animals mutely reproducing the world as they find it, or degenerate into a condition lower than that of beasts by turning against their own kind. *Saṁsāric* repetition is not a mechanical law of nature. It is human beings who birth and rebirth the world (society) by their repeated practices. They leave behind the heritage of their actions benign or baneful to the generations that follow them. Human beings are not the pure products of conditions; neither are they sovereign agents who are totally independent of conditions. The Buddha taught that conditions are not results of chance, the fates, or the creation of gods. Human conditions have conditionally co-arisen, and thus come into being through the action of other beings. The processes that produce suffering in the world can be reversed. What has been constructed can be unconstructed, if through proper investigation one tracks down the conditions that gave birth to it. This is the basis of the Buddha's optimism. To understand karma as collective action is to understand the necessity of collective action for freedom.

KARMA AS LIBERATIVE PRAXIS

The mutually conditioning constructing-constructed (*saṅkhāra-saṅkhata*) foregrounds the dual character of human agency and has anticipated by centuries Marx's concept of praxis as defined in his *Theses on Fuerbach*. Humans are neither passive objects of circumstances nor are they wholly free subjects of circumstances. They find themselves in conditions made by other human beings, and therefore, they can change them through right understanding of the conditions that gave rise to them. The interaction of human beings with "nature" has historically been not mere contemplation but active appropriation and transformation. This is not just a philosophical notion. It was everywhere evident in the age of the Buddha.

From around the eighth century BC, intrepid pioneers had transformed the rainforests of the Majjhimadesa, or "The Middle Country" of Northeast India, into arable and habitable lands by collective action. The transition to agriculture and sedentarism enabled the development of advanced technologies like metallurgy and irrigation agriculture so that the land yielded two or three crops a year. Surplus production created conditions for the development of a host of ancillary technologies that enhanced and diversified the productive capacity of human beings. The mighty elephant and the wild buffalo had been tamed to serve human ends. The region produced fine textiles that had become famous throughout the then civilized world. The tragic irony of human history is that so-called material progress has not been accompanied by a corresponding development of human moral sensibilities. This was everywhere manifest in the society of the Buddha's day. Greed and violence were the ruling values of the time. Humans had mastered the powerful forces of external nature, but had become the slaves of craving (*taṇhā dāso*). However, in the very capacity to develop techniques for regulating the forces of nature towards envisaged ends, the Buddha discovered the key to resolve the problem of suffering. He developed a "technology" (theory and practice) for human beings to understand themselves, overcome their passions, and channel their energies to realize wholesome ends. The false dichotomy between "value-free" science and technology and moral values was abolished.

The human situation is a hundred thousand times worse today than it was in the Buddha's day. Unimaginable luxuries for the few and unrelenting misery for the many have become a monstrous global phenomenon, leading even to the degradation of the living environment of the entire planet. The fundamental challenge of the Buddha's noble ethical practice is more urgent today than when it was first proclaimed. Harnessing of nuclear energy, space travel, mass instant communication, and all the marvelous masteries of science mean little if the same ingenuity cannot be deployed to lift the burden of suffering from the shoulders of millions who belong to the same species and inhabit the same planet.

A world in which two-thirds of its people starve while the rest wallow in luxury and go on seeking more must be lacking an essential degree of global compassion and justice. Things will not change unless humans discover their humanity, apply the creative potential of their species-being to the sphere of morality, learn to overcome themselves, and become compassionate to others. The perennial relevance of the Buddha's teaching on the human capacity for creative action and the moral implications of this capacity will be evident if we substitute the Buddha's examples below with the achievements of today's applied sciences.

> Canal diggers divert the waters,
> Smiths hammer shafts into shape,
> Carpenters fashion the wood,
> The wise tame themselves. (Dh. 145)

References

Balandier, Georges. 1972. *Political Anthropology*. New York: Pelican.

Chalmers, Robert. 1894. "The *Madhura Sutta* Concerning Caste." *The Journal of the Royal Asiatic Society*. London: The Royal Asiatic Society.

Foucault, Michel. 1970. *The Order of Things*. London: Tavistock.

The Book of Gradual Sayings (*Aṅguttara Nikāya*). 1932–36. Translated by F. L. Woodward and E. M. Hare. London: Pali Text Society.

Jennings, J. G. 1947. *The Vedantic Buddhism of the Buddha*. London: Oxford University Press.

Kalupahana, David J. 1976. *Causality: The Central Philosophy of Buddhism*. Hawaii: University of Hawai'i Press.

Marx, Karl. 1973. *Grundrisse: Introduction to the Critique of Political Economy*. Middlesex: Penguin Books.

Marx, Karl. 1975. *Marx/Engels Collected Works* (*MECW*). Vol. 5, Theses on Feuerbach, The German Ideology and Related Manuscripts. Moscow: Progress Publishers.

Marx, Karl. 1977. *Capital: Capitalist Production as a Whole*. London: Lawrence and Wishart Ltd.

The Middle Length Discourses of the Buddha: A New Translation of the Majjhima Nikāya. 1995. Translated by Bhikkhu Nanamoli and Bhikkhu Bodhi. Boston: Wisdom Publications.

The Middle Length Sayings (*Majjhima Nikāya*). 1954–56. Translated by I. B. Horner. London: Pali Text Society.

Nanajivako Bhikkhu. 1990. "Kamma: The Ripening of Fruit." In *Kamma and Its Fruit*, edited by Nanaponika Thera. Kandy: Buddhist Publications Society.

Nyanaponika Thera, ed. 1990. "Kamma and Its Fruit." *Wheel Publications 221/224*. Kandy: Buddhist Publication Society.

Pali English Dictionary [*PED*]. 1925. Edited by T. W. Rhys Davids and W. Steede. London: Pali Text Society.

Sanskrit English Dictionary [*SED*]. 1899/1960. Edited by Monier Monier-Williams.Oxford: Oxford University Press.

The Sutta Nipāta. 1881. Translated by V. Fausböll. In Vol. X, *The Sacred Books of the East*, edited by F. Max Muller. Oxford: the Clarendon Press.

Wijesekera, O. H. 1951. *Buddhism and Society*. Colombo: M. D. Gunasena.

AN AWAKENED VISION:
DR. B. R. AMBEDKAR'S STRUGGLE TO RE-ETHICIZE INDIAN SOCIETY

MANGESH DAHIWALE

INTRODUCTION

Although the words and terminology of Brahmanism and Buddhism look alike, they are functionally counteractive. For example, the idea of "karma" in Brahmanism refers to ritual action, while in Buddhism it refers to ethical action. In this way, the Brahmanical worldview of society is diametrically opposite to the Buddhist worldview. "Dharma" in Buddhism refers to the natural karmic law of ethical action and the Buddha's teachings on benevolent conduct, which create the basis for a democratic social system. However, "Dharma" in Brahmanism strikes at the basis of democracy by speaking of the religious "duty" of following the principles of graded inequality in *varṇa* or caste. According to Dr. Bhimrao Ramji Ambedkar, born on April 14, 1891 in Mhow in Madhya Pradesh, Indian history and the history of caste is nothing but the conflict between these two worldviews of Buddhism and Brahmanism. He noticed that caste as human inequality based on birth and maltreatment meted out to one class of people by another has been sanctified by so-called sacred religious texts, such as the *Vedas*, *Smṛtis*, and *Śāstras*. In Buddhism, he not only found the mechanism to create a democratic social system, but also found a mechanism to liberate individuals classed as "untouchables" and "backward."

In order to make Buddhism relevant to modern society, he had two tasks: (1) liberate Buddhism itself from the corruption and distortion injected by the Brahmanical tendency towards ritualism, and (2) liberate his people from mental and social slavery in order to establish a democratic social system. While attempting to liberate Buddhism from the dead wood of the past, he suggested minor changes in the form but none in the content. One important example was his attempt to redefine the role of sangha and the role of the monastic. He was in favor of humanistic Buddhism in lieu of monastic Buddhism. Ambedkar envisioned a just society. A just society is a democratic social system. It is a society based on the principles of liberty, equality, and fraternity. He knew that if the principles of liberty, equality, and fraternity are to be injected into caste-based Indian society, there is a need for sangha, not necessarily monastic, to make these principles a living reality. As he was for humanistic Buddhism, he commented that this order would also include lay persons. This project of constituting sangha to dissolve caste identities could not become reality during his life, as he died a few weeks after administering initiation (*dhamma dīkṣa*) to his followers. However, the signposts he placed indicate beyond a doubt that he wanted to create such sangha and make lay persons the torchbearers of a New Buddhism (*navayāna*) in India.

AMBEDKAR'S VIEW OF CASTE

Ambedkar's Seminal Experiences of Caste

Although Indian society is fragmented into castes, there has been some change due to the movement of Ambedkar and other reformers. Some of his followers have benefited in terms of education and wealth due to his efforts. However, the change is not striking, and many are still subjected to hatred and perish in poverty. Caste-based violence continues to be an all-pervading phenomenon. Even after the abolition of untouchability by law in 1950, violent practices, such as inhuman treatment, raping untouchable women, and so forth, still occur in India. The situation at the time of Ambedkar was worse, and he personally experienced the caste system in its most inhuman form, being born into and brought up in an untouchable family.

A few seminal experiences awakened him to reality of the caste system. The first took place in Goregaon when Ambedkar was a boy of nine. He was to visit his father along with his brother. The location of his father's work place was far from the railway station, and no cart man was willing to take them on a bullock cart. One cart man agreed with the condition that the boys would have to drive the cart while he would sit behind. Throughout this escapade that lasted through the night, the boys went hungry, because they could not get pure water to drink, even though they had plenty of food. Their inability to get water was of course due to the fact that untouchables were barred from using public wells. This incident had a very important place in Ambedkar's life, and it left an indelible impression on his mind.

His worst experience of the caste system took place in Baroda when he was to become the military secretary to the Baroda State. He could not get accommodation in Baroda, because he was an untouchable, though highly educated. He found quarters in a Parsi boarding house and assumed a Parsi name. At work, the Brahmin clerks and subordinates kept their distance and threw files and papers on him to avoid his touch. Even in the club, he was only allowed to sit in the corner and was not allowed to take part in games. No clear assignment was given to him, though he was a military secretary. When the Parsis discovered his identity, they besieged his boarding house and threatened to beat him. Eventually, the owner expelled him, and he had to leave Baroda.

The third seminal experience took place in Chalisgaon, where no horse carriage driver was willing to take Ambedkar from the railway station to the place where a meeting was to be held. After a long wait, a carriage was finally brought. The driver and he were the only two occupants of the carriage. The carriage had not gone two hundred paces when there was almost a collision with a motorcar. Ambedkar was surprised that the driver, who was paid for hire every day, should have been so inexperienced. The accident was averted only because of the loud shout of a policeman. They somehow arrived at the culvert on a river. Around it there were no walls as there are on a bridge. The carriage was thrown down on the stone pave- ment of the culvert, and the horse and the carriage fell down from the culvert into the river. So heavy was the fall that Ambedkar was knocked senseless. As a result of this he received several injuries. His leg was fractured and he was disabled for several days. On inquiry, Ambedkar was told the real facts. The delay at the railway station was due to the fact that the carriage drivers were not prepared to drive with a passenger who was an untouchable. They felt it was beneath their dignity. The Mahar untouchables could not tolerate that their leader should walk to their quarters. A compromise was therefore arrived at: the owner of a carriage would give it on hire but not drive. Although they could not find someone to drive it, the Mahars thought this to be a happy solution, evidently forgetting that the safety of the passenger was more important than the maintenance of his dignity. It was then that Ambedkar learned that even a menial Hindu carriage driver looked upon himself as superior to any untouchable, even if that person be a barrister-at-law like Ambedkar.

There are many more incidents such as these from Ambedkar's life. These few, however, are sufficient for any person to understand the suffering experienced due to the practice of untouchability and caste. Many people in contemporary India still suffer from this system of graded inequality. They are living the life of degraded human beings. In the end we must ask, why is it necessary for them to suffer so much and occupy such positions in the social system?

Ambedkar's Analysis of Caste

Understanding the origin, genesis, and mechanism of caste in India is a very complex problem. Many able minds have tried to penetrate it, including Ambedkar who began work on this issue as early as 1916. He attempted to link the many chains in the history of India in order to show how the caste system evolved. In Ambedkar's understanding, the prime factor responsible for the evolution of the system of untouchability was the religious persecution of Buddhists, while other social-psychological factors are secondary. The existence of caste in India is due to the notion of inequality imposed by religion, which gives rise to social and cultural practices and prejudices. If these social and cultural practices cease, caste could be annihilated. This is a simple formulation of the quite complex issue of caste.

The life and work of the Buddha marks the flowering of the axial period in India in the sixth century BC. This period was one of great turmoil as smaller tribal societies were transforming into larger settled ones and eventually mighty empires. It has been shown that these smaller, pre-imperial societies were not based on a graded system of inequality or caste (Chakravarti 1987). This is not to say that there was no class system. Further, these societies often exhibited unethical and immoral aspects, like incest, alcoholism, war mongering, and the savage practice of ritual sacrifice (*yajña*). Thus, the revolutionary role of the Buddha was, first, in clearly proclaiming that the happiness of humans and society lies in ethics and not in rituals. Ambedkar understood the Buddha's awakening under the bodhi tree as a true revolution. "It was as great a revolution as the French Revolution. Though it began as a religious revolution, it became more than a religious revolution. It became a social and political revolution" (*BAWS* III, 153).

The Buddha's revolution that culminated in the emergence of the mighty empire of Ashoka (r. 270–232 BC) further strengthened the Buddhist worldview based on liberty, equality, and fraternity; a universal message that went beyond the Indian subcontinent. Under Ashoka, equality of punishment irrespective of the social standing of the criminal emerged. The priestly class was given the same treatment as that of the common people. Although Ashoka prevented worship of clan deities (*kula devata*) that served as the basis of income for Brahmins, he was ecumenical and promoted inter-religious tolerance. He did not persecute Brahmins, yet Brahmins lost their social prestige as the majority of the people abandoned the animal sacrifices that Brahmins officiated. A rule of law was established, and even animals received good treatment, as noted by the famous Chinese pilgrim Hsuan Tsang.

In *Revolution and Counterrevolution in Ancient India*, Ambedkar explains that after the establishment of the rule of law, Brahmins lived as a depressed class for the nearly 140 years of the Mauryan empire. Pushyamitra Sunga of the Samvedi Brahmin clan then conspired to destroy Buddhism as the state religion and to make Brahmins the sovereign rulers of India with the political power of the state behind it through murdering Ashoka's grandson, Emperor

Brhadratha, in 185 BC. After his accession, Pushyamitra launched a violent and virulent campaign of persecution against Buddhists and Buddhism. Thus, the counterrevolution against Buddhism began with the emergence of the Brahmins under the Sunga Dynasty.

At the same time, various major Brahmanical texts were written in order to counter Buddhism. According to Ambedkar, these texts are the true sources of inequality and were largely post-Mauryan developments. For example, Ambedkar showed that the *Code of Manu* (*Manu Smṛti*) was written by Sumati Bharagava after Psuhyamitra's revolt in 185 BC. The *Code of Manu*, which served as a law of inequality, was drafted and enforced with the newly acquired state power by the Brahmins, while the myth of the first cosmic being, Purusha, which tells of the divine origin of caste, was interpolated into the *Ṛg Veda*. According to Ambedkar, the *Manu Smṛti*, the *Bhagavad Gītā*, *Śaṅkarācārya's Vedānta*, the *Mahābhārata*, the *Rāmāyana*, and the *Purāṇas* are all post-Mauryan texts that serve as sources of inequality.

It should be noted, however, that the Buddhists of ancient India did not accept this worldview all at once. Perhaps they never did, as is evident from the continuous struggle between the Brahmins and the untouchables (former Buddhists) of modern India. The hatred and contempt preached by Brahmins was directed against Buddhists in particular and not against other groups. After the Mauryan period, most Indians who had upheld Buddhism slipped back into Brahmanized Hinduism. Other Indians who did not follow suit became untouchables, like the "broken men." The "broken men," according to Ambedkar, were the remaining peoples of the broken and defeated tribal groups of ancient India. Ambedkar wrote about this concept of "broken men" and how they came into being when the primitive societies were breaking up and transforming into the larger settled societies of imperial India. Brahmanism never tried to absorb these Buddhists into the caste system but rather shut them right out of it by making them untouchable and all that it stood for, such as no education, no means of economic development, etc. Untouchability was thus only born sometime around 400 AD, as these "broken men" were not able to abandon beef eating when cow killing was made a capital offense by the Gupta kings. In this way, the cow politics of present day India has its roots in the counterrevolution of the Brahmins against the Buddhists. Untouchability was thus born out of the struggle for supremacy between Buddhism and Brahmanism on a variety of levels from political power to social convention.

This is not to say that Buddhism was destroyed all at once. The struggle went on until the Muslim invasion in 1200 AD. The Muslim invasions played a decisive role as the Muslim invaders killed Buddhist monks or caused them to flee India. According to Ambedkar, "Religion like any other ideology can be attained only by propaganda. If propaganda fails, religion must disappear. The priestly class, however detestable it may be, is necessary to the sustenance of religion. For it is by its propaganda that religion is kept up. Without the priestly class religion must disappear." Due to this onslaught, the Buddhist Sangha in India underwent a great change in its composition. A disorganized system of married clergy with families who were called *aryas* developed. They took the place of the bhikkhus and began to cater to the religious needs of the general community. They eventually attained the status of bhikkhus through the performance of some sacraments. They officiated at religious ceremonies, but at the same time, in addition to their profession of priesthood, they earned their livelihood through such avocations as masonry, painting, sculpting, gold smithing, and carpentry. These artisan-priests, who were in later times larger in number than the bhikkhus, became the religious guides of the people. Their avocations left them little time and desire for the acquisition of learning, for deep thinking, or for devotion to meditation and other spiritual exercises. They could not be expected to raise Buddhism to a higher position through their endeavors, nor could they check its course towards ruin through the introduction of salutary reforms. It is obvious that this new Buddhist priesthood had neither prestige nor learning and was a poor match for the rival Brahmins (*BAWS* III, 151–437).

The upheaval caused by the Muslim invaders in the Buddhist community lasted for a while. However, the Muslims did not destroy or challenge its principles or doctrines, which governed the spiritual life of the people. On the other hand, the Brahmanic invasion changed the principles that Buddhism had preached for centuries as universal ones of a spiritual life. According to Ambedkar, the Brahmanic invasion of Buddhist India is significant but usually neglected by the historians of India. Buddhist India is not a myth or construction of Ambedkar. This is supported by material evidence (Rhys Davids 1903). However, the concept of Vedic India or the Golden Vedic Age is truly a construction of recent times by Hindu nationalists. The neo-Brahmanism of the post-Mauryan period brought the real changes in the political and social structure.

Through the medieval and colonial periods, the struggle against Brahmanism continued, though it was very much weakened due to the forces of time. The saint-poets of the fourteenth century onwards, such as Kabir, Nanadnar, Cho-kamela, and Tukaram, came from untouchable castes or backward classes and reflect "Buddhist" sentiments. Their teaching is marked with anti-caste and anti-Brahmanistic ideas. They ridiculed the *Vedas* and the religious texts of Brahmanism. They praised the ideals of liberty, equality, and fraternity. This influenced untouchables in south India who also realized in the beginning of the twentieth century that they were Buddhists and began their now well-documented movement (Aloysius 2004).

This deep-seated caste-based hatred is responsible for most of the problems and evils in India today, including the degradation of women. The creative energy of the country is imprisoned in the caste system. The life and mission of Ambedkar was to annihilate caste and create a new society based on the principles of liberty, equality, and fraternity. He also knew that the solution lay in making people aware of their social history and why they were condemned to such a life. He wanted to usher India into an era of enlightenment, or "Right Enlightenment" (Nanda 2002). This enlightened vision is the preface and key to everything else in conquering ignorance (the origin of suffering) and in the higher life (the end of suffering). For developing this enlightened vision, Ambedkar felt one needed to realize and understand the law of causality (*paṭicca samuppāda*), "This is, that is; with the arising of this, that arises. This is not, that is not. With the cessation of this, that ceases."

AMBEDKAR'S "AWAKENED" VISION

The New Buddhism

Ambedkar likened Indian society to an orange. If one removes the artificial rind of Hinduism, what remains is a fragmented society with mutually conflicting groups called castes that run into six thousand in-kind. Ambedkar did not strive for positional change in the whole system of graded inequality. He wanted to bring structural change to Indian society. He concluded that the contemporary state of degradation in India was due to the triumph of Brahmanism over Buddhism—the victory of a worldview that sanctifies a graded inequality amongst living beings over one that prizes ethical conduct towards all such beings.

David Brazier in his thought-provoking book, *The New Buddhism*, raises some very important points by questioning what the real project of the Buddha was after his enlightenment. He stresses that the Buddha had a vision of an ideal society that he shared with his disciples and thus awakened them to the reality of the world. This vision he termed as *bodhi*, that is, awakened vision. This vision of an awakened society moved the Buddha to turn the wheel of the dharma and to express his enlightenment experience to others to make this awakened society a reality (Brazier 2001).

Ambedkar also challenged traditional Buddhist positions and views. While he accepted that the Buddha was centrally concerned with suffering and the end of suffering, he did not define suffering based on the traditional eight types of suffering. His set of sufferings includes suffering due to humans' own wrongdoing and suffering due to inequality to other humans. In *The Buddha and His Dhamma*, he reformulates the life and teachings of the Buddha so that they can speak to contemporary Indian society and the modern world. For him, the function of the dharma is twofold: to purify one's mind and to reconstruct the world. In short, the purpose of the dharma is to transform an individual into a buddha and to transform the world into a sangha. In the preface to *The Buddha and His Dhamma*, Ambedkar speaks of the purpose of the dharma as the creation of *dhamma rajya*, an ideal society based on liberty, equality, and fraternity. It is clear that Ambedkar was trying to revive the Buddha's original project of the reconstruction of world. He called this vision *Navayāna* or the "New Buddhism," which is a universal model applicable to all societies.

Steps Towards an Awakened Society

In the early years, Ambedkar was still struggling with his spirituality and slowly defining for himself this awakened vision. Therefore, most of his work for the liberation of his people came within a framework of activism concerning laws, committees, and commissions in British India. For example, he gave evidence before the Southborough Committee for franchise and representation to the Indian legislatures in 1919. This was his first successful campaign without any mandate from his people. He successfully gained representation for depressed classes in the legislative assembly in Bombay. He was invited to participate in the Round Table Conference during 1932–1934 in order to discuss the future constitution of India, which he subsequently drafted. At this conference, he clashed with Gandhi, who denied the independent political rights of untouchables by deliberately trying to keep them in the fold of Hinduism. He also submitted a memorandum to the Cabinet Mission Plan in 1946 on behalf of the All India Scheduled Caste Federation (AISCF) in order to guarantee civil and political rights for them in free India.

The limited effect of such work within the system led Ambedkar to increasingly work outside of it as well. He began initiating mass protest movements, such as the Mahad Water Tank Movement (1927) and the Kalaram Temple Entry Movement (1934). He consciously created conditions for the illiterate people around him to become aware of the reality of the caste system. These conditions included writing books addressing various issues, editing several newspapers, launching political parties, and forming social organizations.

After clashing with Gandhi on the issue of the political empowerment of untouchables, Ambedkar realized the futility of changing the minds of the high caste Hindus. Although Gandhi outwardly showed his commitment to the untouchables, his real purpose appears to have been political. He wanted to ensure numerical power to Hindus (i.e. high-caste Hindus) vis-à-vis Muslims. These events led Ambedkar to renounce the systemic container of Hinduism. From May 30–31, 1936, at Dadar in Mumbai, he delivered a lengthy speech entitled "What Way Liberty?" In this historic speech, he detailed the path leading towards liberty and gave a call to conversion. He did not make it clear as to which religion he was going to convert. However, at the end of this speech, he gave a clarion call to his people, which echoed the teaching of the Buddha, to "be your own light and refuge".

While thinking over what message should I give you on this occasion, I recollected the message given by the Lord Buddha to his Bhikkhu Sangha just before his *mahāparinibbāna* and which has been quoted in *Mahāparinibbāna Sutta*:

"Once the Bhagwan, after having recovered from illness, was resting on a seat under a tree and his disciple Venerable Ananda went to the Buddha. Having saluted, he sat beside him and said, 'I have seen the Lord in illness as well as in happiness. But from the present illness of the Lord, my body has become heavy like lead; my mind is not is peace. I cannot concentrate on the Dhamma, but I feel consolation and satisfaction that the Lord will not attain the *parinibbāna* until a message is given to the Sangha.'"

"Then the Lord replied, 'Ananda! What does the Sangha expect from me? Ananda, I have preached the Dhamma with an open heart, without concealing anything. The Tathāgata has not kept anything concealed as some other teachers do. So Ananda, what more can the Tathāgata tell the Bhikkhu Sangha? So Ananda, be self illuminating like the sun. Do not be dependent for light like the Earth. Believe in yourself; do not be dependent on others. Be truthful. Always take refuge in the truth and do not surrender to anyone.'"

I also take refuge in the words of the Buddha to be your own guide. Take refuge in your own reason. Do not listen to the advice of others. Do not succumb to others. Be truthful and take refuge in the truth. Never surrender to anything. *If you keep*

in mind this message of Lord Buddha at this juncture, I am sure, your decision will
not be wrong. (*BAWS* XVII, 147)

In order to realize an awakened society, Ambedkar saw that an inner
revolution among his people needed to take place in tandem with the social
and political work of gaining equal rights for untouchables. This internal
revolution he found in the act of conversion from the dependency and
subservience of being an untouchable in Hinduism to the independence and
empowerment of a Buddhist identity and complete development as a human
being. In this way, Ambedkar began to develop a vision for his people in order to
make them realize the importance of the Buddha Dharma. He saw that religious
reformation is often a precursor to political emancipation. In his *Annihilation
of Caste*, he cited such examples in the revolutions of Protestant Europe, the
first Mauryan ruler Chandragupta, and the contemporary revolution of Guru
Nanak and the Sikhs in Punjab. He concluded that the emancipation of the
mind is a necessary preliminary for the political emancipation of the people.

Ambedkar's Vision of Dharma and Practice

❖ Vision of Dharma

Dharma is the perfection of life: In *The Buddha and His Dhamma*, Ambedkar
describes the path of the bodhisattva and presents the sublime teaching
of non-attachment through quotes from the dialogue between the Buddha
and Subhuti in the *Diamond Sutra*. In this sutra, the six perfections (*pāramī*) of
giving, morality, patience, energy, meditation, and wisdom are taught as
not only practices for the individual but also ones to instigate others to do.

Dharma is to live in nirvana: Ambedkar strongly affirmed the nature of
nirvana as experienced here in this life and in this world. He wrote that
the Buddha clearly rejected notions of nirvana held by other schools of
thought at the time. Specifically, the Buddha saw that the Brahmanistic and
Upanishadic notions of the salvation of a soul made nirvana into a goal
achieved after death. Ambedkar quotes the famous Fire Sermon (*Ādittapariyāya
Sutta*, S.iv.19) to show how the Buddha's notion of the extinction of the passions,

and not physical death, made nirvana into a much more practical this-worldly goal. Nirvana or "awakened vision" tells one of the difficulties in the realization of the Eightfold Path. The chief of these difficulties are the five fetters (saṃyojana) or five underlying tendencies (anusaya). The third fetter of dependence on the efficacy of rites and ceremonies is especially important in this context. Ambedkar felt that no good resolutions, however firm, will lead to anything unless we shed ritualism. By ritualism, he meant the belief that outward acts associated with priestly power and holy ceremony can afford one assistance of some kind. It is only when we have overcome our ties to salvific ritual that humans can be said to have fairly entered the stream of liberation and have a chance to sooner or later win victory.

Dharma is karma—the instrument of moral order: Ambedkar clearly stated that the moral order of the world (kammaniyāma) does not depend on a creator God or any other gods. The moral order may be good or bad but this depends on humans and nothing else. The Buddha discovered that the world (loka) revolves due to karma. There are three worlds: the sensual world, the form-ish world, and the formless world. The state of nirvana, where the law of karma is not operative, is a way of being and acting beyond these worlds. However, the world in which most of us live most of the time is the world of sensual pleasures. The mental states in the sensual world are destructive because enormous strife and suffering come about due to competition for sensual desires. This world is made up of sounds, forms, colors, tastes, tactile objects, ideas, concepts, etc. Sometimes, the ideas or concepts are just imposed by society, such as caste or graded inequality in India.

Caste as a consciousness comes into being due to social practices and conventions and is wrong view (micchā diṭṭhi). It is a mental and social conditioning whereby the individual is crushed. Individuals have little or no choice. Clearly, this goes against the Buddha's teaching of karma and the power of intention (cetanā). The intention or mental state behind an action indicates its moral quality and action per se does not determine the nature of karma. As mental states precede actions by body and speech, positive mental states lead to positive actions of body and speech and negative mental states lead to negative actions of body and speech. Thus, the law of karma emphasizes personal responsibility and positive action, not passivity to harmful social conventions. In this way, it clearly does not support the idea that birth in a lower caste is the deserved result of one's unwholesome past actions.

❖ Practice—purification of mind, body, and speech by meditation and morality

Thus Ambedkar made it explicit that purification of mind, body, and speech is the dharma. Ambedkar emphasized the training of the mind in meditation, as did the Buddha, for developing intention or thought, which leads to right states of consciousness. He paraphrases the *Sallekha Sutta* (M.i.40) as follows:

> You are to expunge by resolving that, though others may be harmful, you will be harmless.
>
> That though others may kill, you will never kill.
>
> That though others may steal, you will not.
>
> That though others may not lead the higher life, you will.
>
> That though others may lie, traduce, denounce, or prattle, you will not.
>
> That though others may be covetous, you will covet not.
>
> That though others may be malignant, you will not be malignant.
>
> That though others may be given over to wrong views, wrong aims, wrong speech, wrong actions, and wrong concentration, you must follow (the Noble Eightfold Path in) right outlook, right aims, right speech, right action, right mode of livelihood, right effort, right mindfulness, and right concentration.
>
> That though others are wrong about the truth and wrong about deliverance, you will be right about truth and right about deliverance.
>
> That though others may be possessed by sloth and torpor, you will free your-selves there from.
>
> That though others may be puffed up, you will be humble-minded.
>
> That though others may be perplexed by doubts, you will be free from them.
>
> That though others may harbor wrath, malevolence, envy, jealousy, niggard-liness, avarice, hypocrisy, deceit, imperviousness, arrogance, forwardness, association with bad friends, slackness, unbelief, shamelessness, unscrupu-

lousness, lack of instruction, inertness, bewilderment, and unwisdom, you
will be the reverse of all these things.

That though others may clutch at and hug the temporal nor loose their hold
thereon, you will clutch and hug the things that are not temporal, and will
ensue renunciation.

I say it is the development of thought which is so efficacious for right states of
consciousness, not to speak of act and speech. And therefore, Cunda, there
must be developed the thought to all the foregoing resolves I have detailed.
(BAWS XI, 285–286)

This sutta can be interpreted as one's own resolve to transform oneself
into a buddha even when the world around is steeped with various vices.

* Morality and Ethics (*sīla*)—the bridge between the individual and the
social or the foundation of a just society

The highest realization in Buddhism is the emancipation of the mind,
which Ambedkar also understood as liberty. The antithesis of liberty is
slavery. According to the Buddha, there are two kinds of slavery: inner and
outer. In a well-known encounter, a deity is said to have asked the Buddha:

A tangle inside, a tangle outside,
This generation is entangled in a tangle.
I ask you this, O Gotama,
Who can disentangle this tangle?

The Buddha replied:

A man established on virtue, wise,
Developing the mind and wisdom,
A bhikkhu ardent and discreet:
He can disentangle this tangle. (*Saṁyutta Nikāya* 2000, 101, S.i.13)

Liberty is freedom from any control and, in return, demands no will to control others. The ethics of Buddhism ensures this freedom from control. Therefore, *sīla* is the foundation of a just society. It is universal and not marked with sectarian feeling. If it does, it will only protect the "group interest" and according to Ambedkar, will become anti-social. *Sīla* is right or ethical behavior by one person towards another. Thus, Ambedkar wrote that religion is personal, while dharma as the practice of *sīla* is interpersonal. Therefore, society cannot do without dharma or righteousness.

In this way, Ambedkar clearly shows an understanding of the difference between the type of morality belonging to personal power and threat and the type belonging to collective power and personal responsibility. He makes the observation that the former type belongs to religion, which is concerned with the relation between humans and God. This type of morality helps to maintain peace and order and "is attached and detached as the occasion requires" to protect the interests of a particular group (Sangharakshita 1986, 156). In the latter understanding of morality, Ambedkar speaks not of religion but of dharma. "Morality is Dhamma, and Dhamma is Morality. Morality and Dhamma arise from the direct necessity for man to love man. It is not to please God that man has to be moral. It is for his own good that man has to love man" (Sangharakshita 1986, 156).

This dharma is the universal morality that protects the weak from the strong and that safeguards the growth of the individual. It gives common models, standards, and rules. Finally, it ensures that liberty and equality can be established. "The only remedy lies in making fraternity universally effective. What is fraternity? It is nothing but another name for the brotherhood of men that is another name for morality. This is why the Buddha preached that dharma is morality, and as dharma is sacred so is morality (Sangharakshita 1986, 157).

This morality, however, is not just a set of ideals, but part of the threefold training of the mind in morality, concentration, and wisdom. For Ambedkar, training in *sīla* is formalized for non-monastics in the practice of the five basic precepts (*pañcasīla*) and the "taking of refuge" in a ceremony called *dīkṣa*. In the institutionalization of the *dīkṣa* ceremony for untouchables converting to Buddhism, Ambedkar included taking the five precepts as well as twenty-two additional vows. He made this ceremony of taking refuge central to his vision of a new Buddhist identity for the lay Buddhist movement he led among untouchables. He recognized the fundamental need of a very conscious statement of Buddhist identity for his community as it renounced Hinduism and embraced Buddhism. In order to face the oppressive system of caste society in India, this new Buddhist identity could not be fuzzy or passive, especially since there was no monastic order to lead and defend the community. He also felt a strong lay community was imperative to reestablishing a proper ordained community in India, since he saw the existing monastic order, especially in Theravada countries, as corrupt (Sangharakshita 1986, 123).

AMBEDKAR'S MOVEMENT FOR JUSTICE

Just Society through a Model Society (sangha) of Just People

The vision of an awakened society led the Buddha to set in motion the wheel of the dharma. The Buddha set in motion the wheel of the dharma when he awakened five disciples in Sarnath. According to Ambedkar, the Buddha organized the bhikkhu Sangha to make this just society a living reality and to set a model for the society to imitate.

> But the blessed Lord also knew that merely preaching the Dhamma to the common man would not result in the creation of that ideal society based on righteousness. An ideal must be practical and must be shown to be practicable. Then and then only could people strive after it and realize it. To create this striving, it is necessary to have a picture of a society working on the basis of the ideal and thereby proving to the common man that the ideal was not impracticable but on the other hand realizable. The Sangha is a model of a society realizing the Dhamma preached by the blessed Lord. (*BAWS* XI, 434)

According to Ambedkar, the code of the bhikkhu, the *pāṭimokkha*, was formulated to make the Sangha an ideal society. Thus, the bhikkhu must always be seen as subordinate to and enfolded into the sangha or ideal society. The training of a bhikkhu/bhikkhuni is aimed at making him/her a perfect citizen of the ideal society. In another sense, the rules of the monastic are not meant for making a perfect being, but for creating a servant of the society who will be committed to ending suffering and to living the ideals of liberty, equality, and fraternity. The monastic should not be indifferent to the suffering of lay people. S/he must fight for establishing an ideal society.

Since the Buddha established the sangha in order to lay the foundation of an awakened society, he preached his dharma *to all* without distinction, to monastic as well as to lay people. Ambedkar felt there was no difference between a monastic and a lay person as far as the practice of the dharma goes. The distinction, however, is in the degree of involvement in the preaching and propagating of the dharma, essentially of time and commitment. Monastics are the full-timers, having neither the worldly responsibilities of marriage nor private property. On the other hand, lay persons are the part-timers, ensconced in worldly duties. As the full-timers have no private property, the part-timers have had to support them with *dāna*. The part-timers have mainly given alms, and provided abodes and robes to the full-timers. The Buddha put in place these dependencies, which are also freedoms, as a check and balance mechanism to ensure that the full-timers should not betray the mission. The part-timers could complain to the larger sangha about the misconduct of any of the full-timers. Thus, the bond of alms between monastic and lay person was instrumental in the successful spread of the dharma.

However, this bond of alms was taken to extremes when the lay emperor Ashoka supported and interfered in the matters of Sangha. The history of the disappearance of Buddhism in India is the history of the gradual weakening of this bond of alms and the disappearance of the nucleus of the Buddhist society, the monastic Sangha. How could any teaching survive with the destruction of its organization and propaganda base? Buddhism eventually disappeared, because although the lay sangha strove hard, they could not give their best energies and could not organize themselves effectively.

Despite his often strong criticisms, Ambedkar did not wish to do away with the monastic Sangha. On the contrary, he saw the Sangha as having an important role in the awakened society. His ideal society was the Buddhist Sangha. However, here is a departure from the tradition. He wanted lay persons to be part and parcel of the new Sangha. With this basic view in mind, Ambedkar expressed his views on the reconstruction of the Sangha to suit modern society.

Firstly, he felt that the absence of a dhamma *dīkṣa* for lay followers was a grave omission. Throughout history, the bhikkhus have been initiated and organized but the lay sangha has not. Except for a few insignificant exceptions, the dharma is common to both. Ambedkar wanted to correct this anomaly and so accepted the challenge to initiate his own lay followers in the dharma. He also suggested the creation of lay preachers who could go about and preach the Buddha's Dharma among the people and look after the new converts to guide their practice, rather than creating newly ordained monastics or depending on foreign monastics for this purpose. He felt these lay preachers must be paid and that they could be married. He wanted to restructure the Sangha so as to fit it in the modern society. Unfortunately, Ambedkar did not live long enough to build a movement to actualize this new understanding of the role of monastics in an awakened society.

However, the British monk Sangharakshita, who met Ambedkar thrice and helped lead the neo-Buddhist movement in India after his death, did develop Ambedkar's basic concept further. He has integrated Ambedkar's criticisms of the bhikkhu Sangha in the creation of his new orders, the British-based Friends of the Western Buddhist Order (FWBO) and the Indian-based Trailokya Bauddha Mahasangha (TBM) order nurtured by Dhammachari Lokamitra. In the spirit of Ambedkar's notion of married lay preachers who would spread the Buddha dharma about India, Sangharakshita has developed an intermediate form of Buddhist practitioner, called a *dharmachari/charini* or "dharma-farer," which dissolves the dichotomy between lay and monastic. Sangharakshita's order has sought to intensify serious training for those interested while not creating a distinction of superiority between those who choose less arduous courses. This flexibility of practice models has significantly allowed those with a high level of training to maintain a lay appearance, thereby facilitating involvement in social activities. The uniting factor of the different levels of practice is the commitment to social service within the community and society. Sangharakshita's vision is one of a decentralized community of people sharing the same spiritual commitment without the need for ecclesiastical structure (Sponberg 1996, 90).

Ambedkar also had other concrete ideas for the creation of an awakened society based on the Buddha Dharma. He had planned to establish a Buddhism and Religions Seminary where persons who wished to become preachers could be taught Buddhism and trained in the comparative study of other religions. He suggested the introduction of congregational worship in the Buddhist temple every Sunday followed by a sermon. *The Buddha and His Dhamma*, itself, was an attempt to create a "Buddhist Bible"—a single volume work that could be a constant companion of the convert. Like the lay preacher, the Buddhist Bible represents a middle way intended to bridge the gap between the lofty ideals of monastic practice and learning and the daily needs of the larger lay sangha.

Ambedkar and the Future of His Movement

Ambedkar made many provisions to create the dharma as a living force in India. Besides his emphasis on the dharma, which he wanted to make the heart of his movement, he knew the importance of social awakening and politics. After his conversion, he planned to constitute a political party, The Republican Party of India. The aim was to ensure the social, political, and economic justice enshrined in the preamble of the constitution of India in order to create an ideal society. Society, according to Ambedkar, cannot do without dharma nor without just government.

> Society has to choose one of the three alternatives: Society may choose not to have any Dhamma as an instrument of government. For Dhamma is nothing if it is not an instrument of government. This means society chooses the road

to anarchy. Secondly, society may choose the police, i.e., dictatorship as an instrument of government. Thirdly, society may choose Dhamma plus the magistrate wherever people fail to observe the Dhamma. In anarchy and dictatorship liberty is lost. Only in the third liberty survives. (*BAWS* XI, 316–317)

According to Ambedkar, the norm or the criterion for judging right and wrong in modern society is justice. Justice is ensured when the society is based on the principles of liberty, equality, and fraternity. The system of grading people as in the caste system will always lead to injustice. Ambedkar saw no solution in communism or capitalism, the two political currents dominant during his day. He found a solution in Buddhism. He said:

> Man must grow materially as well as spiritually. Society has been aiming to lay a new foundation that was summarized by the French Revolution in three words: fraternity, liberty, and equality. The French Revolution was welcomed because of this slogan. It failed to produce equality. We welcome the Russian Revolution, because it aims to produce equality. But it cannot be too much emphasized that in producing equality in society one cannot afford to sacrifice fraternity or liberty. Equality will be of no value without fraternity or liberty. It seems that the three (liberty, equality, and fraternity) can coexist *only if* one follows the way of the Buddha. (*BAWS* III, 462, italics and bracket added)

He saw the ideal society as one full of channels for conveying change taking place in one part to other parts. In an ideal society, he remarked, there should be many interests, consciously communicated and shared. There should be varied and free points of contact with other modes of association. In other words, there must be social endosmosis. This is fraternity, which is only another name for democracy. Democracy is not merely a form of government. It is primarily a mode of associated living, of conjoint communicated experience. It is essentially an attitude of respect and reverence towards fellow beings. Finally, this reconstruction of the world is possible through dharma. Dharma is essentially and fundamentally social. In this way, his ideal society is based on the universality of dharma, which consists of liberty, equality, and fraternity. In the All India Radio broadcast of his speech on October 3, 1954, Ambedkar clarified the usage of these terms: "Positively, my social philosophy may be said to be enshrined in three words: Liberty, Equality, and Fraternity. Let no one, however, say that I have borrowed my philosophy from the French Revolution. I have not. My philosophy has roots in religion and not in political science. I have derived them from the teachings of my master, the Buddha" (*BAWS* XVII, 150).

The sad part of Ambedkar's movement, however, has been the lack of recognition in the entire movement of the role of dharma (the practice of liberty, equality, and fraternity). As a result of this, the social organizations and political parties based on Ambedkar face the problems of caste and conflict. They fall asunder due to organizational problems. The success of Ambedkar's movement lies not just in education and agitation but in how effectively his followers organize themselves; that is to say how they use fraternity as a principle to make fraternity universal. Ambedkar wanted to establish universal fraternity that was not to be based on sectarian attitudes and caste prejudices. He wrote:

There are two forces prevalent in society: individualism and fraternity. Individualism is ever present. Every individual is ever asking "I and my neighbors, are we all brothers, are we even fiftieth cousins, am I their keeper, why should I do right by them?" and under the pressure of his own particular interests acting as though he was an end to himself, thereby developing a non-social and even an anti-social self.

Fraternity is a force of opposite character. Fraternity is another name for fellow feeling. It consists in a sentiment which leads an individual to identify himself with the good of others whereby "the good of others becomes to him a thing naturally and necessarily to be attended to like any of the physical conditions of our existence." It is because of this sentiment of fraternity that the individual does not "bring himself to think of the rest of his fellow creatures as struggling rivals with him for the means of happiness, whom he must desire to see defeated in their object in order that he may succeed in his own."

Individualism would produce anarchy. It is only fraternity, which prevents it and helps to sustain the moral order among men. Of this there can be no doubt. (*BAWS* III, 44)

There are many offshoots of the political party of which Ambedkar himself planned and wrote a constitution. Their main motivation is anti-Brahmanism and anti-caste. However, most of them are trapped in their own prisons of caste or the interests of their group, and therefore, have become anti-social. Dharma is the way to break the prison of caste and prejudices. Dharma is to extend fraternity both horizontally and vertically in the social structure, and hence, the dharma can help in overcoming caste identities.

In conclusion, the most unfortunate part of Ambedkar's movement was his untimely death. He died just after the great conversion movement in 1956. Most of the ideas in his mind died with him. However, he left enough material and blueprints for his millions of followers to follow and organize themselves as an ideal society to set up a model for the world. The reentry of Buddhism to India after a gap of hundreds of years has been very dramatic. Buddhism has come back as a mass movement among the untouchables.

The success of the Buddhist movement depends on the organization of a sangha of full-timers and part-timers. This sangha must transcend caste and should not get trapped in one caste or group. It needs to integrate with the larger Indian society by breaking isolation. This sangha should exemplify liberty, equality, and fraternity to live and act in harmony within itself. There is a necessity for trained *dhammasevak* (servants of the dharma). The *dhammasevak* must have at the same time a strong sense of history and should be ready to go beyond the great wall of caste. The new servants of the dharma must passionately fight for practicing and propagating liberty, equality, and fraternity. In short, dharma can re-ethicize Indian society, but it depends on how the followers of Ambedkar understand and situate the dharma in the various movements organized under his name and philosophy.

References

Aloysius, G. 2004. "Transcendence in Modern Tamil Buddhism: A Note on the Liberative in Popular Religious Perceptions." In *Reconstructing the World: B. R. Ambedkar and Buddhism in India*. Edited by Surendra Jondhale and Johannes Beltz. New Delhi: Oxford University Press.

Ambedkar, Bhimrao Ramji. *Dr. Babasaheb Ambedkar Writing and Speeches [BAWS]*. Vol. I–XVIII. Mumbai: Education Department, Government of Maharastra.

Brazier, David. 2001. *The New Buddhism*. London: Constable Robinson.

Chakravarti, Uma. 1987. *The Social Dimensions of Early Buddhism*. New Delhi: Oxford University Press.

The Connected Discourses of the Buddha: A New Translation of the Saṃyutta Nikāya. 2000. Translated by Bhikkhu Bodhi. Boston: Wisdom Publications.

Nanda, Meera. 2002. *Breaking the Spell of Dharma and Other Essays*. New Delhi: Three Essays Press.

Sangharakshita. 1986. *Ambedkar and Buddhism*. Glasgow: Windhorse Publications.

Sponberg, Alan. 1996. "TBMSG: A Dhamma Revolution in Contemporary India." In *Engaged Buddhism: Buddhist Liberation Movements in Asia*. Edited by Christopher S. Queen and Sallie B. King. Albany, NY: State University of New York Press.

Rhys Davids, T. W. 1903. *Buddhist India*. London: T. Fisher Unwin.

THE "POSITIVE DISINTEGRATION" OF BUDDHISM: REFORMATION AND DEFORMATION IN THE SRI LANKAN SANGHA

JONATHAN S. WATTS

INTRODUCTION

Buddhists often pride themselves, and attempt to distinguish themselves from the monotheistic Abrahamic traditions of the West, for not having a history of religious holy wars based in fundamentalist understandings of doctrine. However, it is hard to ignore the political violence and ethnic war in Sri Lanka of which Sinhala bhikkhus have been a driving ideological and cultural force. Apart from Sri Lanka, we can find numerous examples in Buddhism of the Sangha, the state, and the dominant ethnicity being fused into a force for power and control over diverse populations.

An investigation into the Buddha's teachings *within the context* of the social, political, and economic conditions of his time as well as the achievements of Ashoka, the great Buddhist monarch who united India under one rule, show something different: the creation of a society in which religious, economic, and political power were kept in a steady state of "flux-balance" in which "dharmic" civilizational ethics bound people together in communities of reciprocity. Of course, one of the testaments of history is that the most ideal models often erode with time, and so did these, as Buddhism spread and lost its differentiation from state and economic structures.

This chapter attempts to make sense of the complex trajectories of Buddhist history in India and Sri Lanka so that we can come to understand how Buddhism in Sri Lanka has become a source for violent ethno-nationalism and to decipher alternative movements that are trying to rebuild the Buddha's and the Ashokan ideal of a civilizational dharma.

SOCIETY IN BALANCE: THE "POSITIVE DISINTEGRATION" OF NOT-SELF (*ANATTĀ*) AND ETHICS (*SĪLA*)

The time of the Buddha (563–483 BC) was one of great change and dynamism in the upper and middle reaches of the Ganges valley in northeast India. The advent of the Iron Age in the eighth century BC spurred a whole series of revolutions in human lifestyle and social organization, principally in the transformation of agricultural methods to open vast tracts of land for surplus production. The towns and cities mentioned in the Buddha's discourses, such as Savatthi, Vesali, Patna, and Rajgir, all lay on the very dynamic and bustling trade route to the northwest reaching up into present-day Pakistan and Afghanistan and linking up with the Silk Road. They also connected to trade routes going south into the hinterland towards modern-day Mumbai. The factor that held people together along these trade routes from the east to the northwest and to the southwest was not common ritual or language but "a whole aggregate of common needs satisfied by reciprocal exchange" (Kosambi 1969, 120).

What was emerging here was a *civilizational* process, in that numerous peoples of different origins and cultural practices were being bonded together to create *qualitatively* new economic, political, cultural, and, to be certain, religious forms. From the political standpoint, there was an increasing need for a single state that to the west could maintain and develop trade routes bypassing tribal custom and rule while still collecting regular taxes, and to the east could exploit natural resources (specifically iron and copper ores) while conquering and assimilating the peoples who lived on this frontier. This need fueled the consolidation of the sixteen principal territories of the seventh century into two tribal assembly republics (Licchavi and Vajji) and two absolute monarchies (Kosala and Magadha) by the end of the sixth century.

Chakravarti notes that, "In this movement towards expansion and consolidation, the keynote was politics unhampered by moral restraint" (Chakravarti 1987, 8). The stakes were high and the riches of conquest certain with vast natural resources to the east and hungry consumer markets to the west. The Magadhan and Kosalan royal families, with relatively lower-caste backgrounds and no tribal assemblies to restrain them, had perfect profiles to engage in the ruthless statesmanship that was required to break down the tribal republics and consolidate power over the region. Their exploits are found all over the Pali *Tipiṭaka*; such as King Vidudabha of Kosala massacring the Buddha's own people, the Shakyans, in part out of revenge for being cheated by the Shakyans who regarded him of unfit birth for marriage with one of their princesses and gave him instead a low-caste wife (Dh.A.i.346–49, 357–61; J. i.133); and the infamous Ajatasatru of Maghada who not only imprisoned his parents and killed his father (*Sāmaññaphala Sutta*, D.i.85) but abused the Buddha's consultation and sent a Brahmin minister to infiltrate and destroy the Licchavi Republic from within (*Mahāparinibbāna Sutta,* D.ii.74).

Unfortunately, the new cultural and spiritual movement of the age, of which the Buddha was a principal force, had not caught up with the practice of state-craft. Ajatasatru eventually won the day against the Kosalans, and Magadha became the seat of the first great Indian empire known as the Mauryan dynasty. It is this form of statecraft that slowly became codified over the next two hundred years in the well-known Machiavellian political text, the *Arthaśāstra*, written by a Brahmin minister of Chandragupta Maurya at the end of the fourth century. *Arthaśāstra*, "the science of material gain," meant the means used to attain the ends needed no justification and held no pretense to morality or altruism (Kosambi 1969, 142). In contrast to the civilizational ethics of the Buddha that espoused debate and democracy, the *Arthaśāstra*'s "advice on state policy could be effective only if kept secret, reserved for a chosen few" (Kosambi 1969, 120–21).

While the political landscape was becoming less diverse with the swallow-ing up of tribal republics by absolute monarchies and the final establishment of a single state in the Mauryan Empire, the economic and cultural land-scapes were complexifying and flowering into new, qualitatively different levels. The religious parallel to this political consolidation would have been a new, single, exclusive religion. However, in this dynamic new environ-ment, that would have only been possible with an immense use of force. Vedic Brahmanism could not offer such a unifying religious force, because it had become an increasingly ill-suited and obsolete spirituality to the new classes of property-owning, agrarian farmers and urban-based merchants (*setthi*). The two new classes found the requisitioning of cattle and other animals without payment for Vedic sacrifices (*yajña*) an intolerable waste (Kosambi 1969, 102).

Vedic Brahmanism with its secret knowledges and its mythic legitimization of class duties offered one enticing social model to match the political model of the *Arthaśāstra*. However, the economic dynamics demanded a social ethic that would free people to engage in a process of reciprocal exchange across geographical, ethnic, and class boundaries. Thus, into this new society emerged multifarious new spiritualities, the most prominent to us now being the Ajivikas, the Jains, and, of course, the Buddhists. To this new age, the Buddha offered a new set of cosmopolitan and universal ethics that spoke out against the ritualism and waste of Vedic sacrifice (*yajña*) as well as the mythic legitimization of caste and patriarchy; addressed the issues of poverty, resource management, and good governance while embodying these ideals in the maintenance of his own religious community; and communicated this message in an everyday language and plain style without mysticism or lengthy speculation. As Kosambi concludes, "To have propounded it at a time of Vedic *yajña* to a society that had just begun to conquer primeval jungle was an intellectual achievement of the highest order" (Kosambi 1969, 113).

As we can see in other chapters in this volume, the Buddha challenged aspects of Brahmanism that had significant impact on the social order. Principally, the teaching of not-self (*anattā*) exposes the ethical pitfalls of a one-way causality derived from a creator God or eternal Self. When causality, as the flow of power or energy, is understood as emanating from an immutable and unconditioned centralized force, like a creator God, there is a natural tendency to recreate social relationships and organizations based on this worldview, such as the fourfold caste system. Such social relationships are not only centralized but also hierarchical and prone to autocratic forms of power. The tribal republics of the Buddha's native region with their less-stratified, two-class system are known to have explicitly rejected the Vedic beliefs, customs, and social practices that were predominant in the Kuru Pancala region to the west (Swaris 2008, 91). The Buddha's modeling of the monastic Sangha's governing procedures along the lines of the congresses of these republics shows that he not only rejected Vedic beliefs of a creator God or eternal Self but also rejected the social order that evolved out of these beliefs. The struggle between the Brahmin's *dharma* of ritualized karmic action and the Buddha's *dhamma* of ethical karmic action was also a battle between two types of social order—one based on autocratic feudalism and the other based on egalitarian democracy.

On the other hand, certain aspects of the Buddha's monasticism represented important changes in the ascetic *samaṇa* culture of his day, which for centuries had consisted largely of small, loosely organized bands of wanderers. For example, creating a monastic order with well-defined rules not only for internal conduct but also for relating to non-monastics was a significant new development (Chakravarti 1987, 54; Seneviratne 1987, 41). The Buddha's acceptance of land from wealthy patrons, upon which permanent dwellings could be built for the monastic order, also represents a middle way between the nomadic life of the traditional *samaṇa* and the Brahmin priests' use of donated lands for agricultural production and personal profit (Chakravarti 1987, 57). As the following chapter explains, the Buddha developed the fourfold sangha as a community of reciprocal exchange based on generosity (*dāna*) and intentional ethical action (*kamma*) that involved doing good (*puñña*). Certainly, the role of the Buddhist bhikkhu and bhikkhuni was to occupy a space apart from the normal social milieu. However, it appears that the Buddhist monastic order was a significant new cultural form, balancing differentiation from mundane life with integration into a larger social system of relationship. Like the developing economic order across the region that also emphasized reciprocal exchange, the Buddha's new religious order was a civilizational movement designed to bring people together in communion while honoring their diverse needs for individual cultivation.

Viewed in this way, we can understand this era as a time of "positive disintegration," which means a growth in diversification and differentiation (in this case, a greater variety of social classes and spiritual movements) as well as integration and consolidation (economic expansion and administrative and political consolidation). Although the era was full of conflict and the drive for power, new types of thinking (differentiation) as well as cooperation (integration) were also emerging. For the Buddha, it was a time of opportunity to select and integrate the best of the opposing currents of Vedism and *samaṇa* yoga while adding his own new insights to differentiate and develop a new spiritual culture. This new insight was not just his realization of not-self (*anattā*) but also the moral and ethical practices that *necessarily* flow out of this realization.

The radical interdependence of not-self that denies an original source of power means that Buddhist ethics cannot be authoritarian or rigid. In this way, we see the Buddha in various discourses repeatedly addressing moral issues in a fluid manner within the context of complex social relationships. He developed different sets of moral norms to guide the maintenance of various communities; for example, the guidelines for a moral king (*dhammarāja*) in the *Cakkavatti Sutta*, for the householder in the *Siṅgālovāda Sutta* (D.iii. 180–93), and for republican congresses in the *Mahāparinibbāna Sutta* (D.ii.74). This third discourse, which includes his final words, expands these republican principles by establishing similar ones for the maintenance of an ideal egalitarian community, the order of monks and nuns. Rather than legitimizing the use of power by some over others, all of these systems support the conditions for responsible communication through mutual respect, self-restraint, and the proper use of speech. When these conditions are met, all members of a community become potential centers of power able to create or prevent change (Brown 1990, 170). In this way, we see how *the way* of not-self is not a cosmic or philosophical claim but rather is indivisibly an ethical claim about how humans should relate to one another in familial, communal, and social contexts.

On a broader sociopolitical scale, the Buddha's ethical vision points to the need to both differentiate and integrate the religious and the secular, the personal and the social. The two spheres of church and state should exist as distinct but interconnected parts of a whole, rather than being rigidly kept apart as in modern secular society. This balance is articulated in the modern democratic ideal of the checks and balances between the judiciary, executive, and legislative branches. Such differentiation and integration creates a steady state or "flux-balance" when the proper tension between opposing forces is maintained (Macy 1991, 73), which I refer to as "positive disintegration." The Buddha appears to have had something like this in mind in the way he viewed the balance between the ruling elite (*khattiya*), economic elite (*seṭṭhi*), and religious elite (*brāhmaṇa*). During the Buddha's time, the *seṭṭhi* were the most prominent lay followers of the Buddha supporting the material needs of the monastic community. This close alliance obviously exerted some check on the power of the ruling elite. At the same time, however, many of the members of the monastic community came from these ruling families, as did the Buddha himself, while very few came from the *seṭṭhi* class (Chakravarti 1987, 134). Perhaps the potential for these former aristocrats to be drawn back into political affairs is another reason for the Buddha's strong prohibition of political involvement by the monastic community. Indeed, he makes it very clear that these two vocations are to be kept separate, and instructions are made to the monks to stay well clear of political matters (*Brahmajāla Sutta,* D.i.7–8). Thus the Buddha's separation of the religious from the political can be seen not as a retreat from society but rather as a result of his understanding of the need to maintain a healthy social system by differentiating the domains of church and state. His further balancing of religious and economic concerns fills out this picture of what we would consider today an ideal civil society that harmonizes church, state, and market through a variety of ethical relationships.

THE GROWTH OF MYTHIC DUALISM AND THE SHIFT IN ORGANIZATIONAL CULTURE

The Monastic Tension and the Myth of the Ascetic

As the monastic order continued to grow after the death of the Buddha, patronage from political and economic elites led to building great monasteries. During the apex of Buddhism as a civilizational force—from the time of Ashoka (r. 270-232 BC) to its demise in India in the ninth century, these monasteries played a significant role in the aforementioned transnational trade, being located in key areas along the trade routes and serving as rest stops, supply houses, banking houses, and venues to sell goods. Not only along the famed northwest trade route into Central Asia but also to the east coast and the deep south, we see the same process at work, namely "inland and overseas trade with civic development under the stimulus of large monastic foundations that accumulated as well as supplied capital" (Kosambi 1969, 191).

The seeds of the development of these great monasteries are found in innovations that took place during the Buddha's life. The first was the establishment of the rains retreat and the temporary halting of the monks' wandering lifestyle, which supported non-materialistic habits by preventing settled residences and places to store goods and materials. In part as a response to this need, both royal and business patrons came forward and offered the Buddha and the Sangha lands, such as the well-known Deer Park and Jetavana Grove. These lands became the basis for the great monasteries that developed after the Buddha's demise, and increasingly a new style of bhikkhu life emerged around them, one focused on a sedentary life of study called *gantha dhura*. The monks who attempted to maintain the original and more ascetic style of the wandering bhikkhu were called *vipassanā dhura*, "vocation of meditation." As we have seen in other matters, the Buddha had a keen sense for flux-balance, and the style of mendicancy that he developed contained unique aspects of material simplicity combined with social engagement. While the *gantha dhura* increasingly lost their foundations in a materially simple life of wandering, the *vipassanā dhura* lost their connection with community by removing themselves as much as possible from what they saw as the corrupting influences of social contact.

The result of this split in monastic vocation also had implications for the way the dharma was understood. As explained in my previous essay in this volume, the mistake of conceptualizing nirvana as an ontologically different state of being, instead of a deconstruction of ignorant consciousness, turned the realization of nirvana into something which Buddhists believed, and basically still believe, can only be accomplished in this life by the most advanced meditation masters, while everyone else must endure countless rebirths awaiting this ideal condition. This tendency was certainly present among the *gantha dhura*, who had become removed from the mendicant lifestyle and more focused on intellectual analysis of the dharma. Neither were the *vipassanā dhura* able to avoid the tendency completely. The Buddha clearly rejected Upanishadic and various *samaṇa* paths, because their focus on world denial and extreme asceticism reflected their understanding of liberation as something ultimately not available in this physical existence. The *vipassanā dhura* and much of Buddhist forest monasticism in general fell into this trap by considering that nirvana was best attained through massive amounts of secluded meditation.[1]

As the period of the Buddha, the perfectly self-enlightened one, and his enlightened disciples became more of an historical memory and the schism between the *vipassanā dhura* and the *gantha dhura* grew deeper, nirvana became an increasingly distant and mythical ideal, not only for the lay but also for the monastics themselves. I use the term "mythical" here not to diminish the genuine value of monastic practice but to highlight how the *image* of the ascetic bhikkhu was developed and used in the institutionalization of Buddhism. This myth developed in two important ways: as the sacred poverty of the bhikkhu and as the sacred other-worldliness of the bhikkhu.

The myth of the monk's sacred poverty provided the legitimizing basis for the massive patronage of these monasteries. This myth was based on the belief that the greater the spiritual power of the monk, as demonstrated in a lifestyle of ascetic poverty (*sīla*), the greater the merit (*puñña*) gained by supporting his material needs. The perpetuation and extension of this myth benefited both the political and religious elites. For those who controlled and accumulated wealth, it sacralized their own material prosperity, neces-

---

1. Buddhadasa Bhikkhu, a dedicated forest monk himself, writes in an essay entitled "Insight by the Nature Method" of the fallacies of reclusive meditation as the only means to nirvana. He says that, "The intensity of concentration that comes about naturally is usually sufficient and appropriate for introspection and insight, whereas the concentration resulting from organized training is usually excessive, more than can be made used of . . . In the *Tipiṭaka*, there are numerous references to people attaining naturally all states of Path and Fruit" with "no organized effort" and that "these people did not go into the forest and sit, assiduously practicing concentration on certain objects in the way described in later manuals" (Buddhadasa 1993, 81).

sary for them to be benefactors of the Sangha; and it obviously materially benefited the monastic institutions that grew from this benevolence. As this process developed and monasteries became more materially prosperous, the myth of monastic poverty became more mythical. This was one critical step in over-integrating the religious sphere with the political and especially the economic sphere.

The second myth that developed out of this ascetic ideal was the monk as a "world renouncer," unconcerned and uninvolved with mundane social matters, especially political ones. The Pali Canon includes several incidents in which the Buddha involved himself in mundane social affairs, such as the aforementioned consultation with King Ajatasatru about the conditions by which democratic republics remain prosperous (*Mahāparinibbāna Sutta*, D.ii.74) and the reconciliation of the conflict over water resources between the Shakyan and Koliyan republics (J.v.412–14). Yet we have also seen the Buddha's strict prohibitions on monks getting involved in political matters. Further, during the Buddha's time, we never see any of his royal benefactors trying to adjudicate on the internal matters of the Sangha, which were always ultimately left up to the decision of the Buddha. These boundaries would come under test in the first great Buddhist society under Ashoka who developed a deep and active interest in the welfare of the Sangha.

Ashoka is presented in the Theravadin tradition as the ideal lay follower of Buddhism. As a living example of the mythical Buddhist moral king (*dhammarāja*), he was said to be not only eminently righteous and a benefactor of the Sangha but also a protector and, in turn, a regulator of the Sangha. The seminal, as well as controversial, moment in this relationship concerns the 3rd Buddhist Council held at Pataliputra around 250 BC, roughly twenty years into Ashoka's reign. This council was initiated by Ashoka to settle a controversy over the *vinaya* among increasingly undisciplined groups of the monastic Sangha. The result of the council was a clarifying of the proper doctrine, a purging of the Sangha, and a number of missionaries dispatched to distant lands, including the first mission to Sri Lanka (Goyal 1987, 176–78).

This controversial account, which is not found in non-Theravadin sources,[2] has served as the seminal model for the relationship between the ideal Buddhist monarch (*dhammarāja*) and the Sangha in the development of Theravadin Buddhist states, first in Sri Lanka and then elsewhere through Southeast Asia (Chakravarti 1987, 175). In this model, the Sangha represents the ideal community and serves as a repository of society's moral values. Thus, it is in need of protection and regulation for the sake of the continued prosperity of the state. The integrity and purity of the Sangha depends on its differentiation from mundane society. It could not be sullied by external forces and the temptations of sensuality and power, and so who better to guard this sacred differentiation than the moral king (*dhammarāja*)? Thus, the ideal of religious and political differentiation was warped into a myth of monastic disassociation or world-renunciation that legitimized the state's control over the Sangha, and the Sangha's inevitable politicization (Seneviratne 1987). As with the myth of poverty, this conflation of political and religious spheres had a significant effect on the structure and culture of society.

Ashokan Statecraft as a Model of "Positive Disintegration"

What we can ascertain now from the Ashokan edicts and the advantages of modern scholarship and research is that Ashoka brought in an entirely new form of statecraft to the Mauryan Empire. As we saw earlier, Mauryan statecraft had been defined by the ruthless machinations of the *Arthaśāstra*. Ashoka was infamously a product of this system, his name meaning "without sorrow." An earlier moniker of his was Chanda-Ashoka ("Ashoka the murderer and heartless"), as he ruthlessly consolidated most of the Indian continent from present-day Pakistan, Afghanistan, and parts of Iran in the

---

2. The account is only found in Theravadin Pali texts, such as Buddhaghosa's commentary on the *vinaya* (*Samantapāsādikā*) and the Sri Lankan Pali chronicles, the *Dīpavaṃsa* and the *Mahāvaṃsa*, and not in the Pali *Tipiṭaka*, the Ashokan rock edicts, the texts of the northern Buddhist schools, or Chinese records of the period. However, Ashoka's Schism Edict, which orders the expulsion of those who divide the Sangha, does provide some undetailed evidence of this conflict within the Sangha (Goyal 1987, 176-182).

west, to present day Bangladesh and Assam in the east, and as far south as Mysore. However, his well-known remorse over this bloodshed and his subsequent conversion to Buddhism, or perhaps rather to a spiritual outlook based on dharma, marks the real penetration of the ethical philosophy of the Buddha and the sixth-century new religions into Indian society and culture.

In one of his edicts, the newly dubbed Dharma-Ashoka declares, "Whatever exertion I make, I strive only to discharge the debt I owe to all living creatures" (Kosambi 1969, 159). Based on this sentiment, Ashoka went about creating public works, such as hospitals and free medical care, and resting places and wells for travelers. He institutionalized frequent visits by the monarch to various regions to check on their conditions and a new class of minister called *dharma-mahāmātra*, literally "minister of morality," who was to examine complaints of law-abiding groups and their beliefs. Ashoka banned the *yajña* and fire (*agni*) sacrifices; attempted to replace rituals and superstitions (like using witchcraft to cure plagues) with ethical tenets; and developed environmental edicts to limit the wanton destruction of the forest and wilderness for commercial use. It indeed appears that this period was the final consolidation of the social revolution of the sixth century in which caste-ridden, tribal communities prone to the wasteful pursuits of warfare and animal sacrifice (*yajña*) were transformed into an ethics-first, transnational civilization focused on agriculture, trade, and administration (Kosambi 1969, 162).

Although Buddhists like to romanticize Ashoka as a great benefactor and protector of the Sangha, the records we do have suggest that he was something even more. Numerous rock edicts show an emphasis towards tolerance of those of other faiths as well as making donations to all legitimate communities, for example the Ajivikas, even though they had open conflicts with the Buddhists at this time (Thapar 1994, 14). Although Ashoka may have been most firmly based in a Buddhist sensibility, he seems to have understood it in terms of "Buddhism with a small 'b'" (Sivaraksa 1992); that is, he was more interested in propagating a civilizational ethic called "dharma" rather than a tribal or national one called "Buddhism." This is evidenced in the total lack of explicit Buddhist teachings and terms in edicts found in the non-Buddhist corners of the empire. For example, *dhamma* is translated as "good conduct" or "pious conduct" in the Aramaic and Greek inscriptions found in the northwest parts of the empire (Thapar 1994, 18, 23). Understanding first hand the exhausting and wasteful use of force in dominating remote regions, Ashoka came to embrace *dhamma vijaya*, "conquest through morality," as the way to integrate progressively more diverse groups of people into one civilization. As we have seen before in the Buddha's vision for a new kind of religious order, this follows the model of "positive disintegration" that maintains a steady-state of equilibrium through balancing integration and consolidation with differentiation and diversity.

The Buddha's and Ashoka's Lost Legacy: The Monastic Sangha's Integration with Power and Differentiation from the Lay

The legacy of Ashoka's dharmic statecraft did not have a lasting effect on Indian culture. Within fifty years of Ashoka's death, the Mauryan dynasty was brought down through the classic kind of intrigue of *Arthaśāstra* politics by the Sunga dynasty, which was much more closely aligned with Brahmanistic concepts of caste and divine kingship (*devarāja* or "god king"). Buddhism's great strength as a civilizational ethic to bond together disparate peoples was perhaps also its greatest weakness in terms of serving as a distinct and independent entity. In the polytheistic world of India, we can speak of the tensions between religions, specifically Brahmanism and Buddhism. However, it is anachronistic to speak of religious conflict in these times in the way we would today in India and elsewhere, in which a specific religion has become fused with a particular ethnicity with particular claims to territorial integrity. With Brahmins serving their role at the village level and on the edges of the frontier and the large Buddhist monasteries serving their role as a cosmopolitan force on the trade routes, these two systems could cohabitate until the seventh century in the north and the ninth century in the south (Kosambi 1969, 185).

Another important development that appears to have sown the seeds of Buddhism's decline in India was that the monastic order became too much the focus of Buddhist community life (Reynolds and Hallisey 1987). The *vinaya* and the fortnightly *uposathā*, at which all monastics gathered to review their observance of the *vinaya*, helped to create a systematic organization for the monastic Sangha that the lay sangha never developed. Lay Buddhism thus developed in reference to the monastics and always as a derivative or inferior form of practice. In the Schism Edict, it appears Ashoka had tried to institutionalize a stronger role for the lay sangha stipulating that both a lay person and a *dharma-mahāmātra* must attend and confirm the gatherings of the fortnightly *uposathā*. However, as Buddhism continued to grow through economic and political patronage, Buddhism as an institutional and organizational body became increasingly removed from the common people, with monks mostly confining themselves to scholarly pursuits in large monasteries.

The great monasteries began to decline when they became more of an economic drain than a stimulus, especially in the valuable metals they hoarded in statues and other religious paraphernalia. As the vast resources of metals in the east began to dry up and the international economy began to decline, these monasteries became inconvenient and inappropriate to increasingly localized trade (Kosambi 1969, 185–86). In this way, the great cities of the east declined rapidly, the richness of the civilizational culture faded, and the village became increasingly insular under the petty rule of the village Brahmin who now rarely took higher learning or practice.

By AD 600 the itinerant Buddhist monk covered in rags had been replaced by the fine-robed cloistered monk of the great universities like Nalanda. By this time, the Sangha had also become exclusivist barring aboriginals and other social dropouts from ordaining. As Kosambi further explains, "The civilizing and socializing work of the Buddha and Ashoka was never continued. The tightening of caste bonds and of caste exclusiveness threw away the possibility of finding some common denominator of justice and equity for all men regardless of class, profession, caste, and creed. As a concomitant, almost all Indian history is also obliterated" (Kosambi 1969, 173).

Evidence of the lost legacy of Ashoka is found in the supposedly devout Buddhist king, Harsha Siladitya (r. 605–655) of Kanauj, who fought incessantly for at least thirty years to gain control of most of India. Harsha eventually prevailed over Narendragupta-Sasanka of west Bengal who launched the first hard persecution of Buddhism and cut down the Bodhi tree at Gaya. In Harsha's final conquest, Nalanda was burnt to the ground amidst the carnage (Kosambi 1969, 178–80). By the time Muslim invaders destroyed the great Buddhist universities of Nalanda and Vikramasila around 1200 and dispersed the monastic order, it was not the great conquest of one religious nation-state over another but rather the final act of Buddhism's quiet withering away with the rise of India's feudal culture. The legacy of Ashoka's dharmic civilization not only was lost in time but also could not serve the needs of a society that had lapsed into insular, village-centered feudalism (Kosambi 1969, 196). What we will turn to now is how Ashoka's legacy was redefined for creating ethno-religious nation-states in the Theravada Buddhist world.

SRI LANKA: A CASE STUDY IN REFORMATION AND DEFORMATION

Paradigm Shift in the Pali Chronicles

The legacy of Ashoka's model of statecraft and dharmic civilization continued on foremost in the Pali writings of the Theravadin school, principally in the three Sinhala chronicles written by monks (the *Dīpavaṃsa*, the *Mahāvaṃsa*, and the *Cūlavaṃsa*) as well as Buddhaghosa's *Samantapāsādikā*, written during his lengthy stay in Sri Lanka. What we can see, especially in the chronicles, is the gradual shifting of the Ashokan legacy from one of "positive disintegration" and dharmic civilization to one of over-integration and religious nationalism.

The three chronicles are a form of religious quasi-history recounting the mythical visits of Shakyamuni to Sri Lanka; his quelling of the aboriginal peoples or in some accounts wrathful spirits called the Yakkhas; the establishment of Buddhism on the island by Ashoka's monastic son, Mahinda; the first Buddhist king, Devanampiyatissa; and the exploits of various

Sinhala Buddhist kings, specifically Dutthagamani, who is said to have united Sri Lanka under Sinhala rule after an Ashokan-like military campaign over the Tamils in the north.

The *Dīpavaṃsa* is the earliest of the three, having been compiled over the fourth century AD. Various aspects of the text show it to be in line with the concepts of dharmic civilization. Firstly, in the Buddha's encounter with the wild Yakkhas, they are moved with fear by a display of the Buddha's great spiritual powers, yet his reaction to this fear is compassion. He eventually manifests a new resplendent island for them to relocate to, which they do with great thanks and joy. The Buddha's method of conquest here is *dhamma vijaya*, conquest through morality, and it establishes the model for Devanampiyatissa who receives coronation from Ashoka directly. Together with Ashoka's son Mahinda,[3] he establishes Buddhism as the state religion and creates a reciprocal relationship with the monastic Sangha of patronage and protection, thereby reproducing the Sangha's mythic poverty and other-worldliness. While we can already see a slight tilt here away from dharmic civilization, Devanampiyatissa's reign (250–210 BC) is characterized as one of compassion, peace, and prosperity, in other words, *dhamma vijaya* (Clifford 1978, 41–42).

The *Mahāvaṃsa* that was compiled quite shortly after the *Dīpavaṃsa* in the early fifth century, however, shows a marked departure in such civilizational ethics. In the Buddha's encounter with the Yakkhas, their fear is emphasized, and they are exiled to a distant land through the coercive power of the Buddha. With this basis, the *Mahāvaṃsa* focuses on Dutthagamani more than Devanampiyatissa as the ideal Buddhist ruler. The key, paradigm-changing point in the story happens when Dutthagamani is struck with remorse in the same way as Ashoka at the end of his conquest. However, instead of having a spiritual awakening to dharma that leads to creating a society of pluralism and nonviolence as with Ashoka, Dutthagamani, already an ardent Buddhist, is counseled by eight *arahants* (fully enlightened monks) that his sins are

---

3. Both Devanampiyatissa's direct relationship with Ashoka and the existence of Mahinda as the bhikkhu son of Ashoka cannot be verified by accounts of Ashoka outside of these Pali records.

minor. They tell him that he has killed only one and a half human beings, for the rest were non-Buddhist and therefore "not more esteemed than beasts" (Clifford 1978, 43). In addition to this key episode, we learn that Dutthagamani was first counseled by his father to never fight with the Tamils; that the Tamil ruler was known to be just and morally upright yet simply held "wrong views;" and that Dutthagamani's principal focus for engagement was religious more than political. He is quoted as saying, "Not for the joy of sovereignty is this toil of mine, my striving has been ever to establish the doctrine of the Sambuddha" (Smith 1978a, 57). Finally, in the aftermath of establishing his Buddhist kingdom, Dutthagamani appears to receive greater praise for his ostentatious patronage of the Sangha through building numerous temples and stupas. In comparison to the *Dīpavaṃsa* in which monks restrain Ashoka in his patronage declaring that to allow a son or daughter to ordain in the Sangha is better than lavish gifts to the Sangha, the *Mahāvaṃsa* emphasizes more acts of ritual merit making (Smith 1978b, 86–87).

In this way, the *Mahāvaṃsa* makes a major departure away from Ashokan dharmic civilization and towards Buddhist ethnic nationalism. Even the well-known Sinhala Buddhist nationalist, Ven. Walpola Rahula, acknowledges that the *Mahāvaṃsa's* recounting of the eight *arahants'* forgiveness of Dutthagamani's bloodshed is "diametrically opposed to the teaching of the Buddha" (Rahula 1974, 22). Elsewhere, Rahula recounts that, "This was the beginning of nationalism among the Sinhalese ... organized under the new order of Buddhism. A kind of religio-nationalism, which almost amounted to fanaticism, roused the whole Sinhala people. A non-Buddhist was not regarded as a human being. Evidentially, all Sinhalese without exception were Buddhist" (Rahula 1956, 79).

In the *Mahāvaṃsa*, we begin to see aspects of a more utilitarian form of statecraft along the lines of the *Arthaśāstra*. This marks a critical shift from a Buddhist standpoint in that for even the monk-chroniclers the dharma was not sufficient for attaining the conditions of its own existence and had become more of a goal than a means (Clifford 1978, 43). This trend and the influence of the *Arthaśāstra* are clearly evident by the time of the compiling of the *Cūlavaṃsa* in the thirteenth century. The *Cūlavaṃsa* focuses on the

exploits of King Parakkamabahu (r. 1153–86), who was regarded as a model
Buddhist king along the lines of Dutthagamani, ushering in a great period of
prosperity for the nation and the Sangha. By the eight and ninth centuries,
it is well documented that Hindu influences had begun to permeate both
Sinhala Buddhism and Sinhala statecraft. Specifically, under the influences
of *Arthaśāstra* modes of statecraft, Parakkamabahu used deceit and murder
to consolidate his rule. The full paradigm shift away from Ashoka's is
evidenced in Parakkamabahu's evident lack of contrition and remorse for his
acts, to which even the righteous Dutthagamani was moved (Clifford 1978,
45). Thus, in parallel to Buddhism's decline as a civilizational force in India,
an emerging Buddhist nationalist ethic in Sri Lanka begins to turn back the
clock to the type of statecraft of Gangetic India in sixth century BC that the
Buddha had tried to reform.

The key point in the "positive disintegration" of the Buddha's and Ashoka's
models is the attention to diversification as well as integration. This attention
to diversification is a form of trust and letting go of attachment, hallmarks
of the Buddha's teaching. This is also something evidenced in Ashoka's
dhamma vijaya in which explicit Buddhist culture gives way to a nonsectarian
dharmic culture while ethics replaces force in political administration. In a
religio-ethnic nationalist model, however, fear instead of trust becomes the
underlying force, and integration at the cost of diversification is pursued. A
first sign of the over integration occurs in the monarch and executive power
becoming too close to the Sangha and the religious order through patronage
(i.e. myth of poverty) and protection (i.e. myth of otherworldliness).

Replication of Indian Over-integration

In Sri Lanka and other Southeast Asian Buddhist kingdoms, the influences of
Vedic and Hindu beliefs, specifically through the rising influence of Mahayana Buddhism, further conflated the political and religious by elevating the
king to the status of the Buddha, or more precisely, a bodhisattvic god. The
concept of the *devarāja* ("god king"), based on the Brahmanistic model of a
close association between political and religious elite, is clearly present in

the Angkor period of twelfth-century Cambodia. Through Angkor's influence, the distinction between *devarāja* and *dhammarāja* also became blurred in the development of the emerging state of Thailand next door. In Sri Lanka, the belief that the king had to be not only a Buddhist but also a bodhisattva became strong by about the tenth century (Rahula 1966, 62). For example, the Jetavanarama slab inscription of Mahinda IV (r. 956–72) decrees that according to the Buddha anyone who is not a bodhisattva will not be king of Sri Lanka (Kiribamune 1978, 111). This elevation of the king parallels that of the Buddha under the influence of the Mahayana to a more mythic figure who stands above all Hindu gods and is even depicted sitting upon the sacred seat of Brahma (Smith 1978b, 78–79).

In this way, the myth of the *devarāja* and the myth of monastic poverty and other-worldliness served to collapse the differentiations that the Buddha had envisioned among church, state, and market. In terms of the organization of the lay sangha and monastic Sangha, the same pattern of Buddhism's rise in India replicated itself in Sri Lanka. By the second century AD, monasteries had received large tracts of land that included large and small villages; had female and male servants or slaves for whom the monasteries received land to maintain; and received all the produce within a "revenue boundary" (*lābha-sīmā*) around the temple. By the tenth century, it is known that certain monks received special salaries, attendants, and other expenses for their maintenance and comfort, usually according to the rank and status of their families (Rahula 1974, 31–38). Monarchs in turn became directly involved in the Sangha, making appointments to high ranks, adjudicating conflicts over incumbencies, and regularly purging the order of rogue elements (Kemper 1978, 215). The increasing influence of Vedic culture also permeated the Sangha, which developed rules against the ordination of low-caste persons and eventually developed entire orders associated with single castes. Finally, the nature of practice gradually shifted as well. Monks who specifically acted as teachers received salaries that differed according to subject. *Abhidhamma* studies received the highest rate and *vinaya* studies the lowest. In this way, scholarly and intellectual studies became more valued over practice and meditation, the latter of which was considered appropriate for older and feeble-minded monks (Rahula 1974, 30).

As we saw in the case of India, the split in the Sangha between scholar monks (*gantha dhura*) and meditation monks (*vipassanā dhura*) led to mythifying various aspects that were central to the Buddha's teaching, such as the monastic's voluntary poverty and differentiation from society, as well as the realization of nirvana itself. With nirvana mythologized in the great attainments of the Buddha and his direct disciples, the practice of the average monk became less focused on realizing this seemingly unattainable goal and more on the ritualized practice of the monastic *vinaya* and the rote memorization of the suttas (Ray 1994). For the lay person, the goal of enlightenment became so distant that further *saṁsāra* in the form of more favorable rebirths became the main goal, which could be achieved through the fetishized merit making of ritualized generosity (*dāna*) in providing for the monastic's requisites. Rahula himself states that

> "Merit" (*puñña*) was the investment that ensured security in the next world. The Sangha is called *puññakkheta*, "merit-field," where one could sow seeds of merit and reap a good harvest in the next world . . . That was one reason why the kings and the people were so anxious about the unblemished purity of the Sangha . . . If the monks were bad, it would be harmful not only to the monks themselves personally, but also to the whole nation—not only in this world, but in the world to come as well. (Rahula 1956, 79)

The result of this development was that the Buddha's notion of karma as intentional (*cetanā*) ethical action transformed back into a Brahmanistic-like conception of ritual action by which to gain heaven and avoid hell. This organizational development fed into the larger socio-political one in which the monarch, instead of being "the People's Choice" (*Mahā-Sammata*) as in the *Aggañña Sutta* or an ethical ruler (*dhammarāja*) as in the *Cakkavatti Sutta*, became a divine ruler (*devarāja*) who was "a repository of merit linking the kingdom to the cosmos and possessing, both in his person and in his office, a relationship to the invisible world by which his body and his actions were made sacred" (*Search of Southeast Asia* 1987, 60). Transferring the mythical qualities of an enlightened bhikkhu onto the monarch helped to create various state-sanctifying rituals conflating the state, the religion, and the people.

The Nation-State: A Second Shift Away from the Ethic of "Positive Disintegration"

The Sinhala Pali chronicles made explicit efforts to conflate the Sinhala people, the Buddhist religion, and the island state of Sri Lanka into one indivisible unit. Contemporary interpretations of these chronicles have deepened this conflation on the basis of our own modern conceptualization of the nation-state that do not fit with the reality of the nature of states in those eras. For example, Dutthagamani's great crusade against the Tamils in the north looked nothing like the present conflict between the bounded nation-state of Sri Lanka against the LTTE and Tamil separatists in the north. Dutthagamani came from the deep south from one of a number of smaller kingdoms and moved his way northward conquering other Sinhala and non-Tamil communities before finally reaching the northern Tamil kingdom of Elara.

The original, pre-colonial political systems of Sri Lanka and the other Theravada Buddhist kingdoms were not like the bounded nation-states we use as reference today but rather "galactic polities" with center-oriented societies that had shifting boundaries. Although the central state structure often exhibited the over-integration of religious and political power discussed above, the technical inability to regulate vast areas and large populations engendered a "devolutionary process of power parcelization" with checks and balances on patrons and clients (Tambiah 1992, 173–74). This lack of strong centralization allowed for diversity and differentiation throughout a system in which minority populations found their places in multi-ethnic areas on the edges of such kingdoms. Where the state was weak and economic patronage simpler and smaller, Buddhist communities could exhibit stronger ethical tendencies alongside the ritualistic ones. In the more rural, localized societies away from the center, Buddhist institutions and monks were closer to the people and could use their influence for more ethical ends in a variety of social roles supporting the integration of society (Ariyaratne 1996, 137). Such societies perhaps resemble most closely the ideal of the early sangha in which monks and the common people lived closely together, before the advent of the great landed monasteries.

This system of governance in Sri Lanka changed greatly under the period of colonization (1517–1948), especially under the British, beginning in 1802. The British and the Europeans, having already undergone their own process of transformation from "galactic polities" to circumscribed nation-states, proceeded to implement one of the key aspects of the modern nation-state: centralized bureaucratic administration. Unlike their administration of Burma where there was much greater tolerance of regional and local identities, the British over-integrated Sri Lanka and administered it as one mass society (De Silva 1998, 18). The centralized nature of British administration created a state with no space for the regional autonomy of local people, as evidenced in Colombo becoming the only major mercantile center (Tambiah 1992, 180). The problem with this drive towards administrative efficiency, as David Loy points out in *A Buddhist History of the West*, is that "bureaucratic role identification minimizes personal relations by maximizing functional relations." Such administration is a victory of means over ends, form over content; an artificial ordering of parts united by fear that engenders distrust in others and precludes the possibility of mutuality. Since bureaucracy is the antithesis of community, the citizens are broken down into alienated atomized "populations" (Loy 2002, 100–101).

In the shift from the "positive disintegration" of Ashokan dharmic civilization towards the over-integration of early Buddhist nationalism, we saw how ethics as the basis of administrating to a diverse population, in other words *dhamma vijaya*, was replaced by the stigmatization of foreign elements and the coercive conquest of them, along the lines of the *Arthaśāstra*. The well-known British style of divide and rule reproduced the ethos of the *Arthaśāstra*, and the use of modern law in such bureaucratic administration took coercive fear to another level as such law replaced mutuality and ethics as the only effective means to address conflict.

The consequent effect of the system on the monastic Sangha was palpable and traumatic, to say the least. The colonial occupation that replaced the Kandyan monarchy and eventually sent it into foreign exile destroyed the reciprocal relationship between the Sangha and its ultimate protector and patron. Over the first forty years of colonial rule, the British took away Buddhism's special status as national religion and established a new administrative and self-governing structure for it. As the general population began to be increasingly educated in Christian colonial schools, the bond between lay, especially upper-class lay, and the Sangha declined, as did the role and status of the monk in society. While loosening its ties to the state was probably a healthy thing for the Sangha, the process went too far with the colonial government supporting rapidly expanding Christian influence on the island. The result for the Sangha was a deep alienation from its previous roles in politics, education, and culture. Like the village Brahmin in the increasingly insular and provincial village culture of medieval India, the Buddhist monk was reduced to a local ritualist while falling into lay lifestyles, such as even maintaining families (Rahula 1974, 90).

In conclusion, a state of "positive disintegration" has a dynamic and harmonious balance of integration and diversification based in ethics and trust, but when this balance tilts, it deforms into what we might call the twin forces of centralization and alienation based in regulation and fear. The imposition of colonial rule on Sri Lanka took a society already tilting towards this latter imbalance—in the conflation of the entire island of Sri Lanka with Sinhala Buddhist kingdoms—and pushed it to a deeper but somewhat different level of extreme—in which the population as a whole was alienated from its own self-government and from control over its own cultural identity.

The Buddhist Revival towards Reintegration

Cultural identity was indeed a key issue and focal point for the modern Sinhala Buddhist reform movement that began in the late nineteenth century. This period marked the creation of Buddhist educational activities in an attempt to reassert Sinhala Buddhist identity among the masses, to raise the educational level of Buddhist monks, and to empower them to once again become relevant actors in society. Two major monastic colleges, which would be at the forefront of the Buddhist nationalist movement a century later, were established at this time: the Vidyodaya Pirivena founded by Ven. Hikkaduve Sri Sumangala in 1873 and the Vidyalanka Pirivena founded by Ven. Ratmalane Sri Dharmaloka in 1875. Shortly afterwards in 1880, the American Colonel Henry Steel Olcott arrived in Sri Lanka and with Sumangala and others started the Buddhist Theosophical Society. Together, they began opening Buddhist schools in several districts in the country, such as Ananda College in Colombo in 1886, which became the leading English Buddhist school (Rahula 1974, 93–94). These Buddhist schools established a tradition of Sinhala Buddhist education and played an important role in linking education, religion, and ethnicity.

One of the most important figures who inherited the work of the Theosophical Society from Olcott was a young, upper-class, Christian-educated Sinhala boy named Don David Hewaviratne (1864–1933). As a young man he took on the lifestyle of a mendicant, adopted the name Anagarika Dharmapala, and became a central figure in the Sinhala Buddhist renaissance. Like similar reform movements in Thailand and among untouchables in India that would follow in the 1930s, Dharmapala's new Buddhism emphasized quintessential modernist themes, such as rationalism, material development, and engaged public service while heavily criticizing traditional ritualism and merit making. Although he strongly rejected his modern Christian education, he was no doubt a product of the modern colonial era and his common themes of cleanliness, discipline, and morality have led some to dub his movement "Protestant Buddhism."

The key point in Dharmapala's vision is what I will call the concept of "reciprocal merit." As other chapters in this volume have shown, within the traditional merit-making system, the lay sangha gives material sustenance to the monastic Sangha, while the monastic Sangha offers back some spiritual edification, principally in the traditional dharma talk. The role of the monk in merit transfer is generally quite passive or indirect. That is, if a monk maintains and develops his spiritual powers or perfections (*pāramī*) through observing the *vinaya*, studying the suttas, and perhaps meditating, merit is transferred to the person who supports such a monastic through the merit-making ritual, such as on alms round or in a robes offering ceremony. However, for Dharmapala and other modern Buddhist reformers, this notion of merit making not only did not conform to the original teachings of the Buddha and his intent for the monastic Sangha, it also was a serious impediment to the material development of the people and the nation. They felt that the people's resources were being wasted on constructing religious edifices and institutions rather than on meeting the basic needs of the people, which were often more dire than the monks'. Instead, these reformers reinterpreted the ritual act of merit making in more reciprocal terms, whereby monks became leaders and supporters for the material as well as spiritual needs of the lay sangha. In this way, the traditional idea of the monk as a passive provider of merit, or as a "field of merit" (*puññakkheta*), was turned on its head, and the monk was transformed into a much more active source of merit through social service. It appears these reformers were trying to recover the original meaning of *puñña* as "doing good," rather than as making ritual merit.

The subsequent movements that followed Dharmapala's work in the late nineteenth century and early twentieth century picked up on his economic emphasis in the promotion of rural regeneration through a self-sufficient, largely agricultural economy (Seneviratne 1999). They also picked up on the critique of secular modernism and colonialism and the promotion of political independence and national integrity (for which economic independence was essential). As noted earlier, the differentiation or alienation between lay and monastic due to the myths of poverty and other-worldliness encouraged the development of ritualistic merit making as the core of Buddhist practice, especially for the lay sangha. Dharmapala and others narrowed this distance between lay and monastic and reintegrated the monk into society by reformulating the monk's reciprocal and material merit in terms of social service. Unfortunately, this did not turn out to be a clean and neat solution to the problem of ritualistic merit making. Instead, a new problem arose: how should this new ideal of "social service" be defined? For one group in

Sri Lanka, epitomized more by the monks of Vidyodaya University, it meant returning to the periphery of the state and to the people at the grassroots in order to work for their economic and spiritual well-being. For another group, epitomized more by the monks of Vidyalankara University, this meant rediscovering their place at the center of the state in order to rebuild the sacred trinity of state, people, and religion that had been destroyed by colonial imperialism.

Movement towards the Center: The Over-integration of the Monk

As Dharmapala grew old and increasingly lived in India where he campaigned for the restoration of the temple at Bodh Gaya to Buddhist ownership, F. R. Senanayake and D. B. Jayatilake became important leaders in the Buddhist movement. Also acting as elite leaders of the political reform movement, they endeavored to push the Buddhist movement towards a less nationalist and more civilizational sentiment. Senanayake's younger brother, D. S. Senanayake, eventually became the first prime minister of independent Sri Lanka. He quickly moved to reinstate the connection between the state and the Sangha through the administration of Buddhist properties by the government as part of the state's obligation to Buddhism.

However, this circle of leadership was also sensitive to draw the distinction "between a government of Buddhists and a Buddhist government, in brief, a careful demarcation of the boundaries between state power and religion" (De Silva 1998, 80–81). Senanayake worked to ensure that the independence constitution had the key elements of a secular, but what I might rather term "civilizational," attitude towards religion and the state. The new independence constitution recalled the Ashokan ethic of ecumenicalism by enjoining the state to treat all religions alike and prohibiting the state from discriminating between persons on the basis of religion. Yet it went a step beyond the Ashokan model by defining the limits of the power of the state in religious affairs. That is, the state would not be an adjudicator in conflicts within the Sangha, thus removing one of the elements that perpetuates the Sangha's myth of other-worldliness through state protection and regulation. In this way, Senanayake became one of the most influential advocates of a Sri Lankan nationalism that emphasized the common interests of the island's several ethnic and religious groups. The result was that the immediate post-colonial order emphasized pluralism, ethnic harmony, and secularism (De Silva 1998, 21, 82).

This movement, however, was met with serious dissent by certain members of the Sangha who had been strongly influenced by the socialist and nationalist movement of the Sangha in Burma. In the 1930s, a number of Burmese monks who had studied Marxism in India traveled to Sri Lanka where they radicalized certain parts of the Sinhala Sangha. These elements launched a campaign against Senanayake's secular constitution, emphasizing a closer association with the state and Buddhism (De Silva 1998, 81, 84). The All Ceylon Bhikkhu Congress was one organization that represented the opinions of many of these left leaning monks, who also tended to be young. On January 26, 1946, a representative of the group, the aforementioned and oft quoted Ven. Walpola Rahula, held a public discussion with Prime Minister Senanayake on the question of the role of monks in politics (Bechert 1978, 203). From this discussion, Rahula wrote *The Heritage of the Bhikkhu* in which he argued that the monk's role in social service is an essential part of the development of the nation, and this included being active in political matters. *The Heritage* spawned a major ideological battle over the role of monks in politics, which took place in the highly politicized environment of post-independence Sri Lanka.

With the election of S. W. R. D Bandaranaike as prime minister in 1956, we see a reversal of the civilizational sentiments of the Senanayake period and the coming together of the elements of ethno-nationalist Buddhism. In 1951, Bandaranaike resigned from his cabinet post in the first post-independence government and formed the Sri Lanka Freedom Party (SLFP) in order to exploit the rising Sinhala nationalist movement that championed its own language and religion as the foundation of the new Sri Lankan nation. Bhikkhu activists were welcomed and came to hold influential positions on the party's executive committee (De Silva 1998, 86). When Bandaranaike came into power, the link between religion and ethnicity cultivated in the

Buddhist schools founded in the nineteenth century was extended to politics. People were not just Buddhists; they were Sinhala Buddhists. The youth who were educated in the Bandaranaike era were called "The Children of '56" (*panashaye daruwo*), and there was a growing sentiment that everyone in the state schools should be educated in the tradition set out by Olcott's Sinhala Buddhist colleges (Navaratne 2008).

In 1958, the two Buddhist monastic colleges, Vidyodaya and Vidyalankara, became fully accredited, four-year universities open to all students, lay and monastic alike. During this period, the distinction between Vidyodaya as progressive and nonpolitical and Vidyalankara as reactionary and political was not so clear-cut. This was a time when being a Buddhist, especially a monk, and a political activist was an exciting and important role in creating the new post-colonial society. As monastic colleges, both schools contributed to Bandaranaike's landslide victory, while their monks campaigned on stage pushing for the "Sinhala only" policy of a single official language.

This optimism, however, proved to be short lived. Bandaranaike was able to push through "Sinhala only" legislation, yet fully implementing it became much more problematic and difficult. As in the Ashokan and subsequent Buddhist monarch paradigm of involvement in Sangha affairs, Bandaranaike set up the Buddha Sasana Commission in 1959. It ended up recommending a set of laws to control entry into the Sangha, supervise education and residence of bhikkhus, regulate engagement in social and political activities, and regulate their paid employment outside temples. However, what turned out to be a chance to effectively regulate the Sangha, which was growing more undisciplined, failed under increasing monastic factionalism. By this time, the growing spectacle of bhikkhu activists getting caught in political infighting and using their new found powers for financial gain and influence-peddling started to turn the public against them. This counterreaction reached its zenith with the shocking assassination of Bandaranaike by one of his own bhikkhu activists in a confusing conspiracy of motives (De Silva 1998, 89–93).

While monks did return as early as 1966 to overtly political activities, the sense of trust, optimism, and positive leadership was difficult to rekindle amongst the larger Sinhala public, and the Sangha movement itself fell victim to its own historical divisions, which were being exacerbated by new modern influences. As Rahula himself relates, Vidyodaya and Vidyalankara provided modern educations for monks to be in tune with the times. When they became public universities in 1958, many students, both lay and monastic, were coming from poor, rural areas. They could get good modern educations, but the economy was not developed enough to provide them jobs that fit their modern liberal arts training (Rahula 1974, 108–113). They were educated and empowered but with no access to power, because the mostly Christian educated elite had inherited control of the society from the British. In this way, the same kind of resentment and righteous anger that fueled Dharmapala and the leaders of the anti-colonial Buddhist movement manifested in a post-independence, ethno-nationalist Buddhist movement directed against not just Tamil Hindus but also against Western capitalists and their "clients" who ran the Sri Lankan government.

This situation also fed into the fault lines of caste in the Sangha, which in Sri Lanka is divided into subsects based on four castes. It has generally been the case that the most vocally political monks tend to be from lower castes and poorer, less educated backgrounds, while the ones from the more prestigious sects, who are still quite influential, do not get involved in politics. Through politics, these low-caste bhikkhus are able to gain the status and prominence that they cannot gain within the Buddhist hierarchy (Navaratne 2008). By the 1970s, a large number of monks from both Vidyalankara and Vidyodaya had joined the Marxist Janatha Vimukti Peramuna (JVP) party. They were attracted by the promises of an egalitarian socialist society that seemed to mirror the earliest ideals of the Sangha, which were based in the republican principles of the Buddha's own Shakyan republic. These monks became an integral part of the JVP, criticizing the widening gap between rich and poor with the opening up of the economy in 1977; campaigning for increased scholarships for students and salaries for teachers at universities; and mobilizing youth for the cause. These monks also attacked the excesses of the establishment monks, accusing them of neglecting their patriotic duties because of corruption from rank, property, and temple building. In this way, they tacitly accepted the threats and violence against these monks by the JVP (Tambiah 1992, 97–99).

During this time, the secularization and modernization of the bhikkhu continued to grow. *The Contemporary Generation of Monks* (*Vartamana Bhiksu Parapura*) written in 1970 by Ven. Horatapala Palita, a product of this new, secularized, urban monastic education, took Rahula's *Heritage of the Bhikkhu* another step in articulating the life of the new, modern Sinhala bhikkhu. In this small book, Palita not only specifically stated that "social service" meant participation in political matters, but also called for a monastic council to revise and update the *vinaya* to better conform with the existing reality of modern society. Even more radically, he called on monks to take gainful employment and cut their economic dependence on the laity, which he deemed "an injury to self respect, an insult to being human" (Seneviratne 1999, 208). By the 1990s there were numerous examples of monks living in private residences with their own form of economic support, creating popular art like nationalistic war songs, and establishing major entrepreneurial development projects through wealthy, overseas connections to countries like Japan. This last development continues to cause major problems in the growth of a civilizational culture in Sri Lanka because of the careless economic support by foreigners, especially foreign Buddhist groups, for bhikkhus with ethno-nationalist tendencies.

The basic impetus to reestablish the Buddhist monk as a meaningful actor in civil society can be viewed as an important retrieval of monastic *sīla* as engaged ethical conduct, as opposed to mechanistic observance of the *vinaya*. However, this social engagement has come at the cost of proper monastic training—a common critique of newly ordained monks who are quickly put into monastic schools and never properly trained by their preceptors in the lifestyle of a bhikkhu (Seneviratne 1999). The focal point of Buddhist practice towards nirvana, which became distant with the early schism of monastic practice into scholastic-oriented (*gantha dhura*) and meditation-oriented (*vipassanā dhura*) lifestyles, has become even more remote as the standard lifestyle of a bhikkhu has been endangered by the nebulous, unrooted vocation of "social service" in a modern consumer society.[4] In trying to become a master of this new world, the bhikkhu has unfortunately become a product of it—in opposition to the true meaning of "other-worldliness," which means to be in the world but not of it. While many of these monks have espoused the romantic vision of the socialistic and Buddhistic, traditional rural Sinhala village, they themselves have abandoned it for urban secular educations. By focusing on their political and economic upliftment, they have lost touch with their monastic training (*sīla-samādhi-paññā*) and the reciprocal bond of *puñña* with their lay community—the true basis for an authentic dharma revolution.

From a socio-political point of view, the over-integration of monks and Buddhism into modern Sri Lankan society has had more tragic effects. As we have seen, one of the key aspects of the "positive disintegration" of a civilization is the flux-balance between the integration and differentiation of church and state. While this is an ideal that is seemingly ensconced in the code of the modern secular nation-state, the dogged propensity for modern nation-states to mutate into tribal nationalisms indicates a fundamental flaw in its design. As David Loy articulates, although the modern nation-state did away with the divine king (*devarāja*), his mythic power lives on in the form of the state itself, like a disembodied ego (Loy 2002, 95). In this way, the Sinhala Buddhist nationalism of Dutthagamani continues to fuel a civil war that has cost hundreds of thousands of lives and the subsequent severe retardation of the Sri Lankan economy.

This is no better evidenced than the tragic regime of Ranasinghe Premadasa (1989–93), who when he came into power consciously tried to replicate the trappings of the great Sinhala Buddhist kings. On January 2, 1989, he took the oath of president in the octagon of the Temple of the Tooth, one of the holiest Buddhist sites in Sri Lanka, while openly espousing the *dhamma*

---

4. There is a slow but growing interest in forest monks, like Ven. Kiribathgoda Gnanananda, who are becoming more engaged in society and offering unorthodox teachings, saying, for example, that according to the Buddha it may be possible for anyone who follows the dharma to reach nirvana in this lifetime.

vijaya of Ashoka and his role as both a temporal and spiritual leader. Like Ashoka, he supported other religions, yet had a clear preference towards Buddhism creating a Ministry of Buddha Religion with himself as the head minister, a post he held concurrently with the Ministry of Defense (De Silva 1998, 109–110; Bond 2004, 79–80). In this way, he seemed to have fashioned himself more in the mode of the hero of the *Mahāvaṃsa*, Dutthagamani. He crushed the JVP rebellion through an extended series of ruthless violence and human rights abuses, which included monks—an act taken against his own people. His death at the hands of a Tamil suicide bomber certainly resembled more the intrigues of sixth-century BC *Arthaśāstra* politics than the heroic conquests of Ashoka or Dutthagamani.

Indeed, because of the aforementioned design flaws of the nation-state, modern Sinhala Buddhist nationalism is far more virulent than the imagined one of the *Mahāvaṃsa* and *Cūlavaṃsa*. If we reexamine deeply this history, we see a devolutionary political system in which the center was never able to absolutely control the periphery and accommodated greater local management. It was a culture that incorporated numerous heterodox systems from the bodhisattva model of kingship of Mahayana Buddhism to the secular Indian statecraft of the *Arthaśāstra* to the organization of the Sangha along caste lines. Bhikkhu activists, like Rahula, not only contradict themselves when they advocate the adaptation of the *vinaya* to allow monks to live better in the modern world yet deny the same kind of flexibility that would allow for a decentralized, pluralistic civilizational Sri Lanka, they also become victims of their own rhetoric. They are outspoken critics of the violent forces of Western political, cultural, and religious imperialism, yet articulate the same exact kind of sentiment in advocating a Sri Lankan society in which Sinhala Buddhists are "first among equals." While this kind of rhetoric not only does not fit with the Buddha's and Ashoka's civilizational ethics, it also reflects more Western concepts of the modern nation-state than even those of the traditional Sinhala Buddhist kingdoms, which accommodated diversity far better. Taking the ideology of Dutthagamani one step further, this qualitatively new form of Buddhist "nation-statism" is summed up in this slogan written by one nationalist monk: "It is not to be king that I bear weapons. I defend my land as Gamunu's [Dutthagamani's] son. Country, religion, race are my triple gem" (Seneviratne 1999, 274).

Movement towards the Periphery: The Reintegration of the Monk

In the decline of Buddhism in India, we saw that the over integration of the Sangha with the state and economy through large, wealthy monasteries alienated it from the lay sangha. This retarded the development of lay Buddhism and eventually helped to secure Buddhism's demise in India when the great monasteries collapsed. In the original vision of the Buddha, however, the lay person occupies a crucial role in the sangha, because the bhikkhu renunciate is dependent upon him/her for material sustenance. This system of reciprocal exchange elevated the lay person "to partnership with the monk in a common existential ecology, biology, and spiritual culture" (Seneviratne 1999, 345). Unlike Brahmanism or medieval Buddhism, the lay person is not made out as a "spiritual outcaste" unable to secure their own enlightenment and dependent on the priest for ritual salvation. The reciprocal aspect of this "partnership" also ensures that the monastic Sangha can neither flee from the world to search for their own personal form of enlightenment like *vipassanā dhura*, nor can they become too worldly as an elitist priestly class allied with political and economic powers like *gantha dhura*. In this reconsideration, the various schisms and disjunctures found in Buddhism, such as between lay and monastic and between personal practice and social engagement, can be mended and the divergent interpretations of the Buddha's essential message can be brought to wholeness.

The reformation of lay-monastic relations along these lines was more successfully realized by the other stream that came out of the early Buddhist revival movement of the nineteenth century. There was a mutual connection and influence between Dharmapala and Vidyodaya monastic college, which was established by Hikkaduve Sri Sumangala. Sumangala was the first patron of the Mahabodhi Society under which Dharmapala began his career. At Vidyodaya, the social activist and rural regeneration ideas of

Dharmapala held greater influence as opposed to the political aspects of the socialist agenda that became the dominant influence at Vidyalankara, of which Walpola Rahula was to become a central figure. Dharmapala and the Mahabodhi Society gave land to the monks connected to Vidyodaya to help them start such rural development projects (Navaratne 2008). However, the movement did not really come to life until the 1930s when universal suffrage made politicians suddenly interested in the fate of the rural peasant and the support that could be garnered from them through rural development. The monks that had been educated in the two large monastic schools in Colombo, particularly from Vidyodaya, were thus well placed to provide a bridge between the urban political elite and the rural masses, and thereby discover a different way of reintegrating themselves back into modern Sri Lankan society (Seneviratne 1999, 59).

The first important monk of this generation was Kalukondayave Pannasekhara (1895–1977), who tempered the nationalist anger in the early Buddhist movement's critique of the colonial system by shedding political elements from his work. This, in turn, made him very pluralistic in working with communities that were not always Sinhala or Buddhist (Seneviratne 1999). Another important monk was Hendiyagala Silaratana (1913–82) who developed a broad and comprehensive theory of social activism. He felt that as a renunciate, the monk is free to primarily serve the people. Recalling the idea of reciprocal *puñña*, Silaratana felt that monks owe more to the laity than just ritualism and acting as fields of merit. Monks should actually stop meditating for certain periods and focus on material service to the laity. He noted that, "What in every religion is called merit (*puñña*) is what is done for the good of the world. That is what we mean by morality (*sīla*)" (Seneviratne 1999, 112). He also criticized the laity for detracting from monks' social service work by demanding too many rituals or putting pressure on them to build monasteries in order to fulfill their desires for merit making. He believed that when a monk rebuilds the morality of the people by constructing a village school instead of a temple, he creates a type of reciprocal *puñña* as positive action that secures "success in both worlds" (*ubhayalokartha*) (Seneviratne 1999, 123).

In the divisive political situation that developed in post-independence Sri Lanka, this movement faced a crisis in that many of the monks newly educated at these monastic colleges were drawn to the political aspects of the Buddhist revival movement. In this way, the monks became increasingly cut off from the people. It was into this gap that lay Buddhists from the original Buddhist schools stepped forward. Some of the lay teachers at the schools, most conspicuously A. T. Ariyaratne, felt that social service should be an important part of a lay Buddhist education. They also felt the need to close the growing gap between youth educated in the cities and their roots in the rural villages.

These lay Buddhists were able to capitalize on the national rhetoric of serving the people by initiating work camps (*shramadāna*) of these students with local villagers for some basic need in the village. These camps were based in the ancient tradition of *attam* in which the monks would ring the temple bell and everyone would show up to work together for the community, such as fixing a road or someone's damaged roof. This is the sharing (*dāna*) aspect of *shramadāna*, which literally means "the gift of labor." From his simple roots as a teacher at the Nalanda Buddhist school, Ariyaratne created the Nalanda Social Service Movement in 1958 that eventually became the Sarvodaya Shramadana Movement, the largest and most conspicuous example of progressive Buddhist social development in the world. Ariyaratne was a product of the early Buddhist revival. He understood the progressive civilizational ideas presented by Dharmapala and these early monks like Silaratne. However, he went far beyond Dharmapala in being able to consolidate, systematize, present, and then manifest these ideas in concrete social, not political, action.

One of Ariyaratne's greatest and most important skills has been his ability to understand Buddhism in civilizational terms, more as dharma than Buddhism. It was this skill that allowed him to attract Sinhala Buddhists, Tamil Hindus, and other minorities, as well as secular, Western development experts to build the movement into a huge enterprise that by 1985 was said to be active in over eight thousand villages, one-third of all the villages in Sri Lanka (Bond 1996, 136). In 1961, Ariyaratne spent time in India under Gandhi's heir, Vinoba Bhave. His grasp and subsequent use of Gandhi's pan-Indian civilizational ethics—such as truth, nonviolence, humility, and equanimity—enabled Ariyaratne to expand the appeal of his work to international circles, as well as draw in progressive Tamil Hindus within Sri Lanka. In the way Ashoka was able to preach dharma under a variety of terms to the different people in his empire, Ariyaratne was able to sell dharmic development to: (1) secular, international development experts as participatory community development; (2) Sri Lankan Tamil Hindus as Gandhianism; and (3) Sinhala Buddhists as a progressive new social order that would revive and reinvent the golden era of Sinhala Buddhist kingdoms. I use the term "reinvent" because the Sarvodayan vision is one more closely aligned with the welfare ethics of the Ashokan empire and the participatory and democratic ethics of the republican congresses of the Buddha's day rather than the nationalistic values of the ancient Sinhala monarchies that broke down the "positive disintegration" between religious and political spheres through state patronage and protection of the Sangha.

In this way, Sarvodaya created a vital venue for the overly politicized monks to find a more progressive expression for their beliefs. After the incidents of 1956, many monks became disillusioned with party politics and wanted to get involved in development work. One such prominent example was Ven. Henpitagedera Gnanasiha. He was part of a group of Buddhist scholars who tried to reinterpret Buddhist teachings and history to support a progressive socialist model that rejected the ritualism of Hinduism, caste, and class, while supporting the welfare of the people (Tambiah 1992, 108). However, his activism also led him to be associated with an aborted coup d'etat in 1964. In the last ten years of his life, though, he stepped out of politics and became active in Sarvodaya's work (Tambiah 1992, 105). Further, large numbers of young monks, who had joined the JVP in the early 1970s but became disillusioned by their secular Marxist sentiments and violent methods, got involved with Sarvodaya. By the 1970s and 1980s, almost all Sarvodaya centers were located in temples, and meetings were usually full of monks who also acted as leaders (Navaratne 2008).

However, the "positive disintegration" (the balance between integration and diversification) between these three camps (Sinhala Buddhist, Tamil Hindu, secular Western) proved increasingly hard to maintain. By the 1980s, increasing numbers of Western academics and foreign funders began to exert their agendas on the organizational structure of Sarvodaya, which had been a participatory, member-built organization. With the influx of large amounts of foreign capital, Western-style strategic and planning methods became more important. This enabled Sarvodaya to grow exponentially, but it also decreased the space in which monks had acted as community leaders. At one point, Sarvodaya started a bhikkhu training center, in part to increase their training in strategic and planning skills, like writing funding grants and doing cost benefit analysis. The problem with this training, it appears, is that the monks did not have parallel training in dharma and practice. The result with many of them was that once they got such training, they were enticed into leaving their robes and continuing on as managers in regular society. The training center now hardly functions, and many temples have lost their best and brightest monks who have used this training to advance themselves in secular society.

Further, in the 1970s when the ethnic conflict started boiling up, most of the northern Sarvodaya staff left and built an organization called Gandhian, which eventually morphed into a militant Tamil group called PLOT in the late 1980s. They felt that Sarvodaya was beginning to impose Sinhala Buddhist values and social structures on them. While it is clear that Sarvodaya began de-emphasizing its Gandhian roots in favor of its Buddhist ones, it appears there was a clash of values between Tamil Hindu social dynamics of caste and Sarvodayan values in which everyone was expected to cook, eat, and work together equally. Though Ariyaratne has tirelessly campaigned against the civil war and organized mass peace meditations of hundreds of thousands of people, once the war started, it was difficult for the organization to remain active in the north and east. It has now come to function more as a rehabilitation NGO serving as a conduit for international organizations to channel funds to the region.

CONCLUSION

Although the work of Sarvodaya has been seminal and inspiring, the core problem that we have seen in Sri Lanka remains to be addressed: the role of the monk and lay-monastic relations in an *urban environment*. Indeed, Sarvodaya's impact in urban areas has been muted. The movement has always been strongest in more traditional, rural areas, struggling to have impact in more urban communities. While examples of progressive Buddhist movements for social regeneration can be found easily in rural areas in Sri Lanka and Thailand as well, for the most part, nationalism, secularism, and consumerism have become the dominant themes of urban Buddhism. Looking outside of the Theravada tradition, we can see numerous attempts in Japan to develop new forms of urban Buddhism. However, rather than confront the monastic issue, they have done away with it by creating completely lay denominations. Meanwhile, mainstream "funeral Buddhism" resembles a modern form of Brahmanism with its ancestor rituals and conspicuously wealthy and secularized priests. Taiwan appears to offer another possible solution with its vibrant monastic Sangha and large numbers of fully ordained bhikkhunis. Though not focused on structural change, the Taiwanese Sangha's commitment to social work has generally embraced civilizational attitudes and steered clear of the kind of nationalist and political engagement of the Sangha in Sri Lanka. This contrast is all the more striking within the context of the struggle of Taiwan to gain political legitimacy apart from mainland China.

What is ironic in assessing the failures of urban Buddhism in Asia is that the original Sangha created by the Buddha was particularly well suited to the new demands of the urbanized, pluralistic societies developing at that time. The monastics were a new breed of renunciant combining dedicated spiritual practice with a connection to the everyday lay world. The Buddha spoke directly about economic ethics to the new business classes and created an economic community of reciprocal exchange as the basis of lay-monastic relations. Finally, the class and gender pluralism of the Sangha established an ethic of respect and tolerance for the rest of society to live up to. Today, the challenge not only for Theravada sanghas, but for the Mahayana sanghas as well, is to reclaim Buddhism as a pluralistic, multicultural civilizational force and to shed the chauvinistic and nationalist elements that have grown over the centuries.

In this chapter, we have seen that some of the keys for this reconstruction are:

First, to reinvigorate the monastic Sangha: From an educational standpoint, monastic education must be on par with, but not the same as, modern levels of secular education. This reform seems to have been somewhat successful in Sri Lanka. However, spiritual training is a second decisive factor in order to reinvigorate the monastic Sangha, and this is an area where we have seen great failure in Sri Lanka. It is the monastic Sangha's *central responsibility* to recapture the essence of nirvana as an insight available to all through dedicated practice.

Second, to empower and firmly establish the lay sangha: The modern Japanese experiment in establishing exclusively lay orders has been an important step in this direction. Ambedkar in India and many of the new Buddhist sanghas in the west have also done significant work to establish lay sanghas as genuine communities of practice. It is vital for the lay sangha to not be overly dependent on the monastic Sangha and to be well established in the core disciplines of ethics, contemplation, and insight (*sīla-samādhi-paññā*) rather than focusing on ritualized merit making.

Third, to properly reintegrate the lay and monastic sanghas into a genuine fourfold sangha, after first establishing the independent reinvigoration and differentiation of both as outlined above: As we have seen in this chapter and others in this volume, such a fourfold sangha is rooted in *dāna* as reciprocal generosity, *puñña* as compassionate action or "doing good," and *sīla* as a mutually empowering set of ethical relationships. By reestablishing these principles, Buddhism can begin to heal the dualism between Hinayana/Mahayana and develop egalitarian communities in which the pursuit of nirvana is a practical and realizable endeavor.

References

Ariyaratne, A. T. 1996. *Buddhism and Sarvodaya: Sri Lankan Experience.* New Delhi: Sri Satguru Publications.

Bechert, Heinz. 1978. "S. W. R. D. Bandaranaike and the Legitimation of Power through Buddhist Ideals." In *Religion and Legitimization of Power in Sri Lanka*, edited by Bardwell L. Smith. Chambersburg, PA: Anima Books.

Bond, George D. 1996. "A. T. Ariyaratne and the Sarvodaya Shramadana Movement in Sri Lanka." In *Engaged Buddhism: Buddhist Liberation Movements in Asia*, edited by Christopher S. Queen and Sallie B. King. Albany, NY: State University of New York Press.

Bond, George D. 2004. *Buddhism at Work: Community Development, Social Empowerment and the Sarvodaya Movement.* Bloomfield, CT: Kumarian Press.

Brown, Marvin T. 1990. *Working Ethics.* Berkeley CA: Regents Press.

Buddhadasa Bhikkhu. 1992. *Paṭicca Samuppāda: Practical Dependent Origination.* Translated by Steve Schmidt. Surat Thani, Thailand: Dhammadana Foundation.

Buddhadasa Bhikkhu. 1993. *Handbook for Mankind.* Translated by Rod Bucknell. Surat Thani, Thailand: Dhammadana Foundation.

Chakravarti, Uma. 1987. *The Social Dimensions of Early Buddhism.* New Delhi: Oxford University Press.

Clifford, Regina T. 1978. "The *Dhammadīpa* Tradition of Sri Lanka: Three Models within the Sinhalese Chronicles." In *Religion and Legitimization of Power in Sri Lanka*, edited by Bardwell L. Smith. Chambersburg, PA: Anima Books.

De Silva, K. M. 1998. *Reaping the Whirlwind: Ethnic Conflict, Ethnic Politics in Sri Lanka.* New Delhi: Penguin Books.

Gomez, Luis O. 1987. "Buddhism in India." In *The Encyclopedia of Religion*, edited by Mircea Eliade. New York: MacMillan Publishing.

Goyal, S. R. 1987. *A History of Indian Buddhism.* Meerut, India: Kusumanjali Prakashan.

Kemper, Steven E. G. 1978. "Buddhism without Bhikkhus: The Sri Lanka Vinaya Vardena Society." In *Religion and Legitimization of Power in Sri Lanka*, edited by Bardwell L. Smith. Chambersburg, PA: Anima Books.

Kiribamune, Sirima. 1978. "Buddhism and Royal Prerogative in Medieval Sri Lanka." In *Religion and Legitimization of Power in Sri Lanka*, edited by Bardwell L. Smith. Chambersburg, PA: Anima Books.

Kosambi, D. D. 1969. *Ancient India: A History of Its Culture and Civilization.* Cleveland: Meridian Books.

The Long Discourses of the Buddha: A Translation of the Dīgha Nikāya. 1995. Translated by Maurice Walshe. Boston: Wisdom Publications.

Loy, David R. 2002. *A Buddhist History of the West: Studies in Lack.* Albany, NY: State University of New York Press.

Macy, Joanna. 1991. *Mutual Causality in Buddhism and General Systems Theory.* Albany, NY: State University of New York Press.

Navaratne, Harsha. 2008. Private interview conducted in Bangkok, Thailand.

Obeyesekere, Gananath. 2002. *Imagining Karma: Ethical Transformation in Amerindian, Buddhist, and Greek Rebirth*. Berkeley, CA: University of California Press.

Rahula, Walpola. 1956. *History of Buddhism in Ceylon*. Colombo: M. D. Gunasena and Co.

Rahula, Walpola. 1974. *The Heritage of the Bhikkhu*. New York: Grove Press.

Ray, Reginald. 1994. *Buddhist Saints in India: A Study in Buddhist Values and Orientations*. New York: Oxford University Press.

Reynolds, Frank, and Charles Hallisey. 1987. "Buddhism: An Overview." In *The Encyclopedia of Religion*, edited by Mircea Eliade. New York: MacMillan Publishing.

In Search of Southeast Asia: A Modern History. 1987. Edited by David J. Steinberg. Honolulu, HI: University of Hawai'i Press.

Seneviratne, H. L. 1987. "Samgha and Society." In *The Encyclopedia of Religion*, edited by Mircea Eliade. New York: MacMillan Publishing.

Seneviratne, H. L. 1999. *The Work of Kings: The New Buddhism in Sri Lanka*. Chicago, IL: University of Chicago Press.

Sivaraksa, Sulak. 1992. *Seeds of Peace: A Buddhist Vision for Renewing Society*. Berkeley, CA: Parallax Press.

Smith, Bardwell L. 1978a. "The Ideal Social Order as Portrayed in the Chronicles of Ceylon." In *Religion and Legitimization of Power in Sri Lanka*, edited by Bardwell L. Smith. Chambersburg, PA: Anima Books.

Smith, Bardwell L. 1978b. "Kingship, the Sangha and the Process of Legitimization in Anuradhapura Ceylon: An Interpretive Essay." In *Religion and Legitimization of Power in Sri Lanka*, edited by Bardwell L. Smith. Chambersburg, PA: Anima Books.

The Sutta Nipāta. 1987. Translated by H. Saddhatissa. London: Curzon Press.

Swaris, Nalin. 2008. *The Buddha's Way to Human Liberation: A Socio-Historical Approach*. Nugegoda, Sri Lanka: Sarasavi Publishers.

Tambiah, Stanley J. 1992. *Buddhism Betrayed?: Religion, Politics, and Violence in Sri Lanka*. Chicago, IL: University of Chicago Press.

Thapar, Romila. 1994. "Ashoka and Buddhism as Reflected in the Ashokan Edicts." In *King Ashoka and Buddhism: Historical and Literary Studies*, edited by Anuradha Seneviratna. Kandy, Sri Lanka: Buddhist Publication Society.

GOODNESS AND GENEROSITY PERVERTED:
THE KARMA OF CAPITALIST BUDDHISM IN THAILAND

SANTIKARO AND PRA PAISAN VISALO

INTRODUCTION

The custom of making merit (*puñña*)—lay people providing monastics and temples with material requisites—constitutes the core of popular Buddhist worship and practice in Theravada Buddhism. The *dāna* (generosity) embodied in providing these requisites is the key concept in this practice, which is one of the three main methods of making merit. *Dāna*, however, has broader meanings and applications. For example, as one of the Ten Perfections (*pāramī*), it is the simplest yet also the highest practice of perfection for the bodhisattva, and is thus equally suitable to lay and monastic alike. When we understand *dāna* in this broader and deeper way, it transforms from a ritual act of merit making into an ethical act of doing "good," the literal meaning of *puñña*. If we want to understand sangha as authentic community life, rather than in the more narrow terms of the male monastic Sangha, we need to see *dāna*

Portions of this paper are based on Santikaro's article "Practicing Generosity in a Consumer World," which appeared in *Hooked!: Buddhist Writings on Greed, Desire, and the Urge to Consume*, edited by Stephanie Kaza (Boston: Shambala Books, 2005).
Santikaro and Pra Paisan Visalo have been long-time partners in the struggle to reform Thai Buddhism. Both have been deeply influenced by the pioneering efforts of the late Buddhadasa Bhikkhu and Pra Dharmapitok (P. A. Payutto). They are not only concerned to rectify erroneous understandings of core dharma principles, but also working to see that these principles play a guiding role in the development of Thai society. This chapter is an attempt to bring together their written perspectives on the nature and significance of *dāna* (generosity) and *puñña* (goodness/ merit) into one essay. While the two halves of this chapter were written separately, we hope the reader will find enriching the shared perspectives of these two spiritual friends (*kalyāṇamittā*).

in such a way—as a reciprocal act of circulating "the gift," being the glue that bonds lay and monastic, male and female, senior and junior, together.

Unfortunately, *dāna* and *puñña* have often not been understood in this way. In the period of high economic growth in certain Theravada Buddhist regions over the last thirty years, capitalism has exacerbated the ritualistic nature of *dāna* and *puñña*. Especially in Thailand, capitalism has intensified the shift from understanding *puñña* as goodness to merit by commodifying it in terms of money. In this way, *dāna* is no longer an act of service but the money to buy such services. The sense of reciprocity—of circulating "the gift"—is being lost, while materialism, individualism, and alienation increase. When wealth rather than character or service to others becomes the basis for being a good Buddhist, various forms of social injustice such as patriarchy and economic discrimination are legitimized. This chapter examines these problems and also considers the potential for authentic *dāna* and *puñña*. It concludes by looking briefly at a movement developing in Thailand to restore merit making as the gift of service.

DĀNA: TEACHINGS AND IDEALS

Let's begin with a quick summary of traditional teachings on *dāna*. Then we can better understand how the practice of giving has changed, as the understanding of *puñña* has been perverted by capitalism. In early Buddhism, *dāna* is explained in various ways. It is commonly described as the first of three bases of good, meritorious activity (*puññakiriyavatthu*) (D.iii.218; A.iv.239; Iti.51). Along with *dāna*, ethics and virtue (*sīla*) and mental cultivation (*bhāvanā*) are generally considered the three basic practices for householders. They are not considered equivalent to the Noble Eightfold Path and lead at best to happy rebirths (A.iv.239). On the other hand, monastic practice is usually described in terms of the three trainings (*sikkhā*), which place more emphasis on meditation and wisdom, are equivalent to the Noble Eightfold Path, and can lead to ultimate liberation. Thus, the *puññakiriyavatthu* formulation puts more stress on pre-meditation aspects believed more accessible and suitable for householders. Because mainstream Theravada considers Buddhist lay people incapable of awakening liberation since they lack the required monastic renunciation, they are taught to focus on accumulating *puñña* for the sake of better rebirths, a practice that will eventually develop into the purity of monastic renunciation in some vague future. The effect is that *dāna* is commonly seen as the main practice for householders, while study and meditation, as well as keeping a more refined ethical discipline, are the concerns of monastics. Traditionally this has meant that householders are givers of *dāna* and monastics are recipients. These cultural forms have guided Southeast Asian Buddhism for centuries and may have been effective within their conventional limits. Nonetheless, the *puññakiriyavatthu* and three trainings overlap and are both suitable for sincere Buddhists, whether monastic or lay.

Another understanding of *dāna* places it among the perfections (*pāramī*).[1] Both Theravada and Mahayana list *dāna* first among the "virtues for crossing over" the seas of egoistic becoming to reach the further shore of nirvana. A remarkable passage in Ven. Buddhaghosa's *The Path of Purification* (*Visuddhimagga*), a Theravada classic, presages the Mahayana in its explanation of the *pāramī*:

> For the Great Beings' minds retain their balance by giving preference to beings' welfare, by dislike of beings' suffering, by desire for the various successes achieved by beings to last, and by impartiality towards all beings.[2] And to all beings they *give gifts*, which are a source of pleasure, without discriminating thus: "It must be given to this one; it must not be given to this one." And to avoid doing harm to beings they undertake the precepts of *virtue* .... Through *equanimity* (*upekkhā*) they expect no reward. Having thus fulfilled the Perfections, these [divine abidings] then perfect all the good states classed as the Ten Powers, the Four Kinds of Fearlessness, the Six Kinds of Knowledge Not Shared

---

1. Generosity (*dāna*), virtue (*sīla*), renunciation (*nekkhamma*), discernment (*paññā*), energy/persistence (*viriya*), patience/forbearance (*khanti*), truthfulness (*sacca*), determination (*adhiṭṭhāna*), good will (*mettā*), and equanimity (*upekkhā*).
2. In other words, the Four Divine Abidings (*brahmavihāra*) of friendliness (*mettā*), compassion (*karuṇā*), sympathetic joy (*muditā*), and equanimity (*upekkhā*).

[by disciples], and the Eighteen States of the Awakened One. This is how they bring to perfection all the good states beginning with giving. (Buddhaghosa 1991, 352–3; Vis.ix,124)

To free ourselves from suffering, and to live a life of compassion, we must give. What a beautifully simple and powerful perspective! We start by giving what comes relatively easy and gradually learn to hold nothing back, not even ourselves.

JĀTAKA OF *DĀNA*

The *Jātaka* are Buddhist versions of standard folk tale material. Primarily ways to make moral points, they purport to tell of the Buddha's former lives as a bodhisattva—for example, as a hare who immolates himself in a starving Brahmin's fire to feed the ascetic and sustain him on his path. In another *Jātaka* story, the Bodhisattva is a prince who offers his own blood so that a starving tigress may nurse her cubs. Giving occurs without calculation; recipient and donor are both elevated within the path of perfections. However, offering one's flesh and blood is not the ultimate charity, for that occurs under the bodhi tree when all clinging to "self" is released.

Ultimately, we perfect the virtue of generosity by giving all that we have, and then ourselves—all of ourselves—until nobody is left. The *Vessantara Jātaka*, the final and most famous of all the birth stories, illustrates the unlimited giving of the bodhisattva. This tale has had an incalculable influence on the cultures of Southeast Asia; anyone seeking to understand these Buddhist cultures must know this story. It describes a life focused on giving until it hurts, with *devas*, parents, and all of nature supporting, even requiring, altruism. The drama of Vessantara's life illustrates the great emotional complexity and turmoil in giving away social position and responsibility, wealth, family, children, and finally his beautiful, loyal, and beloved wife, Maddi. The dramatic tension becomes high as those dearest to him suffer as a result of his giving.

At the age of eight, Vessantara thought to himself:

All that I give comes from without, and this does not satisfy me; I wish to give something of my very own. If one should ask my heart, I would cut open my breast, and tear it out, and give it; if one should ask my eyes, I would pluck out my eyes and give them; if one should ask my flesh, I would cut off all the flesh of my body and give it. (*Jātaka* 1981, J.vi.486)

As he matures into manhood, Prince Vessantara is given immense wealth many times over. Whatever he is given, Vessantara passes it on. Gods and kings collude in giving him even more—to give away! Finally, he is asked for and willingly bestows the auspicious white elephant that arrived with his birth. The people of Sivi cannot accept the loss of this sacred, rain-bringing, battle-invincible elephant to a rival polity. Though they can find no fault with Vessantara, they demand his banishment, and his father, the king, gives in to the mob's demands. So Vessantara begins to suffer for his generosity.

The price is an ascetic life for himself, his wife, and their children—and the real punishment for this big-hearted giver is seven months of nothing to give. Isolated in the forest, he finds himself unable to perfect himself further in the practice of giving. Our exiled ascetic hero's first big chance to give is to the evil Brahmin Jujaka, whose wife demands Vessantara's son and daughter as her slaves. Vessantara can only but give. The children's parting from their father and longing for their mother (away gathering food) is heartrending for all. Maddi arrives late to find the children gone and her husband in dumb silence. The pathos is touching, disturbing. Yet the story makes it clear that Vessantara had to do what he did. That is never questioned. It is his purpose in life, necessary for his future realization of Buddhahood.[3]

Later, when Maddi's turn comes, the suitor is the god Sakka, disguised as a Brahmin. Vessantara gives her away immediately, and she obeys. However, this is merely a test, arranged by Sakka to help move the story along to its

---

3. Not that he was aware of future awakening (nirvana); this is retrospectively added to the story, as so often happens.

climax. Maddi is returned as soon as Vessantara and she have passed the test. The children, however, undergo abuse, beatings, and hard work from Jujaka, who accidentally takes them back to Sivi and ends up ransoming them to Vessantara's father. The tale ends happily with Vessantara reinstated in Sivi and everyone reconciled except Jujaka, who gorges himself to death. Having passed the tests and fulfilled his destiny, Vessantara enjoys boundless wealth to give away until the end of his days.

From the perspective of this final *Jātaka*, *dāna* is the final *pāramī* to be perfected. Thus, *dāna* is both first and last. What is often portrayed as the most basic virtue turns out to be the culmination as well, the last perfection fulfilled before the bodhisattva is ready for his final birth. This shows that the spirit of *dāna* runs throughout and perfects all the *pāramī*. For the bodhisattva, there is no tolerance, wisdom, and compassion without wholehearted unlimited giving. One must give completely of oneself in order for compassion and the other perfections to be realized.[4]

DĀNA FOR THE SAKE OF COMMUNITY

Shakyamuni Buddha's own life story is marked throughout by generous giving and receiving. In the traditional accounts, his great awakening depends on the *dāna* of Sujata, a serving girl, and Sotthiya, a grass cutter. Her sweet milk rice and his fresh cut grass sheaves give the Buddha-about-to-be strength and comfort for the supreme final effort. To these are added gifts of nature— a cool river for washing away accumulated ascetic grime, a friendly forest in which to meditate, the shade of trees, and the songs of birds. Finally, the Naga snake king provides his great hood for protection from weather and malevolent forces. Thus, the Buddha's supreme human effort was not entirely individual; it depended upon the collective circulating charity of many beings. In return, liberated from personal concerns, the Buddha gave his entire life in service of the dharma.

---

4. I take this to be an early example of *bodhicitta*, so much emphasized in the Mahayana.

The teaching of *dāna* continued through the Sangha founded by the Buddha. Monks and nuns walked mindfully out of forests and ashrams, across fields, through the pathways of villages and streets of cities, stopping at houses to beg silently. Not merely a stereotype, the practice still survives today in Southeast Asia and helps sustain Buddhism as a living reality. We can picture the shaven head of a nun or monk gently bowed over a bowl as a village child, housewife, or old man offers a spoon of rice, a dollop of curry, a piece of fruit. *Dāna* is especially powerful when it supports the sangha, which understood according to the original emphasis (*supaṭipanno* "those who practice well") includes women and householders. In this way, the four assemblies of laity and clergy, male and female, interact through the practice of *dāna*, thereby making the religious tradition whole.

The Buddha praised gifts given to a community of serious practitioners (*sanghadāna*) over gifts given to individuals, even the most exalted of all (himself). Giving to the Thus-Gone-One who no longer needs anything is valued less than giving to those who are training in the way, their guides, and the community that will keep this noble way alive. Such *dāna* is for the sake of maintaining the centers of tradition, learning, and cultivation that support all who follow the way, whether home-leavers or householders. Individually, only buddhas fulfill the highest ideal of practice; by including the noble community, even struggling members are uplifted so that they contribute, too.

This is the Sangha of upright conduct

Endowed with wisdom and virtue.

For those people who bestow alms,

For living beings in quest of merit,

Performing merit of the mundane type,

A gift to the Sangha bears great fruit.[5] (*Saṁyutta Nikāya* 2000, 333, S.i.233)

Community, as understood in early Buddhism and as practiced in Buddhist cultures, naturally involves different levels of *dāna*. However, consumerism and other modern forces have made this time-honored approach to community precarious. The Thai experience illustrates this well.

Traditional Buddhism throughout Thailand and Southeast Asia has had an agrarian village base. Here, "doing good" (*tanbun, bun* from *puñña*, "goodness," or more commonly "merit") is the central operative value. The most prominent practice of *tanbun* consists of giving food to the monks, especially when they are out gathering alms, as well as making other donations to the temple. Before capitalism took over in Thailand, such *dāna* was almost always in kind, since there was not much money in village economies. *Dāna* supplied the material goods needed by the monks personally and for daily maintenance of the temple. Because the temple served as community center, "town hall," clinic, counseling center, news exchange, entertainment stage, and market, in addition to its religious and spiritual functions, supporting it meant supporting the entire community and most of its activities. In fact, until modernization, temples were communal property more than monastic property (though this was not the case in all Buddhist societies). Generosity sustained them.

For their part, the monks were expected to live simply and unselfishly, to look after the temple and to uphold traditions. When somebody wanted to talk about a problem, or the weather, the monks would listen. When a ritual, blessing, or chant was needed, the monks would go. They were available around the clock, like country doctors used to be in the United States. Actually, many of the monks *were* country doctors. Being around, being available, and being helpful were central to the life of village monks, including the itinerant meditators who would come and go.[6]

---

5. Here, "Sangha" refers to the four kinds of noble ones, the exemplars of dharmic life and the leaders of the community of the Buddha's disciples.
6. Kamala Tiyavanich's *The Buddha in the Jungle* (Chiang Mai: Silkworm, 2003) provides abundant illustrations of this.

Pra Dharmapitok (P. A. Payutto), the leading Thai Buddhist scholar and writer of recent years, concurs that the core principle of the old system was *bun*, goodness.[7] *Bun* is what circulated within the religious economy of Thai life, back when the divisions between family, economics, community, politics, religion, and personal life were tenuous. Villagers gave what they had to give and considered "good," worthy of giving: their best food, robe material, betel nut, tools, materials for repairing temple property, labor, and craft skills. The monks gave advice, consolations, blessings, rituals, teachings, meditation instruction, leadership, writing, and other specialized skills. Most important, the participation of monks gave religious meaning to daily acts of decency, generosity, and kindness, elevating these from the realm of mutual obligations to spiritual significance.

Bun circulated within fairly large loops connecting infants with grandparents, the better-off with the poor, women and men, temple dwellers, ancestors, spirits, even honored water buffaloes. The temple dwellers might include an old abbot who had been around for years, an itinerant or two, newly ordained "temporary monks" from the village or nearby, novices, nuns, temple boys, and senior citizens. Thus, the giving was seldom binary and tended to circulate widely. As *bun*, *dāna* circulated as the blood of the community so long as its members understood goodness mutually.

THE COMMODIFICATION OF *DĀNA* AND *PUÑÑA*

As noted earlier, Buddhist lay practice has tended toward simplified versions of dharma practice, such as the *puññakiriyavatthu*, in comparison to the more difficult practices recommended for monastics. Since Brahmanistic and Hindu influences have always been strong in Theravada Buddhist countries, it is not surprising that the common Buddhist understandings of karma, *dāna*, and *puñña* have become distorted by such influences. In particular,

---

7. From a Thai language talk given at Suan Mokkh in the late 1980s. To my knowledge, this was never published.

the lay practice of *dāna* has often become limited to making ritual offerings to the monks in order to gain merit (*puñña*) towards a better rebirth. As the monastic-centered tradition continued to emphasize that lay followers, especially women, could not attain enlightenment in this lifetime, lay practice continued to devolve into performing or sponsoring rituals towards securing an advantageous rebirth. "Senior monks discouraged sermons on [essential] principles and teachings such as not-self (*anattā*), dependent origination (*paṭicca samuppāda*), thusness (*tathatā*), and emptiness (*suññatā*). Supposedly, these were too difficult for ordinary people to understand. For the masses, moral teachings based on ancient—and not particularly Buddhist—beliefs about karma, rebirth, merit, heaven, and hell were considered appropriate and sufficient" (Santikaro in Buddhadasa 1994, xvi).

Here, too, the *Jātakas* have played an especially powerful role as myths that influence popular beliefs. For example, the *Mahājanaka Jātaka* (J.vi.35) implies that if one has accumulated enough merit in past lives, one will be spared from misfortune or get lucky in this lifetime, often through the divine intervention of certain gods. However, Pra Dharmapitok (P. A. Payutto) remarks, "Overemphasis on rebirth into heaven realms and hell realms ignores the good which should be aspired to in the present . . . . Good actions are performed for the sake of profit. Overemphasis on past and future lives ignores the importance of the qualities of moral rectitude and desire for goodness, which in turn becomes a denial of, or even an insult to, the human potential to practice and develop truth and righteousness for their own sakes" (Payutto 1993, 50). Such limitations and distortions are to be expected in popular religiosity; they are part of the local culture over which ordinary people have some control. Modernity brings in powerful influences that villagers have little influence on.

Capitalism intensified this shift away from the operative principle of goodness and onto money, that is, from *bun* to *baht* (the Thai currency). Increasingly, donors give *baht* or food purchased with *baht*, rather than prepare food and other offerings themselves. Village skills and handicrafts have suffered, partly because they were not voluntarily practiced and learned at the temple. More time was spent in the fields working on cash crops; economic migration to urban areas increased; and children saw less of their parents. Communal work and shared labor disappeared; even the temples had to start paying. People no longer wandered through or hung around the temple as they used to. Things that did not earn money were devalued. Eventually, Buddhism was expected to aid economic success, magically if not concretely.

In many towns nowadays, monks queue up at dawn before market stalls where ready-made food offerings are for sale. Such commercial food usually includes additives such as MSG and sugar, and contributes to poor health among many monks. Donors queue up on the other side, pay their *baht*, pick up a tray, and take their turn putting food into the waiting monks' bowls (or buckets carried by temple boys, depending on how many offerings are purchased). Then donors and recipients go their own ways. All very efficient, in the wonderful way of consumer capitalism, with donors putting less time and care into their offerings and monks, accordingly, appreciating them less.

Rather than food offered as *bun* in promise of better karmic fruits, *baht* is given in hope of more *baht* (and dollars)—successful business ventures, passing exams for career advancement, winning the lottery. The monks, too, have become more money-minded. Monastic titles are linked to funds raised and spent on temple buildings (not to mention what goes into the envelopes passed under tables, e.g., for permission to travel abroad). Temple services such as the large funeral industry cost money and are treated as investments by temple committees, complete with outsourcing of flowers, coffins, and catering. City monks indirectly probe how much *dāna* will be given—cash in envelope—before deciding what meal invitations to accept. Of course, monks travel, study, and live in the same consumer economy as everyone else and thus need money. Nothing is free any more.

The magical side of popular Buddhism, too, is now much more about money and making money, than about protection from spirits and disease. Amulets are big business. Stories circulate about people getting rich after donating to a certain monk (e.g. Luang Po Khun) or temple (e.g. the infamous Wat Pra Thammakai). Luang Po Khun became famous during the '90s economic boom when rumors spread of people, including royalty, getting rich after making donations to him. The rumors may have been spread by those around his temple who benefited from the large influx of "merit makers."[8]

Wat Pra Thammakai is still dealing with an unresolved scandal concerning misuse of temple funds. The abbot personally invested in gold mines, which he attempted to justify as contributing to business efficiency in producing devotional objects "marketed" (Thammakai uses such terminology themselves) at margins that would make ordinary entrepreneurs drool. Thammakai has unabashedly embraced capitalism, often distorting the Buddha's teaching to win followers amongst the merchant and professional classes. For a while, the abbot was suspended pending resolution of criminal charges. However, these charges were dropped two years ago during the Thaksin regime. There is some speculation that the abbot—believed to be the source of all buddhas by the most cultish of his followers—curried favor with the Thaksin government so that the charges were dropped.

The degeneration of the practice of *puñña* into such crass forms of spiritual materialism also promotes a kind of spiritual classism, reminiscent of the Hindu caste system. In such a system, the rich are better positioned to gain favorable rebirth because of their wealth. Also not unknown in other religions, such as the medieval Christian church's selling indulgences in Europe, rich Buddhists attempt to buy their way into heaven by building large, gaudy stupas and temples. Wat Pra Thammakai again serves as an appropriate example:

> [Thammakai] not only promises worldly achievement to its followers, but also uses marketing techniques to create a demand for merit through "direct sale." Merit is commodified and diversified in different forms for followers to have more choice. Competition is encouraged between volunteers who solicit donations, and rewards are given to those who can achieve the highest amount of donations. These techniques are derived from the idea of its leader that, "Buddhism is an excellent commodity that gets bad sales because of the lack of good marketing strategies." (Visalo 1999, 242)

---

8. Luang Po Khun has been in poor health in recent years and has fallen from the level of popularity he held when this article was written.

Perhaps what is of greatest concern here is the distorted karmic under-standing that rich people have earned their merit and hence deserve their elevated status. This likewise implies, of course, that people who are poor also deserve their situation. This simplistic equation reverses the causality properly taught in Buddhism. Its corrupted logic reflects a deterministic understanding of karma that ignores the role of *structural violence*, for often it is economic and other social factors that force the poor into professions that violate the lay precepts and create bad karma, such as working in slaughter houses (killing), prostitution (unskillful sexuality), fraudulent marketing (lying), drug dealing (use of intoxicants), and downright theft. Generally, monks have little understanding of social factors and merely focus on the individual level and disembodied tenets memorized in their dharma classes.

RECOVERING SANGHA BY MAKING MEANINGFUL MERIT

When the great Thai Buddhist reformer of the past century, Buddhadasa Bhikkhu, was young, his mother taught him a mantra while taking care of the family's rice field. "If birds eat our rice, that is *puñña*. If people eat our rice, that is *dāna*" (so don't be angry with them). Buddhadasa once compared three different types of merit making with how we wash our bodies. The first type, which is like washing the body with muddy water, is done by people who sacrifice the lives of other beings in performing a supposedly merito-rious ceremony. The second type, likened to pouring perfumed water onto the body, is done by people who make merit with a belief that they will be rewarded somehow and be reborn in heaven. The last type, like cleaning the body with pure water, is the highest level of merit making as the person ful-fills the deed selflessly and without any attachment to the result.

Recovering sangha is one way that we can create nonconsumerist breath-ing space. Since monastics have more material resources than society's poor, they, too, ought to consider *dāna* as something they are to give. While this commonly occurs in forest practice temples, it is not common in city temples. On the other hand, lay practitioners need not be limited by old stereotypes.

Their practice of generosity need not be confined to giving only to monks. One can give to other people, and even animals, for this is a practice that can be carried out in various ways.

Traditional Approaches to Reciprocal Merit Making

The attitude that helping other people is also a merit making practice—that offering *dāna* to monks is not the only way to do *puñña*—can, in fact, be found in traditional Thai culture. There are many traditional practices in the North, as well as other regions, that are based on this attitude. For example, *tan tod* is a practice where requisites or *dāna* (*tan*) are offered to poor people by laying them (*tod*) near their houses and then lighting a firecracker to alert the recipients. It is believed that one can obtain as much merit from this practice as offering *dāna* to monks. Unfortunately, such practices have recently fallen into disuse, whereas offering *dāna* to monks still prevails, giving the impression that *puñña* can be obtained only through practice and rituals involving monks. In the past, however, offering *dāna* to monks and acts of community service were never distinguished. Since the temple was the center of community life, utensils offered to monks, for example, were often borrowed by villagers for feasts on various occasions, e.g. at a wedding, ordination, or funeral. As Thailand has modernized, the focus of village activities has shifted from the temple to secular institutions, such as modern schools and other social services provided by the government. Monks have become marginalized and their roles confined to strictly religious rituals like funerals and of course merit making. In this way, *dāna* offered to monks has become more and more confined to their personal use in the temples. In other words, *puñña* involving monks is increasingly divorced from community service.

In 1980, the Coordinating Group for Religion in Society (CGRS) initiated a new form of merit making called *pa pa khao*. *Pa pa* are the Thai words for "forest robe" and *khao* means "rice." This practice is adapted from the traditional one of offering robes to monks (*pa pa*), which is a popular ceremony in which people collect money and offer it, along with robes, to monks for various purposes, e.g. building temples or supporting monastic education. In this new ceremony of *pa pa khao*, rice is collected, as well as money, in order to support rice banks or rice cooperatives in the local villages. Rice banks and cooperatives have been set up in many villages to assist indebted villagers by providing them with cheap rice or rice loans at low interest. In some years, however, due to drought, these projects could not get enough rice to help their members. To address this problem, those living in other villages have initiated *pa pa khao* to raise rice and money for the affected villages. Such practices not only help rice banks and cooperatives to function properly, but also raise funds to support other village projects, such as educational funds for the young and free school lunches.

During the last decade, *pa pa khao* has been increasingly practiced in the North and East. It has become popular because of the belief that much merit can be acquired by doing it. In the more traditional *pa pa*, the ceremony ends when money and robes are offered to the abbot. With the increasing use of cash money in modern merit making, however, *pa pa* has been manipulated for corrupt ends, usually due to lack of transparency in the temple administration, especially the temple's bank account. There is a saying about *pa pa* money that "half goes to temple, and the other half to the (lay) committee." Although the new practice of *pa pa khao* is not impervious to such corruption, there is an important shift in the direction of the money. The abbot, instead of keeping the offering for monastic purposes, gives the rice and money to villagers for community projects. Thus the traditional role of monks in community service, which has been ignored for decades, is being restored and strengthened.

It should also be noted that these practices are initiated by villagers in the surrounding areas, in the spirit of helping fellow villagers who are in trouble. In this way, the practice helps to strengthen the network of local villages and serves as a basis for cooperation among villagers in the area. In addition to sustaining existing rice banks and helping cooperatives to function properly, *pa pa khao*, which is now performed almost every year, plays an important role in supporting new rice banks and cooperatives in various villages. Apart from *pa pa khao*, which assists rice banks and cooperatives, there are also *pa pa nangsue*, which collects books to support rural literacy and education, and *pa pa tonmai*, which collects seedlings and plants for reforestation.

In addition to applying traditional ceremonies for community development, new social programs have been set up based on the concept of *puñña*. *Satcha sasom sap* or "savings with truthfulness" is one example. *Satcha sasom sap* is another type of local savings bank where people keep their savings and receive cheap loans, enabling them to avoid commercial banks and moneylenders. *Satcha sasom sap* was initiated by a monk, Pra Subin Panito, who successfully organized almost three hundred groups in many provinces. More than half of the villages in his home province of Trat have set up such groups. What makes *satcha sasom sap* distinct from ordinary local saving banks is the reliance on Buddhist virtues such as truthfulness. Every member of *satcha sasom sap* is required to make and keep a pledge of truthfulness that the same amount of money will be deposited in the group bank every month. This promise of truthfulness helps to maintain their commitment to the group. The concept of *puñña* is another principle of these groups. Members are told that their participation is a way of practicing *puñña* since their savings can be used to help people in trouble. In the process of making loan decisions, priority is given to people who are in trouble, such as needing money to pay medical bills or school tuition for children.

This is another attempt to revive the traditional virtues of compassion and generosity. In the past these virtues were so integrated into the life of village people that they could be seen in all details of their daily life, such as providing drinking water in front of houses, giving food and lodging to strangers, building shelters for travelers, giving a helping hand with rice harvesting, constructing houses or roads, etc. All these acts of cooperation were regarded as the practice of *puñña*. The systematic organization of *satcha sasom sap*, however, has developed this practice to another level. Rules and regulations are laid out for collective decision making and transparency. Another difference is that money is mobilized, instead of labor as in the past. Further, these funds circulate within the local village economy rather than being siphoned off to distant financial centers. These are examples of applying merit-making practice to structural issues such as supporting community work and reducing poverty.

New Approaches to Reciprocal Merit Making

Ideally, the goal of merit making encompasses three levels. The most basic is to bring about material well-being in the present, encouraging peaceful coexistence in society. A higher level is to elevate one's mind so that the merit maker becomes a better person morally. The ultimate level is to develop one's understanding of dharma so that one is no longer enslaved by the uncertainties of life. This combination of the material, moral, and spiritual dimensions of each meritorious act improves both the individual and his or her society as a whole. This expansive notion of *puñña* is essential for creating social harmony and well-being. It is also the basis of a strong and healthy civil society. In accordance with this, attempts have been made to promote a proper understanding of *puñña* as taught by the Buddha. The Network for Buddhism and Society (*Khrueakhai chaoput puea pra putthasasana lae sangkhom tai*) is one of a few groups in Thailand that have launched programs along these lines during the past few years. It started its campaign by publishing a handbook for *puñña* practice called *Smart Ways of Making Merit* (*Chalat Tanbun*) (Chai Worathammo 2001).

The handbook begins by introducing the reader to the three bases of meritorious action (*puññakiriyavatthu*) mentioned earlier, as well as seven others that are part of the popular tradition: humility (*apacāyana*), rendering service (*veyyāvacca*), sharing or giving out merit [i.e., getting others involved in meritorious service] (*pattidāna*), rejoicing in other's merit (*pattānumodāna*), listening to right teachings of the dharma (*dhammassavana*), teaching the dharma properly (*dhammadesanā*), and correcting one's views (*diṭṭhujjukamma*) (D.A.iii.999). The handbook also suggests new practices of *puñña* and *dāna* that are beneficial to recipients and that contribute to social and spiritual well-being.

For example, one can join a group of friends to cook food for the orphans, the disabled, or the HIV infected. Those with artistic skills may arrange some recreational activities for the underprivileged. One group often neglected is prison inmates who certainly appreciate compassion. Paying visits to the elderly can also teach one about the age-old truth of life's transience. There are no limits to this alternative merit making: sparing free time to teach street kids, reading books to blind people, or volunteering for the community or at a local temple. In fact, the easiest way to make merit is simply to be good to those around us, be they our own parents, children, siblings, or neighbors. A caring gesture or a smile can bridge the gaps among people. Why wait until the last moment of one's life to do good to each other? The true nature of merit making is "opening up"—learning to be compassionate and accepting towards every human being, regardless of differences in social status, religious beliefs, political ideologies, and so on. Discrimination is a form of violence and bad karma, often committed unconsciously and breeding more violence in return. The ultimate merit comes from opening our hearts to each other.

Some people believe that every religious act must involve elaborate rituals. In fact, recitation of prayers and other customary rules are simply tactics to enhance collective harmony and to prepare the bodies and minds of participants before a meritorious act begins, like cleaning a bowl before filling it with water. However, these rituals are not always necessary and, in themselves, do not bestow any sacred power to the performer. Fundamentally, a genuinely meritorious act of giving must provide the recipient with what he or she truly needs. Moreover, the amount of the donation is less important than the good, pure will in wishing well for other beings. Whether we are inviting others to make merit together with us, or are being asked to join in the activity, a meritorious deed is done with a joyful heart, not out of pride, fear, or with a competitive motive. Buddhism emphasizes that a charitable deed should be guided by mindfulness and wisdom in order to ensure that the meritorious deed will yield a wholesome result.

The beginning of *vassa*, the traditional rainy season retreat, was the occasion for launching the handbook mentioned above. Within three years, it received such a good response from the public and media that it was reprinted forty times, amounting to nearly two hundred thousands copies. The handbook has become popular as a gift or souvenir for important events such as birthdays, anniversaries, and funerals. Most people buy this book (or give it to their friends) because it opens their eyes to the proper practice of *puñña*. It helps them to realize that *puñña* can be practiced at any time and has nothing to do with an unintelligible religious ceremony.

In 2003, another handbook was published, a smaller and more concise collection of merit making practice with the title *30 Practices of Puñña for the Well-Being of Life and Society*. At the back of the booklet, the addresses of non-profit organizations are provided for those who want to do meritorious acts by volunteering or donating money. For those who seek spiritual well being, places to do meditation in various parts of the country are also included. The booklet was put on sale at gas stations in Bangkok one week before the beginning of the *vassa*. Again, within a few days the booklet became very popular, with much positive coverage in the media. Nine reprints have already been made, totaling two hundred thousands copies. The fact that both handbooks are still in demand reflects the enthusiasm of modern people to know and participate in creative *puñña* practices that contribute to the well being of both individuals and society. People are showing that they want an alternative to conventional *dāna* practice that is wasteful, ritualistic, materialistic, and just another form of consumerism.

CONCLUSION

Pra Sekiyadhamma (a national network of socially concerned monks) and the Network for Buddhism and Society have been working to expand the practice of these reinvigorated forms of merit making to the national level. This year the Network for Buddhism and Society wants to take a further step in initiating concrete social action, hoping to persuade Thais to make merit by doing voluntary work during the *vassa*. Many non-governmental organizations are participating in this project, which has chosen the issue of children as the central theme. Executives in large private companies are the target group of this campaign. Thousands of volunteers will be recruited from the private sector to participate in various projects aimed at improving the quality of life for children in various ways, e.g. education, environment, media, social welfare, and human rights. This campaign not only aims to create a new attitude towards *puñña* and *dāna* among the Thai public, but also seeks to create a nationwide voluntary movement based on the concept of *puñña*. It is designed to revive the concept of *puñña* as a cultural force for the well being of society as a whole, instead of being limited to temple or religious rituals.

Though such a social movement motivated by *puñña* is not yet well established, there are already many individuals committed to social activities based on the concept of *puñña*. Given the bases of meritorious action (*puññakiriyavatthu*), one can see that *puñña* is essential to all aspects of well being (physical, social, mental, and spiritual) for both the individual and society. Every time *dāna* is offered properly, it not only reduces personal selfishness, but also contributes to social harmony and peace. This also applies to the other bases of *puñña*. If *puñña* is misunderstood, however, one's practice tends to become a Brahmanistic-style offering for divine blessing or a capitalistic exchange for more profit. The tradition of *puñña* is still powerful and has great potential for social reconstruction, especially in countries where Buddhism is prevalent. As this chapter has shown, it can provide an important social virtue for a uniquely Buddhist civil society. However, unless *puñña* is properly understood and practiced, through the proper education and propagation of Buddhism among lay people as well as monks, its potential will not be actualized for the welfare of all.

References

Buddhadasa Bhikkhu. 1994. *Heartwood from the Bodhi Tree: The Buddha's Teachings on Voidness.* Translated by Santikaro Bhikkhu. Boston: Wisdom Publications.

Buddhaghosa. 1991. *The Path of Purification: Visuddhimagga.* Translated by Bhikkhu Nanamoli. Kandy, Sri Lanka: The Buddhist Publication Society.

Chai Worathammo. 2001. *Smart Ways of Making Merit (Chalat Tanbun).* Edited by Paisan Visalo and O. Chettakul. Bangkok: Komol Kheemthong Foundation.

The Connected Discourses of the Buddha: A New Translation of the Saṁyutta Nikāya. 2000. Translated by Bhikkhu Bodhi. Boston: Wisdom Publications.

Itivuttaka: This Was Said By The Buddha. 2001. Translated by Thanissaro Bhikkhu. Barre, MA: Dhammadana Publications.

The Jātaka. 1981. Vol. VI. Translated by E. B. Crowell and W. H. D. Rouse. London: Pali Text Society.

The Middle Length Discourses of the Buddha: A New Translation of the Majjhima Nikāya. 1995. Translated by Bhikkhu Nanamoli and Bhikkhu Bodhi. Boston: Wisdom Publications.

Payutto, P. A. 1990. "Foundations of Buddhist Social Ethics." In *Ethics, Wealth, and Salvation: A Study in Buddhist Social Ethics*, edited by Russell F. Sizemore and Donald K. Swearer. Columbia, SC: University of South Carolina Press.

Payutto, P. A. 1993. *Good, Evil and Beyond: Karma in the Buddha's Teaching.* Translated by Bruce Evans. Bangkok: Buddhadhamma Foundation.

Visalo, Paisan. 1999. "Buddhism for the Next Century: Toward Renewing a Moral Thai Society." In *Socially Engaged Buddhism for the New Millennium*, edited by Sulak Sivaraksa. Bangkok: Santhirakoses-Nagapradipa Foundation and Foundation for Children.

THE KARMA OF STRUGGLE

Karmic Fatalism and Social Injustice

BURMESE BUDDHISM'S IMPACT ON SOCIAL CHANGE: THE FATALISM OF *SAṀSĀRA* AND MONASTIC RESISTANCE

MIN ZIN

Burmese Buddhists seem to still be sleeping in a "magical garden" (to use Max Weber's term) in which tradition is never questioned. Unfortunately, their sleep is full of misery because their dreams have become nightmares.

Theravada Buddhism is the religion of 89 percent of the Burmese people. According to this tradition, the Buddha taught that each thought, word, and act is a karma that has consequences or fruit (*vipāka*). If each idea bears fruit, the fruit that Burmese society grows should be critically examined. The issue of whether there is a correlation between the predominantly Buddhist society and its consequent "un-Buddhist" experiences remains highly controversial and has yet to be resolved.

As is well known, the people of Burma bear unspeakable suffering derived from gross human rights violations, kleptocratic corruption, a media blackout, and the world's top drug industry. The irony in all this is that if the basic Buddhist teaching of the five precepts (*pañcasila*)—to abstain from killing, stealing, engaging in sexual misconduct, lying, and using intoxicants—were observed, as religious devotees recommend, these afflictions would not have occurred in Burma. However, the reality proves that Burma's nickname, "The Golden Land," so called because of the glittering pagodas and temples throughout the country, is nothing more than words. The question of why a Buddhist country suffers from such atrocious misery seems to be bewildering to those who have great faith in the "idea" of karma and its fruit!

Although Burma is not religiously monolithic, popular Buddhist culture has considerable influence on people's attitudes, behavior, and social relationships. Culture is, of course, not the sole determining factor for societal change. However, examining Burmese cultural practices and their relation to power in Burma's social and political context can shed considerable light on the social impact of Burmese Buddhism.

ONTOLOGICAL DISTORTION? THE HEGEMONY OF *SAṀSĀRA* DISCOURSE

In Burmese Buddhism, the concept of *saṁsāra* is widely accepted and can be assumed as part of the Burmese ontological understanding or worldview. *Saṁsāra* is a Pali word combining two elements: *saṁ* meaning "in succession," and *sāra* meaning "going," "wandering." In its ultimate sense, *saṁsāra* is the operation of dependent origination (*paṭicca samuppāda*), that is, the continuous arising of ignorant consciousness (*viññāna*) through the successive coming together of mental factors (*namā*) and matter (*rūpa*). In other words, it is the momentary flux of mind and body, of physical and mental phenomena. However, very few Buddhists, for the most part only Buddhist monks who practice insight meditation seriously and profoundly, are able to appreciate such a subtle meaning of *saṁsāra*. In everyday use and popular belief, *saṁsāra* is mistaken as the material world in which beings live. It is assumed to be the round of rebirth or cycle of life and death, the stream of existence and transmigration.

Thus, the *saṁsāra* notion has become the Burmese Buddhist discourse that binds all Buddhist concepts into a neat package. This *saṁsāra* discourse has been effectively manipulated by the political and religious elite with the consent of the people. It provides not only a frame of knowledge for understanding the world but also implies actual practices for living in it. Burmese (even non-Buddhists living in Burma, in one way or another) are very much influenced by this *saṁsāra* discourse. The realm of *saṁsāra* is almost endless, continuing until one attains nirvana. Thus, Burmese people tend to see themselves against the backdrop of *saṁsāra*. They see themselves as guests in this life. This present life is just a brief transit point throughout one's long journey of *saṁsāra* .

Interestingly, when a funeral ceremony is held in Burma, attendees are offered a hand fan printed with a poem entitled "Guest." It means that you are just a guest in this life. You come alone into this world and return from it alone. Life is very short. Burmese Buddhism says that humans are travelers in the realm of *saṁsāra*, the round of rebirth. We all are subjected to impermanence—the phenomenon of just arising and passing away, or "coming and going." Nothing lasts. Nothing exists that one can hold onto permanently. According to this belief, life is no longer for being enjoyed, cherished, and celebrated. Burmese in general have a strong tendency to treat not only the sadness and misfortune but also the happiness they encounter as part of life's vicissitudes—the natural process of ups and downs, and coming and going in life.

Thus, every experience that happens—one can include personal crises, human rights violations, social injustice, inequality, and what not—is part of the vicissitudes of life and the impermanent nature of the world. Why should one allow oneself to get mad about these unfortunate experiences? "Let them go," they tell themselves. People's sensitivity to these normally unbearable and unacceptable experiences becomes blunt. They develop a stoic acceptance of injustice as they train themselves to put up with the bitterness. They have learned to endure the pain and misery of life. They survive but see no point in resisting. The effect of overemphasizing this philosophy of life is desensitizing and disempowering. People view themselves as passive objects rather than subjects of change and transformation and come to feel powerless.

Obviously, culture is always determined, at least in part, by power. As particular cultural practices gained hegemony through power, successive rulers and the religious elite in Burma have effectively promoted this *saṁsāra* discourse. Acts of making merit (*puñña*) in the form of charity (*dāna*), morality (*sīla*), and so forth, are always appreciated as an investment in one's own *saṁsāra*. The phrase "investment in *saṁsāra*" is a literal translation of the one that many monks in Burma use to describe the merit making ceremonies of lay devotees. Although people may claim that they are actually making an investment in nirvana by creating the conditions for a beneficial future rebirth (i.e. as a monk) through which they may gain nirvana, their intentions are largely confined to the *saṁsāra* domain, rather than actually transcending it.

This *saṁsāra* discourse is very useful in prolonging the status quo, because it mystifies and obscures the causes of injustice and inequality. Last but not least, it is helpful in pacifying the anger and the struggle of the oppressed people. Thus, this overemphasis on *saṁsāra* is the best possible ideology for the Burmese ruling powers. The powerlessness that results from this exploitative and distorted interpretation of popular Buddhist belief by the powers-that-be seems to be prolonging authoritarianism and harsh repression. Burmese people have grown more passive and powerless as the struggle has lingered on for many years.

DOES HISTORY MATTER MOST? THE GENEALOGY OF BURMESE BUDDHISTS' SOCIAL PRACTICE

Without adding some empirical information, the above-mentioned explanation would be insufficient. The conceptualization of the people's mentality and beliefs alone is not enough to understand the reality. Treating the ideological explanation as the sole reason for what is happening in Burma would be an ahistorical approach and run the risk of regarding the conceptual as reality. When one looks at Burmese history, one notices complex events unfolding that appear to contradict the popular Burmese Buddhist *saṁsāra* belief. In other words, there seems to be a tension between Burmese Buddhist teachings and Burma's actual political activism. More accurately, religion always remains an important medium in the formulation of political strategies and identities in Burma. No political practice is possible without involving Buddhism—and Buddhism has been politicized to such a degree that no religious act is apolitical.

Pagodas, as the most visible symbols of religious beneficence, have long played an especially important role in reinforcing claims to political power. In his *History of Burma* (1925), Godfrey Harvey noted that the pagodas built by

Burma's King Bayinnaung in Ayutthaya (in present day Thailand) and other neighboring kingdoms "are still to be seen, and in later ages the Burmese would point to them as proof of their claim to rule those countries." This mindset has persisted to this day, as seen in the current regime's building of pagodas modeled after Rangoon's renowned Shwedagon Pagoda through-out ethnic minority areas as a way of asserting Burmese (i.e. ethnic Burman) sovereignty over these ethnically distinct regions.

Actually, the most illustrative case of Burmese rulers using religion to enhance their political legitimacy is their patronage of the Buddhist monastic Sangha. Successive rulers have exploited the Sangha's historically important role as a unifying factor for state control. The military regime has formed Sangha organizations in villages, townships, and districts. All monks have to obey the orders of their local organization, whether or not they belong to it. Buddhist monks cannot do anything without the permission of the government. Even traditional religious ceremonies (such as novitiate and ordination ceremonies) need prior permission from the government. Aside from the intimidation and severe repression, the regime tries to control the monastic order by awarding religious titles to leading monks who are loyal to the regime and whom the regime wants to co-opt.

However, all of the restrictions and repression only reveal how Burmese Buddhist monks are defiant against the regime. The number of monks, esti-mated at four hundred thousand to five hundred thousand, is about the same size as the army. Therefore, it poses not only a moral challenge to the military but also an organizational one. Throughout history, Burmese monks have been engaged and active in politics, opposing the powers-that-be. Aung San, the Burmese independence hero and father of Aung San Suu Kyi, said that monks must desist from taking an active part in political life. They must refrain from politics. However, the first organization established during the independence movement against the British was the Young Men's Buddhist Association (YMBA), created in 1906 in response to Christian influence. It was especially attractive to young Burmans who had been educated abroad. They staged an effective "no footwear in the pagodas" campaign against the British who wore shoes in the compounds of pagodas.

The first Burmese monk arrested for his political activism was U Ottama, who had lived abroad in India, France, and Japan. He urged people to wear local clothes and use local materials. He was arrested twice and imprisoned for a total of seven years with hard labor. Another monk who was arrested by the British colonial government and died in prison after a 166-day hunger strike was U Wisara. Both influenced many Burmese people who previously had not concerned themselves with politics. However, both were generally viewed as very politicized. Some abbots were critical of them for having "Mahayana tendencies" (i.e. following the bodhisattva model), since engaging in profane politics is contrary to mainstream Burmese Buddhism. Actually, both spent time in India deepening their international political experience and knowledge by joining conferences and activities sponsored by Gandhi's Congress Party. Both were influenced by Gandhi's nonviolent disobedience, rather than by indigenous Buddhist philosophy.

To make a long story short, Burmese Buddhist monks have continued this anti-establishment tendency. From the beginning of the former socialist government in 1962 until now, monks have been at the forefront of massive demonstrations for democracy. When the military ruthlessly cracked down on unarmed protesters in August and September 1988, six hundred monks were among the more than ten thousand people killed. On August 8, 1990, in commemoration of the second anniversary of that democracy uprising, more than seven thousand monks and novices walked through the streets of Mandalay, solemnly and peacefully accepting alms from the people. Soldiers confronted the monks and opened fire, killing two monks and two students while wounding seventeen others. One novice disappeared.

Following this massacre, the Monks' Union (*Sangha Sammagi*) of Mandalay, led by Ven. U Yewata, declared "overturning the bowl" (*pattam nikkujjana kamma*) against the military. A refusal to accept alms is used as a rebuke to lay people, since making merit (*puñña*) through donations (*dāna*) to the monastic Sangha is a basic form of lay Buddhist practice. This powerful religious boycott, which began in Mandalay, spread like wildfire across Burma. Throughout the country, monks refused alms from military personnel and their families and refused to attend religious services organized by the regime. This alarmed and traumatized the ruling junta, because it struck at the heart of the *saṁsāra* discourse by depriving the junta of the ritual and cultural means of recreating their power. The military retaliated by staging a massive clampdown on the Sangha. More than 350 monasteries were raided and more than three thousand monks and novices were arrested. Twenty monasteries were seized and expropriated. Several leading monks died in prison.

Since then, the military has increasingly tightened the control of monks through National Sangha Mahanayaka Council, a centralized administration that was founded in 1980. The regime has bribed senior monks with lavish gifts and prestigious titles so that the abbots would stay away from political engagement, while they have intensified surveillance and intimidation over the younger monks who are politically active and more sympathetic to the democracy movement. Since 1996, opposition activists have been prohibited from seeking ordination in monasteries in order to sever any possible connection between activists and the monastic community. The military has occasionally instigated anti-Muslim riots to distract the political discontent of young monks. The generals have also actively organized large-scale ritual events in which they have mobilized the Buddhist population to take part, such as national veneration of the Buddha's sacred tooth relic in 1994 and a *htidaw* (umbrella) hoisting ceremony in 1999. As Juliane Schober, an expert on Burmese Buddhism, observed, the regime has attempted to "transform a political and national community into a ritual community to ensure stability and prosperity for the nation-state" (Schober 2005, 117).

However, the rough road of Burmese political struggle has not come to a halt. Buddhist monks have continued to defy the authorities. Together with activists, some defiant monasteries have played key roles in providing education to poor children, assisting HIV/AIDS patients, and hosting ceremonial events of the democracy movement.

On August 15, 2007, the junta suddenly increased fuel prices overnight by as much as 500 percent. The hikes resulted in increases in the prices of public transport and of some basic commodities due to such high transport costs. The sharp rise of fuel prices triggered a series of small protests in the capital of Rangoon. The 88 Generation Students Group, comprised of key student activists from the 1988 democracy movement, led walking protests to demonstrate against the junta's mismanagement while calling for lower consumer prices. However, plainclothes security officials and paid civilian thugs handled the protesters with brute physical abuse. At least thirteen activists from the 88 Generation Student Group, including Min Ko Niang, the most well known activist after Daw Aung San Suu Kyi, were arrested.

On September 5, police and civilian hooligans attacked Buddhist monks in Upper Burma who joined the protest against the gasoline price hike. The news of monks being tied up to lampposts and beaten fueled the public's anger in this devout country. Fellow Buddhist monks throughout the nation called on the regime to apologize for their wrongdoing and to start a national reconciliation process, by threatening another religious boycott (*pattam nikkujjana kamma*) if the regime failed to comply. As the junta ignored their call, the monks exercised their boycott, refusing any religious services and donations from the military and its family members.

Thousands of Buddhist monks led marches in several major cities of the country, chanting lovingkindness (*metta*) verses from the Pali Canon and praying for the peace of the country. When students and the general public joined the marching monks, the numbers of protesters reached up to two hundred thousand alone in Rangoon. The chanting voices of the *Metta Sutta* (the Buddha's discourse on lovingkindness) and the sending of *metta* to all beings filled the whole atmosphere throughout Burma, from Kachin State in the north to Mon State in the south and from Arakan State in the west to Karen State in the east. "May you be free from all danger! May you cease in your anger! May your suffering cease! May your heart and mind enjoy peace and serenity!" Through *metta*, the Sangha and its lay followers called for national reconciliation between adversaries and relief for the people's suffering. All in all, the movement struggled to restore a sense of ethics in Burmese politics.

At one point, the monks stopped outside Daw Aung San Suu Kyi's compound where she is confined to house arrest. Suu Kyi came to the gate of her house and paid respects to the thousands of monks who offered blessings to her with their chanting. This symbolic union of political leadership and spiritual movement made the regime extremely concerned. The military generals, who are attempting to institutionalize ill will into the country's constitution in forms of repression and military supremacy, were determined to reject the *metta* within and without. Suu Kyi once rightly observed the lack of *metta* in the regime and its consequential fear. "If there is a lack of *metta*, it may be a lack in yourself, or in those around, so you feel insecure. And insecurity leads to fear" (Suu Kyi 1997, 23).

Fear, of course, leads to violence. The military used deadly force to crush the *metta* movement of the monks and its followers. The soldiers shot the monks and people, resulting in at least thirty-one deaths according to the United Nations. At least six thousand monks were arrested, and hundreds of monasteries were raided. However, the *metta* activists have unconquerable spirit and courage. U Gambira, a leading monk in the September 2007 Saffron Revolution who is now in the military's *gulag*, once told this author that with the collective *metta* of the Sangha, the monks strive to reach their goal in the service of truth (dharma) and the people, no matter how deadly the consequences they might face. Avoiding confronting ill will with *metta* is a betrayal of this dharma.

This is a very unusual statement in the context of traditional Burmese Buddhist teaching. Conventionally, when Burmese Buddhists speak about the practice of *metta*, they use it mainly in their mental contemplation or as a form of meditation. In other words, they don't put much emphasis on *metta* in action; they just develop *metta* in their mind and send *metta* to other people. Otherwise, they simply do recitation. In the September protests of 2007, the monks showed an entirely new approach, demonstrating *metta* on a well-organized action level.

All of these unfolding historical events surprisingly confirm that the actual activism of Burmese Buddhists seems to work against the Burmese philosophical foundation of belief in *saṁsāra*. A compartmentalization or division between the ideal and the real is evident. It appears that Burmese monks engage in societal affairs so actively that it contrasts with their daily preaching, which points in a different direction.

COUNT STRUCTURE AS SIGNIFICANT: THE PITFALLS AND POTENTIALS OF THE LAY-MONASTIC RELATIONSHIP

The activism of Burmese Buddhists does not come from philosophy, but from the structural role of societal leaders, the monks. As a traditional agrarian society, the majority of Burmese people live in rural areas. In the village-bound traditional social life, the monks and monasteries play the leading role in every aspect of people's daily lives. The villagers support the monks materially as a way of making merit (*puñña*), while monks give their supporters not only spiritual guidance but also social, educational, and health-related welfare. Since they want to help their supporters, whose main concerns are with their daily lives rather than with seeking enlightenment, many monks even engage in fortune telling, astrology, and providing protective charms and incantations to lay people. These actions can be seen as a sort of mutual merit making by the monks in return for their daily necessities. However, the ideal focus in these actions is not the more selfish concern of accruing personal merit but the more selfless concern of practicing generosity (*dāna*).

The main idea concerning generosity or any of the ten perfections (*pāramī*), of which *dāna* is the first and foremost, is that there should be no strings attached. The Buddha urged his followers to give without any expectation of personal reward. Basically, the ultimate aim of generosity practice is the transformation of the individual from a self-centered, greed-driven existence to one that is other-centered and greed-free. The Venerable Ashin Thittila of Burma explains the benefits of *dāna* thus, "The object in giving is to eliminate the craving that lies dormant within oneself; apart from which there are the attendant blessings of generosity such as the joy of service, the ensuing happiness and consolation, and the alleviation of suffering." Giving is literally a practice in letting go, one that increasingly flies in the face of the acquisitive tendencies that drive modern society.

Evidence of the importance of charity in Burmese culture is abundant, from the golden glory of the Shwedagon Pagoda (which owes its magnificence to the donations of countless devotees) to the familiar sight of mendicant monks receiving alms. Charity is not only reserved for those who choose the religious life. Rest houses are set up all over the country for the comfort of travelers, and vessels of pure, cool water can be found on every roadside, put there for the benefit of passersby. These distinctive clay water pots are replenished daily, often by local people who have little else to offer, but who remain intent upon contributing something to the well-being of others. "The inclination to charity is very strong" among Burmese, noted Fielding Hall (1898) in his travels through Burma over one hundred years ago. "The Burmese give in charity far more in proportion to their wealth than any other people."

However, even in societies that are not completely consumerist in orientation, true generosity faces serious social pressures. In Burma these days, many observers take a more jaundiced view of "charity." "Everything has gone to pot here," remarked one respected Burmese writer recently. "You can't paint a rosy picture of so-called Burmese beauty anymore. *Dāna* has become a self-serving tool to acquire wealth and power," complained the octogenarian author, who has written extensively on Buddhist literature in Burma. "Even among religious people, *dāna* amounts to little more than sending a money-transfer to the next life." This approach to *dāna* and making merit denigrates the core thrust of the Buddha's teaching by warping practices for present moral and social welfare into essentially selfish ones for future recompense.

Dāna has been misinterpreted by successive reigns and regimes to serve the interests of the ruling elite, who profess to promote the values espoused by Buddhism. Under the current military regime, *dāna* is often represented as a panacea for poverty. In its propaganda, the junta stresses that a lack of generosity, and not poverty as such, is the real problem facing the country's many destitute citizens. "If you say you can't make donations because you lack wealth, you can never expect to become wealthy," reads one typical pronouncement in a state-run newspaper. This Catch-22 may be cold comfort for the poor, but for the regime it makes perfectly good sense. Why blame decades of mismanagement for the country's many economic woes, when the Buddhist scriptures (according to the junta) say that poverty is simply a product of parsimony?

Given the prevalence of such self-serving interpretations of Buddhist principles in public discourse (which is almost totally monopolized by official state opinion), it is not surprising that many Burmese have strayed from Buddhism altogether without realizing it. Many who profess to be Buddhists often direct their charitable offerings according to the advice of soothsayers and astrologers in order to accrue as much merit for themselves as possible. Not only is this practice based on misplaced faith in the powers of pseudo-spiritual fakirs, it also runs contrary to the Buddhist conception of charity as an act free of self-interest.

Even more disturbing, from the standpoint of the social impact of such distortions of Buddhist principles, is the way charity has become a form of bribery or even a means of laundering ill-gotten gains. When business-men want to obtain a license or permit of some sort, they invariably make a donation to a pet project run by one of the ruling generals. For Burma's drug lords, who enjoy a status akin to aristocracy in the country's capital, charity serves as a convenient way to convert illicit profits into social, politi-cal, and economic capital. Thus donation ceremonies, which routinely bring together generals, drug lords, and businessmen, are highlighted daily on the state-run Myanmar TV news programs. Charity funds everything from the restoration of pagodas to the national football team, but ultimately, the real beneficiaries are those who control the flow of finances behind the scenes.

Most ordinary Burmese are well aware of how the system works, and remain troubled by it, even after more than a decade of such abuses. "Steven Law of Asia World Company has offered a huge donation to build schools and fund multimedia classrooms," remarked Rangoon schoolteacher Mya Lwin recently. He added, "We all know where he gets his money from, but what can we do, except hang our heads in shame?" Law is known to be one of Burma's leading narco-billionaires.

While some of these practices are distinctly modern innovations, there is nothing new about Burmese rulers using charity to enhance their politi-cal legitimacy. The current regime has in many ways modeled itself after Burma's pre-colonial kings. This has been most conspicuously the case in its patronage of the monastic Sangha. On a daily basis, the generals make religious offerings that serve not only as a form of personal merit making, but also as powerful symbolic gestures that exploit the Sangha's historically important role as a unifying factor of the state.

The practice of co-opting religious symbolism for political ends literally reaches its pinnacle with the ceremonial hoisting of the *htidaw* (umbrella) on the top of pagodas that have been newly constructed or renovated. This act is regarded as the ultimate merit making event, and yet it has no basis whatsoever in Buddhist doctrine. According to historian Dr. Than Tun, "This practice began in the fifteenth century when a Mon king invaded Burman dominated territory and put a big crown made like his own on top of each pagoda in the land he conquered." As retaliation, "the Burmese king put a likeness of his own crown on top each pagoda when he re-seized his land."

In early 1999, Burma's military rulers held a *htidaw* hoisting ceremony to mark the completion of a major renovation of the country's most sacred religious edifice, the Shwedagon Pagoda. The ceremony, which was treated as one of the most important religious events of the twentieth century, culminated with the generals shouting "Aung Pyi! Aung Pyi!" ("We won! We won!"). Far from sharing in the generals' sense of victory, however, local people were left feeling more defeated than ever. "When we heard what they were shouting, we felt crushed," recalled one Rangoon shopkeeper. "It was not an act of *dāna* but of sorcery. I was also frightened by the thought of this regime remaining in power for years to come," she added.

By far the most appalling misuse of the principle of *dāna* is the widespread practice of forcing people throughout the country to "donate" their labor to public works projects. The regime has repeatedly claimed that such "voluntary labor" is carried out in the spirit of *dāna*, as if there were something spiritually uplifting about being forced to perform backbreaking labor at gunpoint. In some instances, people are genuinely willing to contribute to the upkeep of temples or to projects that directly benefit their communities, but this clearly does not apply to the construction of roads and other infrastructure for the tourism industry, for instance. "In some cases, people do not mind donating their time voluntarily for their religion," observed recently exiled social critic Tin Maung Than. "But the donation of labor for temple construction must be separated from being ordered to give free labor for government projects," he added.

Some scholars have pointed out that the current regime is worse than the pre-colonial monarchy in the way it has conscripted labor. "Even King Mindon, unlike some of his predecessors, insisted on paying for labor by his subjects, and did not require them to attend to court matters while they were busy during harvest time," explained anthropologist Gustaaf Houtman, citing Dr. Than Tun's *The Royal Order of Burma*. King Mindon, who belonged to Burma's last royal dynasty, eventually abolished corvée labor altogether, following the introduction of coinage and a new taxation system in 1868, according to Burmese historian Toe Hla.

Political abuses are not the only issue that makes *dāna* problematic from a modern perspective. There are also economic consequences that need to be considered. Melford Spiro in his study of Buddhism in rural Burmese society (1982), observed that, "The typical upper Burmese village is reported to spend from 30 to 40 percent of its net disposable cash income on *dāna* and relative activities." This may have the positive effect of encouraging hard work and thrift, but, as Trevor Ling points out in his *Buddhism, Imperialism and War* (1979), "It is important to note that the money that becomes available at harvest time, when the farmer sells his surplus, is channeled into what are, from the entrepreneurial point of view, unproductive activities." A Singapore-based Burmese economist, speaking on condition of anonymity, concurred, "*Dāna* monies may have a very low opportunity cost if the donors do not have the skills, knowledge, and opportunities to invest them productively." The tendency to "invest" savings in risk-free religious generosity rather than in risky capital accumulation has the effect of retarding the rate of economic growth, he argued.

Taken to extremes, some might argue that charity as it has been practiced in Burma for centuries is a hindrance to economic development, since it diverts capital away from more "productive" uses. However, the Singapore-based economist concedes that the problem lies less with charity than with the general inefficiency of the Burmese economy. "In this case, it is tied up with the problem of a lack of mechanisms, modalities, and motivation for efficient allocation of financial resources." Although the profit motive, the driving force behind market-based economics, seems to be at odds with the values of Buddhism, it would be a mistake to conclude that Buddhism is inimical to economic growth. The Buddha taught his lay followers that instead of squandering or hoarding wealth, a quarter of one's income should be used for consumption, a quarter saved for an emergency, and a half used for one's business—a very high rate of reinvestment if taken literally (*Siṅgālovāda Sutta*, D.iii.188). The experience of other Buddhist countries also attests to the fact that Buddhism is no impediment to economic progress. "Thai people also devote a considerable percentage of their income to merit making," observed anthropologist Christina Fink. "Yet the Thai economy grew at a rate of more than ten percent a year during the late 1980s and throughout most of the 1990s."

Contrary to the regime's practice of directing its *dāna* almost exclusively towards the Sangha, most learned abbots and Buddhist scholars agree that there is no doctrinal basis for such bias. In his book *Ottama Purisa Dipani*, the Venerable Ledi Sayadaw stated, "Alms giving done for the benefits arising therefrom after selecting the status of the donees and the way to accrue most merit is not a noble meritorious deed." Citing Ledi Sayadaw's teaching, U Shwe Aung, one of Burma's most influential Buddhist scholars, wrote, "Giving alms not only to the Three Gems (the Buddha, the Dharma and the Sangha) but also to the poor is the noblest deed of alms giving." Efforts to assist the poor by providing such necessities as food, medicine, and education, initiated by well-respected abbots like Thamanya Sayadaw, as well as by Aung San Suu Kyi's National League for Democracy and other, smaller volunteer groups, reflect a clear understanding of the spirit of *dāna* as it is taught in the Buddhist scriptures. However, Burmese people seldom make such "secular" donations, in large part because the requisite institutions of civil society are almost entirely absent. Independent civic-minded organizations are virtually nonexistent in Burma today, as any form of popular participation in activities affecting whole communities is regarded as a threat to military rule. The few "volunteer" organizations that do exist in Burma at present operate under the auspices of the regime, and often serve primarily as a means of channeling corporate or private "donations" directly into the hands of the generals or their cronies.

Beyond these immediate political circumstances, however, there are also deeper cultural factors at work that tend to lead to the misapplication of basic Buddhist values in Burmese society. An inordinate attachment to tradition for tradition's sake, without a critical awareness of the basis of many time-honored practices, eventually renders even the best of these practices meaningless. The Buddha's teachings on *dāna* remain as deeply relevant as ever, but only when they are applied thoughtfully can their true value be properly appreciated.

The structural role of the monks as "fields of merit" (*puññakhetta*) and reciprocators of generosity (*dāna*) seriously determines their intervention in the disastrous situation of their supporters. In cities such as Mandalay, where many impoverished Burmese have sold their homes to Chinese immigrants and moved to the outskirts of town, monks have been left by themselves in the city center with no one to feed them. The monks consequentially are very sensitive to the joy as well as the plight of the local people. When local people suffer from heavy taxation, forced labor, rice quota extortion, and relocation, the monks cannot ignore these miseries.

For example, Thamanya Sayadaw U Vinaya, an elderly monk from the Pa-o ethnic group, lives at the foot of Thamanya Mountain, some twenty miles outside of Pa-an, the capital of Karen State. Apart from his accomplishments as a meditator and his other imperceptible religious qualities, the Sayadaw is also revered for his socially oriented charity practice. The grounds owned by Thamanya Sayadaw cover a three-mile radius around the mountain where about seven thousand families live. The Sayadaw owns several vehicles, including heavy-duty trucks that are used for various construction projects, such as building schools and maintaining roads and various public utilities. Aung San Suu Kyi once noted that while the regime forces people to contribute labor to build roads, the Sayadaw achieves his works through voluntary contributions from the people. However, some observers have noted that most people who donate money to the Sayadaw seem to do so in the belief that they will earn greater merit due to his exalted spiritual status, rather than with an awareness of the social value of their contributions.

The most recent and striking example of Buddhist monks actively engaging in relief of societal suffering was their role in the relief operation of the Nargis Cyclone, which hit southwest Burma on May 2 and 3, 2008, leaving at least 140,000 people dead. The military regime not only failed to launch a substantial relief operation of its own, but it also blocked access for private donors and international agencies. Buddhist monasteries ended up being the only major institution that people could rely on for help. Monks cleared up fallen trees, offered shelter in temples, rebuilt houses, and distributed food to survivors. Several monasteries all over the country also sent trucks loaded with relief supplies and volunteers to the affected areas.

Ashin Nyanissara, known as Sitagu Sayadaw and one of the most influential abbots in the country, even went to the storm-stricken delta area and quickly established clinics for cyclone victims. He arranged for generators and water filtration systems to be set up in some affected areas. The military regime moved to curb the monks' efforts, ordering the monasteries to clear out refugees and prohibiting some from receiving supplies from relief organizations. However, monks continued to play the role of conduits for relief supplies due to their wide-ranging structural networks and public trust.

In this way, monks represent "the public conscience." The structural and historical roles of the Burmese monks and their followers require them to be deeply involved in societal affairs and inevitably in politics. This appears to contradict their preaching. This contradiction or compartmentalization produces several disadvantages for Burmese Buddhists, because there is no philosophical underpinning, aside from the structural and historical role of the religion. One of the clearest cultural impacts is the lack of perseverance of the Burmese people. The Burmese temperament can be described with the metaphor of a hay-fire. When you set fire to the haystack, it burns quickly and even aggressively, but it extinguishes quickly, too. Similarly, when all protests are silenced, Burmese just sit back and learn to adjust to the status quo. Passivity, apathy, and even cynicism with politics are increasing, and there is no ideological force pushing them back on track. The Burmese cannot draw power, guidance, or energy from their philosophy. In short, the worldview of Burmese Buddhists does not operate at a functional level.

In this way, there is an inherent inconsistency between the Burmese Buddhist worldview and Burmese practical activism. Burmese Buddhist monks and their followers are being pulled by their ontology in one direction and by their structural/historical role in a different direction. Life seems divided into separate and distinct spheres for Burmese Buddhists. Thus, the Burmese must think critically about how to reduce the gap between the reality and the ideal. Otherwise, the role of Buddhism in Burma's future may become more nominal, perhaps remaining as merely an instrument or ritual for relieving tension, in the approaching waves of wide-ranging industrialization and globalization. Religious values will then not be exercised in daily practice. The compartmentalization between the daily life and the religious life of Burmese people will persist.

PARADIGM SHIFT? THE PRECIOUSNESS OF DULLABHĀ

In fact, there are several counter-hegemonic attempts initiated by some abbots and lay leaders, including U Hpo Hlaing and Daw Aung San Suu Kyi, to reinterpret some particular teachings of the Buddha to apply to modern circumstances and restore relevancy, such as the ten precepts for kings and the seven "conditions that lead to no decline" (*aparihāniya*) (*Mahāparinibbāna Sutta*, D.ii.73). However, it is doubtful that their reinterpretations are based on a fundamental paradigm shift.

Actually, a new paradigm could be found within Theravada Buddhist teachings that can reconcile the reality of today's Burmese Buddhism with its ideal. According to Buddhism, there are five great opportunities that are difficult to obtain or scarce (*dullabhā*). These are:

1. birth as a human being (*manussatta-bhava-dullabhā*)
2. encountering a buddha (*buddhuppāda-dullabhā*)
3. going forth from the life of a lay person and becoming a bhikkhu/bhikkhuni (*pabbajita-bhava-dullabhā*)
4. attaining confidence in the Buddha, Dharma, and Sangha (*saddhā-sampattiyo-dullabhā*)

5. hearing the true teaching (*saddhamma-savanaṃ-ati-dullabhā*)
   (*Chiggala Sutta*, S.v.456; A.iii.441)

Among these five opportunities, birth as a human is the most important. Human life is *dullabhā*. It is very difficult to attain. A human life may attain innumerable merits and is, therefore, regarded as particularly precious. The Buddha did not say that attaining the life of a celestial being is *dullabhā*; instead, he highly valued individual human life. According to Buddhist understanding, human existence is more conducive to enlightenment than divine existence. Thus, every human being holds the preciousness of *dullabhā* life.

If we assume that everyone has his or her own human value, it would have significant social implications. If people appreciated their *dullabhā*, they would not allow others to violate and abuse their human dignity, human rights, and human value. They would become sensitive to injustice, inequality, and oppression. They would have a strong will to fight back against any attempt to dehumanize them. On the positive side, one would take more responsibility for self-betterment—financially, intellectually, and spiritually—because one appreciates life in its *dullabhā*-defined preciousness. This *dullabhā* notion is, in fact, not antithetical to *saṃsāra* but its best compliment for the well-rounded welfare of people. The notion of *dullabhā* can inspire a sense of energy and right effort to take advantage of the preciousness of our present existence, as opposed to the passivity and resignation engendered by the eternal power of *saṃsāra*.

If Burmese Buddhism would shift its emphasis from the *saṃsāra* paradigm to *dullabhā*, the problem of compartmentalization would also be resolved effectively. By emphasizing the present preciousness of human *dullabhā*, Burmese could generate infinite sources of power, energy, and guidance to take a more active role in changing their destiny—not only their political and social destiny but also their spiritual destiny. This paradigm shift would be harmonious and more in accordance with the path that Lord Buddha wanted Buddhists to walk.

References

Ling, Trevor. 1979. *Buddhism, Imperialism and War*. London: G. Allen and Unwin.

Harvey, Godfrey E. 1925/2000. *History of Burma: From the Earliest Times to 10 March, 1824: The Beginning of the English Conquest*. New Delhi: Asian Educational Services.

Hall, H. Fielding. 1898/1995. *The Soul of a People*. Bangkok: Orchid Press.

Schober, Juliane. 2005. "Buddhist Visions of Moral Authority and Modernity in Burma." In *Burma at the Turn of the 21st Century*, edited by Monique Skidmore. Honolulu: University of Hawai'i Press.

Spiro, Melford. 1982. *Buddhism and Society: A Great Tradition and Its Burmese Vicissitudes*. Berkeley, CA: University of California Press.

Suu Kyi, Aung San. 1997. *The Voice of Hope: Conversations with Alan Clements*. New York: Seven Stories Press.

LIBERATION AS STRUGGLE:
OVERCOMING KARMIC FATALISM IN SHAN STATE, BURMA

KHUENSAI JAIYEN

THE PROBLEM OF NONVIOLENCE, KARMA, AND SELF-DEFENSE

The Buddha is well known for his emphasis on nonviolence, as found in the very first precept for all Buddhists, monastic and lay alike, to refrain from doing any harm to any sentient being. As seen in the previous chapter on Burma, the popular understandings of *karma* and *saṁsāra* can be used to create passivity towards suffering, both individual and social. We could consider this kind of teaching positive as it helps prevent the kind of violent, political fundamentalism that has plagued Islam. At the same time, however, these teachings have not prevented some Buddhists in Burma from participating in political movements against the British, and more recently, against their military dictatorship. There are other such cases in which Buddhists have aided anti-state (in China and Japan) or anti-colonial (Vietnam) revolutionary movements. Further, in some places, like Sri Lanka today, Buddhists have actively supported violent warfare.

Still, the core Buddhist teachings, especially the discourses of the Buddha, have a very strong commitment to non-harming and even a pacifist stance in responding to violence. In one such discourse, King Pasenadi of Kosala, a leading lay devotee of the Buddha and "a friend to whatever is good," decided to launch a counter attack upon receiving word that King Ajatasatru of Magadha was already leading an attack towards his kingdom. In the initial encounter, Pasenadi was defeated and the Buddha reflected, "Victory

The author would like to thank Ven. Sao Jotika at the University of London and the Burma Relief Center for providing background material for this essay.

breeds enmity; the defeated one sleeps badly. The peaceful one sleeps at ease, having abandoned victory and defeat" (Saṁyutta Nikāya 2000, 177, S.i.83). In a second encounter, Pasenadi defeated Ajatasatru but took mercy on him and sent him home after disarming his troops. Still the Buddha warned him, "The killer begets a killer; one who conquers, a conqueror. The abuser begets abuse; the reviler, one who reviles. Thus by the unfolding of karma. The plunderer is plundered" (Saṁyutta Nikāya 2000, 178, S.i.85). Here it seems the Buddha is discouraging any form of violent reaction, even a defensive one.

Indeed, in one Jātaka story, the Buddha-to-be offered the ideal model as a king who allowed invaders to conquer his city declaring, "I want no kingdom that must be kept by doing harm." In the end, the conquering king experienced deep pain at the karma of his violent actions and so freed the king and his city. It is said that the first king's nonviolent stance saved numerous lives on both sides by refusing to enter into violent conflict (J.ii.400–403). In this story, we see how an absolute stance towards nonviolence can actually lead to the best kind of victory that does not breed enmity and creates a secure peace. Yet this Jātaka tale is a myth. How many such scenarios can we find in real history?

The common result of such a pacifist stance is what supposedly happened to the Buddha's own people, the Shakyans. They were destroyed by King Pasenadi's son, Vidudabha, because they did not defend themselves (Harvey 2000, 242). This was foreseen by the Buddha, who successfully dissuaded Vidudabha three times, but on Vidudabha's fourth attempt, the Buddha saw the karmic force of the situation as unavoidable. He remarked in the end, "If you regard only the present existence, it was indeed unjust that the Shakyans should die in such a way. What they received, however, was entirely just considering the sin they committed in a previous state of existence [of having thrown poison into the river]" (Dh.A.iv.3). In this story, we see the typical teaching towards karma being applied; that is people experience bad fortune, suffering, and death *directly* as a result of bad karmic deeds in the past.

"BAD KARMA" IN SHAN STATE

As we have seen in other chapters in this volume, such an overly simplified view of karma helps to develop a set of cultural values that legitimize forms of social injustice. This culture not only affirms the self-righteousness of the oppressors but also helps to confirm feelings of worthlessness, passivity, and disempowerment in the oppressed. The people of Shan State in northeast Burma are a tragic example of this culture, developed out of Buddhism, which legitimizes not only structural oppression by outright direct violence.

The Shan share a rich Theravada Buddhist heritage with their fellow Burmans and the ethnically related Thai and Lao. This heritage also has its own distinct aspects with early Mahayana influences as well as texts and a teaching tradition all in their native language. However, since the emergence of military dictatorship in Burma over forty years ago, the distinct and independent nature of Shan Buddhism, and Shan culture in general, has been under attack. Although the Burmese military regime has declared that there is religious freedom throughout Burma, they have actually been preventing ethnic minorities from practicing their culture. In Shan State, Buddhism is traditionally taught in the native language, so the monks have usually taught the people to read Shan. However, monks are not able to do this freely now. The teaching of Shan is restricted throughout Shan State, and even monks must ask special permission from the authorities to teach Shan to villagers in their communities. Even if they are given permission, they are suspected of being subversive.

The military regime wants to assimilate everyone into the Burmese Buddhist system. They have given an order that if monks in Shan State want to become abbots, they must pass monastic exams in the Burmese language. However, the Shan have their own monastic exams, organized by the Shan religious ruling body in Pang Long, although the state does not want to recognize them. The military regime has also introduced a law which stipulates that monks from Burma can only go to study abroad if they are over thirty-five and if they have passed the Burmese monastic exams. This clearly discriminates against Shan monks.

The Shan have a saying: "Where there is a village, there must be a temple and monks." It is deeply rooted in the culture. However, in some parts of Shan State, the regime has forcibly relocated hundreds of thousands of people from the countryside to the towns. The relocated villagers have been forced not only to abandon their homes and fields, but also the temples and monks that form the heart of their community. This has been like destroying the soul of the people. Once the villages were deserted, the Burmese troops looted many of the temples. They stole the Buddha images and decorations, and burned the ancient Shan texts. Nearly all the novices studying at the temples have disrobed immediately, since they have had to follow their families to the relocation sites. Many of the monks have also disrobed out of fear of being killed by the military. The Burmese troops suspect that all Shan monks support the resistance. In March 1997, several monks were killed, including Ven. Yanna from Kengkham Temple, who was put in a sack and drowned.

The military officers of the regime are often seen in the state media taking part in Buddhist ceremonies. This is basically using religion to exert power over others. For example in Shan State, they have been building pagodas in many places. These pagodas are built in the Burmese style, not the Shan style, and have Burmese names. Clearly, they were planning to represent Burmese domination of the area and to subvert traditional religious customs.

In 1997 in Kunhing, Central Shan State, many monks were invited by the Burmese authorities to attend the groundbreaking ceremony to start building the Maha Kanbawza Pyi Nyein Aye Pagoda (meaning "Peaceful Shanland" in Burmese). That year there had been heavy fighting in the area between the Shan resistance and the Burmese military. So in order to pacify the people, they chose to build the pagoda then, at that place, and under that name. The temple was built in the style of the Shwedagon Pagoda in Rangoon. Many Burmese military officers came to the ceremony, including General Maung Aye. The time and date chosen for the ceremony was at nine a.m. on the ninth day of the ninth month (according to the lunar calendar) nine being the auspicious number of the regime. In this way, the regime shows its greater interest in astrology rather than in real Buddhist teachings. During the actual groundbreaking, according to custom, monks and local people should have buried valuables under the pagoda, but they were all kept away during this part. Only the military officers performed the ceremony. The local people were very suspicious and felt uncomfortable. They suspected the officers of putting in something evil. Then afterwards, the local villagers, including children, were forced to build the pagoda. In this way, it seems clear that the religious activities performed by the regime have nothing to do with real Buddhism (Burma Relief Centre, 1999).

As part of this process of "Burmanization," many ethnically Burman monks have been sent into Shan State. These monks, who have links to the military, tend to emphasize patience or equanimity (*upekkhā*) towards the trouble in this region and also use the teaching of karma to explain present sufferings. Some Shan monks have supported the resistance to the military government. However, there is still a prevalent view among the Shan people, inculcated by Buddhism, that to recruit soldiers for resisting the Burmese military is evil, because it means taking part in killing and the creation of more bad karma in the future. In turn, they have developed a sense of fatalism that their suffering is due to bad karma from a past life. The idea of past karma has been used to make the people submissive, so they are waiting for a savior, unable to liberate themselves. Nonviolence (*ahiṃsā*) has been interpreted here as passivity, so instead of fighting for their rights, the people are fleeing.

It is this kind of interpretation of karma and nonviolence that makes one question what is a proper Buddhist response to direct violence, especially in extreme cases such as the systematic rape of women in Burma by the Burmese military. The Dalai Lama at present and the Buddhist movement in Vietnam during the 1960s have been serious attempts to develop a comprehensive and systematic response to violence. However, the results are inconclusive: the Vietnamese movement was crushed and the Tibetan movement was unable to significantly change Chinese policy. In the Shan case, it is clear that the doctrine of karma is being used to warp the idea of nonviolence and non-harming into one of passivity and fatalism in the face of direct violence.

THE *MAHOSATHA JĀTAKA*

Another *Jātaka* story, the *Mahosatha Jātaka* (J.vi.546), offers us a way to explore more deeply this problem of karma and the way to respond to more direct forms of violence. Mahosatha, whose name means "Noble Cure," was the son of Siriwattana and Sumana Devi, whose town was east of Mitthila, the capital of the land of Videha. As he grew, news of Mahosatha's wisdom spread far and wide, and in time the king summoned him to his place to serve as a minister. His presence, however, was resented by other ministers. A scramble for royal favor finally ended with Mahosatha gaining power. Yet he was generous enough to pardon his erstwhile enemies by reinstating them in their former offices. He was appointed regent when it became clear to the king that he entertained no ambition to usurp his throne, and so he set out to do his best in this position.

Mahosatha came to learn through his spies that King Culani of Kapila, about one thousand miles to the north of Videha, was planning to subdue all of the 101 lands far and near and make himself supreme ruler. Mahosatha thus began to face the eventual offensive that was to come to his land and his people. Assisted by his capable minister Kewat, King Culani conquered all the lands except Videha within a span of seven years. Then he launched three successive offensives against Videha, all of which failed, thanks to Mahosatha.

Undaunted, Culani resorted to win Videha by ruse. He decided to offer his daughter to his counterpart as queen but to take him prisoner instead when he came to pay a formal visit to Pancala, the royal capital of Kapila, to ask for his daughter's hand. Foreseeing the scheme, Mahosatha decided to play along by gaining Culani's consent to allow him to set up a temporary citadel on the border between Videha and Kapila. Taking advantage of the proximity of the enemy's capital, Mahosatha constructed a system of tunnels that led to Culani's palace from which he planned to abduct the queen and her daughter.

At last, the date for the wedding was fixed, and King Videha traveled to his temporary residence at the citadel. On cue, Culani surrounded the citadel with thousands of troops and demanded his submission. The defenders, instead of complying with his ultimatum, took hold of Culani's queen, daughter, and close relatives and countered with their own ultimatum to lay down his arms. A truce was eventually declared between the two sides, after which Mahosatha defeated Culani in a duel conducted in private. In sparing Culani's life and honor, Mahosatha forced him to accept the following conditions: to free the enslaved kings, to restore the conquered lands back to them, and to conclude a treaty of peace and amity among the lands.

Thereafter, all the lands and their peoples lived together in peaceful coexistence; and Mahosatha, in his subsequent final life as a prince of northern India, became the Lord Buddha, the supreme teacher of all people.

Was the Buddha Really a Peace Advocate?

It is on this story and the moral behind it that I have modeled my life: to love all human beings but to protect one's country and people; to work for peace but to never hesitate to apply force when it is necessary. Moreover, this *Jātaka* fits in with what I learned during my own three-year quest for a truth in which I could take refuge.

At one point in my youth, I was about to give up the struggle against the Burmese rulers because of our own Shan intra-party intrigues, not unlike those experienced by Mahosatha. In fact, I was suspected of treason and thrown in jail for almost four years by the resistance leadership, namely the Shan United Revolutionary Army's executive council led by General Gawnzoeng. I regard this order for my imprisonment as a mistake that turned out to be a good one, because without that incarceration, I wouldn't have become who I am today.

During this time, my suffering was basically spiritual, because no one abused me physically. I considered myself innocent and felt bitter for being humiliated in this way. It would have been better if they had killed me. My bitterness filled me with bitter thoughts that occupied me day and night. As a result, I gradually lost my appetite and became ill. One day, a medic who was treating me tried to cheer me up, but from the corner of my eye, I saw him shaking his head to other inmates. The meaning was clear: I was going downhill and only a miracle would bring me back to life.

Facing this reality, I began to ask myself whether I should let my illness take care of all my troubles once and for all. Somehow I felt that it would be a shame to go down that way without a fight and decided to take things into my own hands. I reflected that I was ill because I didn't eat; I didn't eat because I had lost my appetite through sleepless nights; and I didn't sleep because my mind was filled with bitter thoughts. The solution, therefore, was to shut my mind off to the bitter thoughts so that I could go to sleep. I then remembered that when I was a child and had trouble falling asleep, I used to count my breathing: inhale-1, exhale-2 and so on until sleep just overtook me. That first night I counted to about eight hundred and fell asleep. The next day I felt better and a little hungry and started to take food. The feeling that I had that day was so nice, so tranquil and yet happy, that I decided to go on with the breathing exercises.

As the exercises progressed, my mind became more lucid. I was able to remember things that I had already forgotten, like when I was two years old, I gave away my gold necklace to a thief who was gently asking for it. My mother later said she felt thankful that the thief had not done anything cruel to me. As I continued to get better, I also learned to read and write Thai, improved my English, and learned to read verses written in old Shan.

Then, just before my twenty-ninth birthday, something happened. I realized that I was not able either to stop my breathing or go on with it indefinitely. Things that start have to end; this is the law of impermanence (*anicca*). I had tried to resist this, the way things go, and so I experienced the law of suffering (*dukkha*). The whole thing was holding me under bondage, because I refused to acknowledge the law of not-self (*anattā*). I pondered this over as I breathed in and out, and suddenly, these three natural truths all came to me. So on my twenty-ninth birthday, I declared what others before me had: "I take my refuge in the Buddha; I take my refugee in the Dharma, and I take my refuge in the Sangha." Since then, I have been born anew.

During this period, I discovered what I call the Seven Triplets, which are as follows:

1. Beings are always looking for prosperity (whether spiritual or material), happiness, and freedom (the choice triplets).
2. But they almost always encounter adversity, suffering, and bondage (the inevitable triplets).
3. The root causes of these inevitable triplets are greed, susceptibility, and ignorance (the causative triplets).
4. The only way to overcome the root causes and achieve the choice triplets is through self-discipline, attention, and learning (the means triplets).
5. One must train oneself in this direction by taking control of one's physical, verbal, and mental actions (the tool triplets).
6. One must not only work for one's good but also that of one's community (nation) and the world (the object triplets).
7. One who is not yet enlightened may slip at times. One must therefore take refuge in the Buddha, Dharma, and Sangha (the refuge triplets).

These triplets were how I came to perceive the Four Noble Truths of the Lord Buddha, who first enunciated them soon after his attainment of enlightenment and later in different wordings but always retaining the original theme.

Coming to the Four Noble Truths, one is inevitably reminded of the Middle Way that the Lord Buddha took pains to highlight. I think many are led to believe that the Middle Way means to avoid the extremes of sensual pleasure and self-mortification only. However, had the Buddha been talking not to a group of austere hermits but to others, say a capitalist and a communist, I'm sure that he would have put it quite another way. The same would have applied when speaking to advocates of peaceful means and those of forceful means.

In this respect, the Buddha and the many Buddhas-to-be from the *Jātakas* employed whichever method was suitable to the occasion. The only criterion was that actions were not affected by greed, susceptibility, and ignorance. He was also careful that actions pointed toward the good of himself (to attain buddhahood), his kin, and the world. Today's catchphrase, "Think globally, Act locally," would have gone fine with the Buddha who counseled to love all beings and to work for the good of kinsfolk (because they are the nearest beings that you have). This did not prevent him from admonishing his followers to not be overly attached to their own kin (e.g. the *Mettā Sutta*, Sn.i.8).

If one still has doubts about the Buddha's stance on peace and force, one should remember that although there is no doubt he was a peace advocate, he was also not above using his own muscleman, Moggalana, for dealing with extremely unruly disciples. The scriptures also name dedicated followers who achieved the path despite being warriors. Maha Siha, the commander-in-chief of Vesali, was credited as being a *sotāpanna*, one who has entered the first stage in the realization of nirvana. I think it is important that we do not judge a person as wicked just because he or she has been forced to use forceful means.

BUDDHISM AND THE SHAN STRUGGLE FOR LIBERATION

Following my release from incarceration in 1978, the leadership allowed us to decide on our own future. Accordingly, some left, but I stayed on. I decided that leaving the struggle would amount to renouncing the Buddha's teachings and example, so I resolved to fight on in the capacity that I was most suited: propagation of the Buddha's teachings in the way that I understood them. Two years later, I was given the job to set up the Institute for Leadership. That was when I was able to convey my convictions to students.

It was General Gawnzoeng himself who supported the Institute for Leadership Project. He and I ended up becoming close friends until his death in 1991 as both of us were firm believers of the Buddha's teachings. We taught the students, most of whom were officers and promising new members of the struggle, about politics, war, administration, history, and conscientization. I personally handled the conscientization in which I focused on the theme that one should consider oneself a Buddhist only if one tries to help one's own people. I taught my students that the same rule applies to other religions. For example, Jesus might have taught about universal love, but he also worked personally for the good of his own people, as did Muhammad.

Furthermore, I taught them that if you want to be free, you have to learn (*paññā*). To learn, you must be able to concentrate (*samādhi*). To concentrate, you need an undisturbed calm. You must, therefore, make and follow rules (*sīla*) that enable you to create and maintain this calm. This method has been effective in all my classes. I have never made rules for the students. They have done so by themselves.

As most Shans are Buddhist, though admittedly bad ones because they just follow their parents' custom of being Buddhist, I was convinced that some, if not all, would get the message. Of course, I wasn't expecting everyone who learned the Buddha's teachings to take up arms. I myself was holding a chalk or a pen most of the time. However, in 1996, one faction of the resistance decided to surrender, but the other, led by most of my former students, have remained to fight on to this day.

I don't think every one of my students wants to become a buddha. Yet I believe most of them would be happy becoming *arahants*, who are in fact little buddhas. Still, as believers they must follow the basics: act for the good of oneself, one's community, and the world. This means that when there is no need or opportunity to act for the good of the community and the world, you have to strive to attain your own good (i.e. liberation). However, when there is a need and opportunity to do good for the community and the world, you must always answer the call. Instead of accepting your situation as karmic fate that must be endured, I want people to engage as Mahosatha did, striving onward tirelessly on the bodhisattva path.

I have always believed that everyone is good at something and that they must make the most of it for themselves, their people, and the world around them. Everyone has a role to play, whether as a farmer, businessperson, soldier, doctor, monk, or teacher. The more we have such enlightened people in every possible field, the quicker the victory of our people will be. In this way, Burmans, Shans, and other neighbors will be able to live together in peace.

References

Burma Relief Centre. December 1999. *Destroying the Soul of Our People*. Newsletter 15. Chiang Mai, Thailand.

The Connected Discourses of the Buddha: A New Translation of the Saṁyutta Nikāya. 2000. Translated by Bhikkhu Bodhi. Boston: Wisdom Publications.

Harvey, Peter. 2000. *An Introduction to Buddhist Ethics*. Cambridge: Cambridge University Press.

THE MEANING AND PRACTICE OF THE BUDDHIST PRECEPTS AS A POLITICAL ACTION FRAMEWORK

UPASEKA YASO

A time comes when silence is betrayal. Even when pressed by the demands of inner truth, men do not easily assume the task of opposing their government's policy, especially in time of war.

- Martin Luther King Jr.

From a very early age, the interconnection of life seemed unambiguous to me. When I was ordered, as a youthful adult by my government (the United States at that time) to undergo obligatory military service, I refused. "Fighting for peace" did not make any sense to me, but this decision was taken at no small personal and social cost. I felt the social stigma of being labeled unpatriotic and that my loyalty to the nation was suspect. I was conditioned from birth by society and school that I should "stand up and make the sacrifice", which I was told to believe is the highest calling of "true men". Songs, eulogies, obligatory anthems, monuments, history lessons—all condemned my choice to not serve in the military and suggested this choice was most likely a manifestation of cowardice.

It took enormous courage and an unshakable belief in the rightness of my personal vision to turn away from this extremely powerful indoctrination and manipulative social teaching. At this time in the early 1970s, I experienced that many ordinary people felt defensive when they discovered I was a war objector. I have since realized that although I was not seeking to challenge them to justify their beliefs, they felt they had to defend themselves against my choice. This was an illuminating but distressing discovery for me of the way in which societies mobilize auto-repression. Mass participation in ostracizing, marginalizing, and humiliating by necessity any member of the group who dares to bring into question the dominant paradigm helps the ordinary person to accept as "normal" policies and practices, which if only briefly reflected upon, would be found to be unacceptable and morally repugnant.

The process of educating members of a society in "the norms" provides for social cohesion and can bring social harmony when all agree and live by the rules. However, this process of socialization is frequently manipulated by the ruling class for their own benefit. There are limits on individual consciousness within the consensus social order. Social criticism of any individual's behavior is hard to bear for any member of a group, but especially for the young. Only through the adherence to a clear set of principles is it possible to remain steadfast in the face of deviant mass behavior. I personally found it quite difficult not to reject society as a whole when I felt rejected for not following the social order. I clearly observed that some other young people became casualties of this social discord, sometimes becoming addicted to drugs or becoming criminals as a result of their inability to stand against such broadly experienced rejection.

VOWS

My decision to refuse military service, even at the cost of my freedom, did not take place in a vacuum. That difficult decision was the result of a great deal of introspection and reflection, which led me to take on several vows for my own personal behavior. One was to become a vegetarian, since I believed that there was a connection between involvement in killing to eat and killing for any other reason. It is thoroughly unnecessary for humans to eat meat to survive, and by killing to eat, or in most cases sanctioning someone else to do our killing for us to eat, a threshold of repulsion against the taking of life has already been breached.

A second vow I defined for myself at that time was to examine all my own personal connections with "systems of death", the most direct of which was my relationship with my own government. Non-participation in the military would be hypocritical if I still paid taxes to a government that used that money to finance its wars and weapons purchases as well as a militant foreign policy. Therefore, I took the additional vow never to pay my taxes and to be public about my reasons for refusal to pay.

BUDDHISM AND DEMOCRACY

I believe that my government should represent my values on the world stage. I also believe that the ideals of democracy and Buddhism are harmonious. When I discover that the actions of my government, or any government, cause suffering, I feel obligated to respond with counter-action. This understanding has led to my participation in a variety of political projects to disrupt the most outrageous of the government actions, especially its production of nuclear weapons. I was responsible with others for the damage, to the extent of several millions of dollars, of material that had only one purpose: the extermination of large quantities of life. I considered these objects to be intrinsically immoral and, therefore, had no qualms of working for their absolute elimination, even by direct action. Property destruction has always fit within my understanding of nonviolent action. For this type of morally guided action, I served time in prison as a "criminal". I finally voted with my feet and now live as a Canadian citizen in British Columbia and in Thailand.

What would one would say to the general of an army who is planning to attack another country? The Buddha dealt with this very situation. His family was fighting over water to build a rice field. He went to them and told them, "If you make war, there will be no end to it. Those who claim victory will be met with hatred by those who lost. Those who won will also feel hatred toward those who lost. Hatred itself will kill you. There is no need for another enemy. Hatred will kill you. - Maha Ghosananda (1913-2007), Cambodian Buddhist monk, story from the *Kuṇālajātakavaṇṇanā* (*Jātaka Aṭṭhakathā*, Ja.536)

BUDDHISM AND ACTION

Buddhism, which I grew into later in my life, has provided me with a framework into which my own initial realizations and understandings of inter-connectedness and complicity are clearly supported. Two key terms of which I have developed deeper understandings, and which govern my actions, I define as follows:

> *Nonviolence:* An *active* term, which means meeting threats to peace and security at the personal, communal, or "national" level with methods that are not violent and directly engage the threat at either the direct, structural, or cultural level.

> *Buddhism:* An *active* term, which is not just a system of belief but a path in which the goal and the method for reaching that goal are indivisible.

Buddhism, whether Mahayana, Theravada, or Vajrayana, share some commonalities, namely: the Triple Gem, the Four Noble Truths, and the Eightfold Path. Together, these provide the Buddhist with an essential core or basis for understanding and practice. An active definition of Buddhism means no one is born Buddhist but becomes Buddhist by conscious choice and action. Becoming a Buddhist can only be undertaken in life once a practitioner becomes cognizant enough to reflect on the result of one's actions. This author's interpretation of basic Buddhist truths in relation to the subject of this chapter are:

> *Triple Gem* means accepting that both the Buddha existed and that the path revealed by the Buddha exists. This path is encapsulated in a set of truths called the dharma, and people who have accepted to attain these truths as fellow wayfarers on the path revealed by the Buddha are the sangha. Ordination is not important in this definition of sangha, however, the distinct choice to follow the path at more than a blind faith level is the determining factor.

Four Noble Truths means accepting and integrating into one's life that there is a path out of suffering and that this path encompasses the *entirety* of the Buddhist life—the Eightfold Path.

Eightfold Path means living one's life within a moral framework to strengthen one's capacity for developing wisdom and liberation. Morality, wisdom, and liberation are indivisible as both path and goal. They do not come in a sequence but rather inter-penetrate and manifest together at progressively deeper levels.

BUDDHISM AND NONVIOLENCE

It is within the living of life in a moral framework and the practice of wisdom that nonviolence is rooted for a Buddhist. If path and goal are indivisible, how is it possible to attain peace through violence?

While wise reflection swiftly reveals the folly of the use of violence, violence is conditioned by three innate forces or potentialities within the human being: greed, hatred, and delusion. It is specifically these latent potentialities that are combatted by the path/goal of generosity, love, and wisdom—in other words, the moral framework for living encompassed by the Eightfold path.

Some livelihoods were pointed out by the Buddha as unsuitable for practitioners of the dharma nearly 2500 years ago, such as the making or selling of weapons and livelihoods that derive from killing of animate life (butchery, soldiering, etc.). To further discourage others, the Buddha counseled the ordained never to accept an offering of support that specifically required the killing of animate life to make that offering.

However, the Buddha was an impermanent phenomenon and could only point the way. It is up to the being living in any age to employ wise reflection and apply the Buddha's insights in the modern day. Humanity has advanced technologically, and this has manifested as new social dilemmas that did not exist in the Buddha's time.

The proscription against killing, or involvement with killing, would clearly require a practicing Buddhist to refrain from any livelihood based on the taking of animate life. However, a more subtle aspect of this teaching is the one that required renunciates to refuse any offering believed to have been specifically killed for them. This teaching educates us about our interconnection to all other living beings and the necessity to reflect upon our complicity in systems of violence of which we ourselves may not be the direct actor but are an indirect supporter or beneficiary. Some things in this realm have changed radically since the time of the Buddha. Most human commerce is no longer carried out directly, but indirectly, through "the market". The market has become the key interconnection for human kind, and a Buddhist must use wise reflection in interactions with this human created institution. Animate life is no longer taken for the direct benefit of a single specific person but for any and all participants in this larger market. In a modern world, this would suggest that practicing Buddhists examine deeply their lifestyle connections to greater society and withdraw as much as possible any support or involvement in systems that take animate life.

Military service, taxes paid to a government maintaining a military force or for the purchasing of weaponry, investing in companies that make weaponry, investing in slaughter houses or companies trading in "livestock" or depending on the taking of life to produce their products (such as leather, skins, and furs) should clearly all be avoided. Of perhaps more difficulty is the question of how a Buddhist should approach modern medicines, when many, but not all, are produced through the sacrificing of the lives of hundreds of thousands of mammals? Only a modest amount of research will reveal that many of these medicines themselves treat diseases that are a result of greed and hatred, such as obesity, stress, and hypertension. The wisest response could be avoidance by lifestyle change, but this carries its own costs and requires the reflected upon judgment of the practitioner.

"Violence never ceases through violence, only through non-violence. This is eternal law." (Dh.5) This truism from the *Dhammapada* continues to inspire through the millenniums. Putting it into practice is far more difficult. One of the key practitioners who revealed the path of active nonviolence as a way of life, as well as a powerful method of political struggle, was Mahatma Gandhi. His key teachings were influenced by Hindu, Buddhist, and Muslim understandings of the interconnection of life. He advised his followers never to cooperate with systems of violence and pointed out that without our support, these systems will collapse. Unreflected upon support by the vast majority of people is what allows most any system of violence to continue.

Wise reflection will usually undercut the urge to perform individual acts of direct violence. However, wise reflection is difficult when our security is threatened. The moment our personal security feels threatened, ordinary people pull back, and become tense and tight. In these situations, we are more likely to have our actions governed by re-action rather than wisdom. If our life has been conditioned by reflection and a moral framework, we are far more likely to be able to cut through the urge to re-act and instead act in a manner consistent with morality—not only at those times when we are confronted with violence but also when we are assaulted by far more common roots of violence: greed, hatred, or delusion. A life lived within a moral framework is much better prepared to respond skillfully in a way that will meet greed with generosity, hatred with nonviolence, and delusion with wisdom.

THE PRECEPTS AS POLITICAL ACTION GUIDES

It is precisely for this type of preparation that the Buddha gave practitioners the Fivefold training in moral conduct (*pañcasīla*). The key areas of the framework are the same for ordained and non-ordained, but the Fivefold framework was expanded into a set of more than one hundred specific rules that were appropriate to situations commonly met by ordained practitioners during the time of the Buddha. The 5 are:

1. *Avoiding lies and speaking the truth.* Truth is the first casualty in war, and violence is fostered by non-truth, secrecy, mistrust, and deception. Truth is liberating by its very nature. Truth can also be used unskillfully,

which is why we are instructed to speak the truth when it is useful and when it is necessary. Sometimes speaking the truth when it is necessary will require personal sacrifice. In the political realm, this requires non-cooperation with corruption and abuse of power by others as well as the defense of human rights for all.

2. *Non-stealing.* How can we foster peace if we are taking something belonging to another? With a somewhat deeper reflection, we may question whether owning, or having what someone else is prohibited from obtaining due to the current social/political order, is a form of theft and a form of violence. Non-stealing can help us realize that there are institutional and structural forms of violence and theft in which we must not participate. This can lead to a satisfying and voluntary reduction in material acquisitions and a deep desire to be generous.

3. *Sexual forbearance.* This precept becomes complete abstinence for a renunciate but requires the taming of sexual greed and reflection on the nature of sexual energy by non-ordained Buddhists. While rape is an obvious form of violence driven in part by unskillful understandings of gendered beings, the use of sexual energy to influence others is a far more subtle and common form of manipulation or coercion. Reflect for only a moment on how frequently this is used to influence commerce, trade, and commercialization between human beings. The sexual objectification of human beings is wide spread, but it takes only a little reflection to see the connection between the commercial objectification and commodification of humans, as well as the increasing global traffic in human beings, sometimes into sexual slavery.

4. *Avoidance of mind clouding substances.* It should be obvious that any substance that clouds the mind is not conducive to wise reflection or action. The pressure of society to use these substances is enormous, and it is the most common way for the human species to deal with stress. Many forms of political violence require alcohol or drugs to manifest, such as torture, due to the ability of these substances to cut human empathy. Both drugs and alcohol, with the exception of medicinal necessities, are areas of economic and social activity that should be avoided by wisdom

advocates. Weapons and alcohol are a particularly lethal combination, and an enormous amount of domestic violence takes place when the two come together with a small quantity of ordinarily dismissable anger or annoyance.

5. *Avoidance of killing.* This is the heart of nonviolence. Do not yourself kill anyone, and do not allow others to kill for you. In some circumstances, prohibit the aggressive actions of others out of compassion for the victim, and if possible, for the karma of the perpetrator. We are all connected.

All five of these actions undercut enormously the power that violence has over an individual and are the basis for a nonviolent and wise life. These will also condition a wise and nonviolent result by our own actions.

BUDDHISM AND REVOLUTION

Wise and deep reflection takes time, which is increasingly difficult to obtain in the fast pace of modern technologically infused life. Decisions are being made in ever shorter periods of time. At the same time, each decision has a greater impact than ever before because of the force multiplier effect of new communications technology and globalization. Wise reflection does not mean rebelling against modern life. It requires that the practitioner reclaim their power and refuse to be mindlessly swept along with the pace of those around them.

Buddhism calls for a revolution in living and our relationship with the world around us, especially in the realm of political power and political economy. Non-reflection on the nature of political power and political decisions in which everyone is involved leaves the ordinary person as a passive supporter of the status quo. Political elites depend on a lack of opposition to the abuse of power to commit immoral acts. An understanding of the inherent indivisibility of all things and the moral Eightfold Path will lead sincere Buddhist practitioners to a path that is politically revolutionary.

BUDDHISM AND DOMESTIC VIOLENCE: USING THE FOUR NOBLE TRUTHS TO DECONSTRUCT AND LIBERATE WOMEN'S KARMA

OUYPORN KHUANKAEW

INTRODUCTION

I was born in a traditional Buddhist community located in a rural area of northern Thailand. "Traditional Buddhist" means that our way of living was closely integrated with Buddhism. Our lives, both as individuals and collectively, from birth to death, were based upon the Buddhist belief system. The temple was the main cultural, educational, and spiritual center of each community. Monks were the main leaders in our religion, while men were the main leaders in the family.

Half of my life I grew up in a very violent family. As a result, I lived in fear and anger throughout my childhood and early adulthood. For so long, I did not trust any man, because if I could not trust my father, the man whom I loved the most, it was very difficult to trust any man that came along later in my life. I lived with anger and rejection toward my father, even some years after his death.

I was a feminist before I became a Buddhist. There was nowhere and no one from whom I could learn to understand the domestic violence that I experienced until I discovered feminism during my studies for a master's degree in my late twenties. Although I knew even at very young age that my father was wrong, that my mother was a good wife and a good mother, and that we were all good children, no one ever told me that I was right. It was a very powerless experience to know that I was right but could not do anything to protect myself and the people I loved.

It is feminism that helps me understand why my father was violent and why no one and no institution helped my family when we were in such suffering. Feminism helps me to understand violence against women and to know why my family and millions of families around the world live with domestic violence. It helps me to know that it is not my fault when I experience gender-based violence anytime, anywhere. This wisdom and strength motivates me to work to end violence against women, particularly domestic violence, because I do not want any women or children to suffer the way I and my family suffered.

I now understand why I was angry when I was working on women's issues. For a long while, the anger and frustration took away my strength until I became exhausted, alienated, and burned out. I started to practice different forms of meditation, because I wanted to have peace and harmony in my personal life. This lead me to become a Buddhist in my early thirties.

I became a Buddhist practitioner long after I became involved in feminist work. Traditional Buddhist culture did not help me understand the suffering that I and my family went through. It did not help me to reconcile with my father. It is only after I learned of the suffering of other women in the Buddhist context that I began to understand how traditional Buddhist culture is one main cause of violence against women. However, when I learned the essence of Buddhism through practice, I found Buddhist teachings to be a path of liberation from my childhood suffering.

During a trip I made to visit the Tibetan community in exile in Dharamsala, I asked a lama if I could visit with some women who had been imprisoned and physically abused by the Chinese. He pointed to a nunnery, where I met one, who happened to be the abbess of the nunnery herself. I was overwhelmed by her radiance of lovingkindness (*metta*) and thought I must be seeing an *arahant*, an enlightened one, in the flesh. I asked what had changed her, and she said it was meditation. When I asked what kind of meditation, she said compassion meditation—for the Chinese soldier that hurt her and for herself—and also meditation on impermanence—to see that the body that was violated is actually impermanent and that the notion of self is but illusory. The depth of her realization and her inner peace was quite different from the refugees I had met before from Burma and Cambodia. From this experience, I felt that I found the tool for the victims of violence to transcend destructive emotions and unjust social structures. The tool to empower them is inner spiritual change.

It is such Buddhist practice that helped me work on my anger with my father. I came to understand my fear, anger, and alienation with men started from the relationship with my father. While feminism helps me understand violence against women through my head, it is Buddhist practice that helps me understand it from my heart. Through Buddhist practice, I cultivate understanding, compassion, and lovingkindness toward my father and myself. It helps me to let go of the anger and fear that lies deep inside me. I know my father through my anger and fear, and I also see his compassion and lovingkindness within me. This is how I reconciled with him and became healed.

Through my life experience, I have learned that the unique principle that feminism and Buddhism share is that wisdom only comes through personal and experiential learning. Feminism says the personal is political, because our experiences are the experiences of society. We talk about injustice, because as women we experience it every single day. Buddhism teaches us that the only way to understand suffering and to attain liberation is by practicing what the Buddha taught and reflecting this through our personal experience in daily life.

Because of this understanding, I became committed to work with Buddhist groups starting first with Buddhist nuns in 1995. My work has aimed to empower them, to raise their consciousness about their suffering, and to support them to find ways to change it collectively. I have facilitated numerous workshops on violence against women with various Buddhist groups in South and Southeast Asia since 1997. These women and men, both ordained and lay, have been from Thailand, Cambodia, Burma, India, Nepal, Bhutan, and include Tibetans in exile. I use Buddhist and feminist principles, methods, and practices as the guiding path to work for peace and justice.

In short, we can say that in his entire life after he gained enlightenment, the Buddha taught only two things: suffering and the way to end the suffering. Therefore, when we do workshops on violence against women with Buddhist groups, we use the Four Noble Truths, the core teaching of Buddhism, as a tool to help participants understand this problem and to work together to find ways to end suffering. The Four Noble Truths consist of suffering, the root causes of suffering, the cessation of suffering, and the paths that lead to the cessation of suffering. Although it is said there are eighty-four thousand discourses that the Buddha used to teach his disciples over forty years, all of them are an expansion of details on this core teaching, the Four Noble Truths and the Eightfold Path.

THE FIRST NOBLE TRUTH: THE SUFFERING OF WOMEN

In my workshops with Buddhist men and women, we draw on a board a picture of an island in the water and discuss with them the nature of the island. For example, it originates deep in the earth; we only see the top part that we call an island; there is the foundation underneath that holds up the island; and if we want to destroy an island we have to remove the earth underneath it.

Then we ask the female participants to identify the forms of suffering that they themselves experience in their family, community, society, or have heard of other women facing. With each form of suffering, we help the participants consider whether the suffering is natural or unnatural. Most of the women that we work with internalize the suffering they are experiencing as natural. They often feel it is a result of their past-life karma, so they cannot do anything about it. Our questions help them see clearly that being a woman is an identity that makes a big difference in their life experience. We write the forms of women's suffering on the island. The following are what participants have identified as forms of suffering that are caused by Buddhism:

+ Monks and religious institutions are silent about gender-based violence.
+ Women are told that they are an obstacle to the monks' celibate life.
+ Women are told, often by monks, that the reason they were born as women is because they did not accumulate enough merit (*puñña*) in their previous lives. Thus, they could not be born in a male form.
+ Women are often told by monks to be patient with abusive husbands. Women who experience suffering, especially sexual violence, are not

able to seek spiritual help from monks, because they are not sure of their safety and the monks' experience in helping them.

+ Women are not allowed to enter certain buildings or areas inside temples. In some temples, paintings about Buddhism depict women as inferior. Some temples write in their chanting books that certain sutras are exclusively for monks and male novices to chant.

+ Women are not usually selected to be part of the temple committee. Their roles are merely to bring offerings to the monks and to cook and clean when there is a temple festival.

+ Women who have aborted their babies are blamed for being religiously immoral.

+ In Thailand, it is common to hear news about a monk who exploits women sexually or financially by misleading them into believing that he has spiritual power to make them attractive to men or to bring back their husband who left them for another woman.

The following are forms of suffering particular to nuns.

+ Generally, nuns do not receive respect even if they have been ordained for a very long time and have undergone long meditation practice or academic Buddhist training.

+ In Theravada and Tibetan schools, women are not yet legally allowed to have full ordination, and young girls are not allowed to take novice ordination.

+ Their identity is not legally and socially accepted; that is, they have no educational or financial support from the government, religious institutions, temples, the public, or their families.

+ They have little or no access to live in a temple with food, decent shelter, or guidance from spiritual teachers. When they do have these facilities, the conditions are usually very poor.

+ When they go for alms in the morning (within the Theravada tradition), they are often treated as false mendicants or beggars.

+ Often, parents force their daughters to disrobe and to return home to take care of them.

- Nuns who live in the temples are totally controlled by the monks. In Thailand, nuns are required to cook for the monks and do the cleaning, often in return for living in the temple. Some temples put signs outside saying, "This temple does not accept nuns."
- In Thailand, some nuns and lay women have been raped or sexually harassed by monks who were their meditation teachers. Some have been verbally, sexually, and spiritually abused by monks living in the same temple.
- The Thai Ministry of Interior does not allow the nuns to vote, saying they are not lay women. However, the Ministry of Transportation charges them full fare, saying they are not ordained, while monks pay only half fare.
- In the Shan State inside Burma, in some communities the nuns are not allowed to pass through or stay in the community, because it is thought that they bring bad luck to the community and the people who meet them.
- In Ladakh in northern India, many nuns still live with their families and work on the farm or as maid of the household with little or no Buddhist training.

Through this exercise, participants are able to see that these are the symptoms of women's suffering that exist in our societies.

THE SECOND NOBLE TRUTH: IGNORANCE AND THE ROOT CAUSES OF THE SUFFERING

After the participants name the various forms of suffering, we ask them to think further about what are the root causes of the existence of this island, what holds it up, and what makes this island of suffering expand. They identify the factors and institutions that cause, sustain, and reinforce the different forms of violence against women, and we write these root causes underneath the island. The root causes are often cited as: patriarchy, religion, politics, war, consumerism, globalization, media, military dictatorship, poverty, education, legal systems, etc. In this chapter, I will discuss only the patriarchal culture and religion.

Description of the Root Causes

It is very important for women to clearly understand the root causes of the violence they are facing, because it helps them to see the big picture of the problem (the structural violence) and to understand that this is neither their fault, their karma, nor is it natural. This understanding is a liberation from self blame, passivity, and faulty acceptance. We share with them that the Buddha taught his disciples to remove the root causes of suffering in order to end suffering. Understanding the root causes and how they reinforce each other also helps women to see the necessity of working together collaboratively to end the problem. The following are cultural and religious factors that cause women's suffering:

+ The misinterpretation of the texts by monks
+ The misinterpretation of the teaching of karma
+ The male dominant culture within Buddhist institutions, state, and society.
+ The poor education of monks

The Misinterpretation of the Text by Monks

The Buddha's teachings were passed down orally and then recorded in the Pali Canon by monks only from a council that was held about four hundred years after the death of the Buddha. When the texts were translated and written into the languages that are spoken today (such as Thai, Burmese, Cambodian, and Tibetan), it was all done by monks. With the internalization of the male dominant culture, it was inevitable that the meaning of the Buddha's teachings was altered, selected, emphasized, and based upon the worldview and the belief system of the writers and translators, and that this did not purely express the true spirit of the dharma, the Buddha's teachings. An example of this is the common situation for women in Thailand to be told orally and in writing that they are the enemies of the monk's celibate life. Venerable Dhammananda, the first bhikkhuni of Thailand, was a well-known scholar of the original texts (as Chatsumarn Kabilsingh at Thammasat University) before she ordained, and she tells the story behind this verbal abuse.

> Ananda, the close disciple and personal attendant of the Buddha, was a very charming monk. He also had much compassion toward women. Many women knew of this kind monk, so many came to see him to seek support. Because Ananda had not attained enlightenment yet, he was impacted by the encounters with beautiful women. The Buddha knew the challenges in Ananda's mind. Then one day the Buddha summoned him and said, "Ananda, if your mind is not yet strong, you should not stay close to women, because the contact could make your mind go astray." The Buddha meant to teach Ananda to watch and to train his mind when he contacted women. He did not teach him to tell the women to keep a distance from him believing that they are the enemy of his practice. He taught Ananda to take responsibility for his own behavior.

A second example is found in the *Garudhamma*, the ten rules written for female monastics to follow. One of them says that even if a bhikkhuni has been ordained for many years, she has to bow to a bhikkhu with fewers years of ordination or even to a young novice who has been ordained for just a day. This is often interpreted by monks that women, even after ordination, have a lower sacredness than the male ordained. Ven. Dhammananda, in her feminist analysis of this particular rule says:

> The Buddha was very progressive as a feminist. Buddhism was born and established in India, whose population at that time was predominantly Hindu. He revolutionized two important discriminatory practices that were deeply rooted in Hindu culture. The first was the caste system. In the Buddha's community, once a person was ordained s/he carried no caste. A man born from a higher caste, once ordained, has to bow to a monk from even the lowest caste who is his senior in period of ordination. The Buddha allowed ordination for women

much later, because he knew that his action would face much resistance, as women were the lowest among all castes. They were listed next to cows in a man's list of possessions. I think if the Buddha did create that particular rule for bhikkhuni it was because he wanted his action to be more acceptable to the public.

Karma as a Cultural Misinterpretation Perpetuated by Monks' Teaching that Reinforces and Sustains Violence against Women

I first heard the word karma from my family when I was quite young. When my father was violent, my desperate mother, unable to protect her children, would cry out loud and keep saying, "What kind of karma have I done? When will this karma end?" My father had many wives and that added more suffering to our family. Eventually, I ended up believing that our family had very bad karma, because other families did not experience as much suffering as we did.

A close friend of mine had a ten-year marriage with a husband who was an alcoholic. With immense suffering, she went to see a monk and ask for spiritual guidance. The monk said to her, "Be patient and keep making more merit (*puñña*) so that one day the accumulated merit will help improve your life." That same monk gave similar advice to her friend whose husband was having an affair with another woman. The monk told her friend, "There is nothing you can do about it. Keep being nice to him. Do not ever challenge his behavior, because you have done bad karma to him in your previous life."

This is what Buddhist women, not only in Thailand, but elsewhere, hear over and over. Here, we can see the problem of monks who generally have no knowledge or experience of domestic relationships and have never been trained in counseling, or in women's or gender issues. With no social knowledge of domestic violence, the monks further reinforce and sustain it by advising the women to be patient and accepting it in order to keep a false peace and harmony in the family. Women not only hear these messages from monks but also from their family, friends, neighbors, and the mass media.

What are the consequences for the women who hear these messages? Firstly, women start to internalize self-blame—that it is totally their fault and they alone, as women, are responsible for this problem. Secondly, women are not empowered by anyone or any institution that will enable them to challenge and change the situation. Thirdly, women will continue to suffer from the abusive relationship. The husband will continue his behavior, because no person or institution takes any action to stop him. The children will internalize the problem by understanding their father's abuse of their mother or his abandonment of them as normal. Thus, when they grow up, boys eventually do the same thing to their wives, and girls accept this violence if it happens to them the same way it did to their mothers.

This notion of karma as understood and internalized by most Buddhists (women, men, ordained, or lay) is the result of the internalization of the male dominant culture. It is viewed as permanent and fixed. Karma in this case only refers to something from a past life and that the people who are abused cannot do anything in this present life to change it except to be patient, accepting, and forgiving (and also to make merit (puñña) to the monks at the temple). This misinterpretation of karma leads to total ignorance.

Structural karma is a higher level of karma that is caused by the social and cultural context in which each individual is living. It is collective, because it is the accumulated acts that are committed by each individual living in the society. This structural karma is very important, much more important than the individual one, as it is a force that influences individual karma. Both karmic interpretations together help us to come to the right understanding about the problem of violence against women.

This structural karma of women's oppression is caused by several factors such as poverty and war, but the main root causes are values and belief systems, roles, and even mental pictures of women and men. These are the images perpetuated by family, school, media, and temple. At the social level, this ignorant and narrow view of karma causes government agencies, religious institutions, and society as a whole to not look seriously at violence against women. Ignorance of the problem leads to the continuation and expansion of violence at every level of society.

A Male-Dominant Culture

An essential component of our workshops includes the understanding of gender roles in their cultural contexts. We want women and also men to be able to separate the Buddha's teachings and the true spirit of Buddhism toward women from the male-dominant culture's teachings and their influence on Buddhism. Focusing on gender roles from their own cultural contexts is also a way to help participants understand male-dominated culture and feminism. This is important, because one way people resist the feminist movement in Asia is by saying that since this theory and knowledge comes from the West, it is not only irrelevant to our culture but will destroy our tradition.

We ask participants to name the images, roles, and expectations of men and women in their society. The following are some of the answers that are very similar in all the countries and ethnicities with which we work.

Men: protector, leader, willing to sacrifice, persons with honor, courageous, trustworthy, strong, smart, decisive, the breadwinner of the family; one who takes risks, likes challenges, and is very determined; one whose roles are in public and in politics.

Women: followers, weak, soft, sensitive, emotional, dependent, polite, gentle, faithful, and sweet; one who is not trustworthy, likes to gossip, and is jealous; as mothers and wives whose main tasks are to raise children, cook, clean, take good care of the family, preserve the culture, and act as good listeners to parents and to husbands.

We ask workshop participants to further consider, "What will happen to the boys when they grow up with such belief systems, training, and education?" They typically answer, "They will be very confident; have much freedom; be leaders; not be able/willing to listen, particularly to women; be self-centered; have large egos; be very controlling; and possibly be very violent."

Similarly, we ask them, "What will happen when girls grow up with such belief systems, training, and education?" They typically answer, "They will become dependent, have no confidence, have low self-esteem, have a narrow worldview, be good followers, and have many fears and worries. Their place will be in the kitchen, and if they work outside the home, their jobs will be in support or service-related work. Their role in public will be as good followers."

Buddhist women and men from many countries in Asia have grown up in this culture. These belief systems are reinforced through training and education from different institutions, such as the family, the village, temples, schools, the mass media, work places, and the political arena. Adult women, no matter what class, educational background, or ethnicity, internalize the belief that they cannot live their lives alone and need a husband to be their leader and protector once they leave their parents' home. To reinforce this belief system, being a single woman or a widow is taboo. Therefore, women married to an abusive husband find it very difficult to think about leaving the relationship because of the messages in their head and all around them. Their fear is understandable because a patriarchal society does not create any support systems for women who decide to leave a marriage. Not even their parents accept them back if they leave their marriage. Particularly for women with children, it is most difficult to leave the marriage because of the economic and cultural conditions. Many of the women with whom we work tell us that they choose to stay in an abusive relationship because they want their children to have a father.

Male Dominance over Buddhist Institutions

The most significant influence of patriarchy within Buddhism is the refusal or the reluctance of the monks and religious institutions in Tibet and most Theravada Buddhist countries (except Sri Lanka) to allow women full ordination. This is in spite of the Buddhist feminist movement on this issue over the last decade. The Buddha allowed women full ordination over twenty-five hundred years ago on the grounds that women are equal to men and have the same potential to attain enlightenment. When the first Thai woman was ordained as a novice in 2002, there was very strong resistance from the monks, religious institutions, and the state. The Thai religious institution's reason for not allowing women's ordination is that there has never been a bhikkhuni lineage in our country. This is the same reason that the religious leaders in Burma, Laos, Cambodia, and Tibet have given to women.

Patriarchy and the refusal of female ordination causes further suffering for women. In northern Thailand, parents expect the son to pay gratitude to them by taking temporary ordination. That action alone completes their expectation of him and his responsibility as a son. The ordination ceremony is very grand and much money is spent. At the time of a parent's funeral, sons may also ordain a day before the cremation so that they can walk in front of the funeral procession to pull the thread leading their parent's coffin. Thus, parents believe that when they die, they can hang on to the yellow robe worn by their ordained son to lift them up to a higher realm. Because a daughter cannot be ordained, her responsibility is to take care of the economic and welfare needs of the parents as long as they are alive. This is a huge and long-term responsibility since many Buddhist countries do not have good social welfare for their elderly citizens. In the north of Thailand this culture leads many poor women from rural areas into the sex industry.

Because of the male-dominated cultures in many Asian countries, there are few or no social services for women, such as counselors or shelters. There is also no protection by law, nor are there legal systems for women who experience violence. Despite the traditional teachings, many women still find religion to be a source of help in their suffering. In general, there is no space for women within the temples, but even if there were, monks rarely have the skills to help them because of their limited understanding of women's life experiences. Thus, it is impossible for women to obtain the spiritual support they need to cope with and relieve their suffering. As a result, large numbers of women who experience violence often suffer alone.

The examples mentioned above show how patriarchy, the foundation for the culture in many Buddhist countries in South and Southeast Asia, has helped establish misogyny, a deep-rooted discrimination, and control over women within Buddhist institutions. When we ask women in workshops which root causes have the most influence in creating violence against them, their answers are usually the culture of patriarchy and religion.

The Poor Education of Monks

When a man wears a monk's robe and has his head shaved, his status and power is further lifted up. In Thailand, most monks come from poor families and take ordination as a way to climb the social ladder, because food, accommodation, money, and other benefits are provided by the community, religious institutions, and state agencies. After ordination, monks are supposed to be trained and supervised for five years under their preceptor (*upajjhāya*), the senior monk who ordains them. However, this is not generally practiced. If some monks go to a Buddhist university, the subjects they learn are mostly Buddhist, intellectual academic study and a few other secular subjects. In general, monks in many Buddhist countries are neither educated in social issues nor capable of applying what they learn to respond to contemporary social problems, let alone issues such as violence against women.

Particularly, when monks do not practice meditation, they are further removed from developing wisdom—a key to understanding suffering and cultivating compassion towards people who are in oppressed situations. Men in robes, with power, privilege, and unquestioned leadership roles, can be socially unaware, ignorant, and uncompassionate, thus becoming an important root factor that causes and sustains violence against women.

THE THIRD NOBLE TRUTH: THE AWAKENED SOCIETY AND THE CESSATION OF WOMEN'S SUFFERING

Before the Buddha passed away he said that Buddhism would continue and flourish when it is taken care of by four groups or assemblies of people: ordained men, ordained women, lay men, and lay women (*Mahāparinibbāna Sutta*, D.ii.105). From his words, it is clearly understandable why Buddhism is currently facing a crisis and in many communities no longer adheres to the essence of the Buddha's teachings. The oppression of women within Buddhism is the main cause of this crisis. The awakened society thus must go back to the Buddha's vision that the four assemblies should be equally involved in sustaining Buddhism. These four assemblies should share power and leadership roles in using resources, transmitting teachings, and leading rituals. They should also work together to interpret and make meaning of the Buddha's teachings that are relevant to their life experiences and society. All Buddhist texts that reflect the true spirit of the Buddha's teachings show no discrimination against women or any minority groups in society.

Women, both lay and ordained, should be respected for their value, religious leadership roles, and spiritual experiences that can be expressed through mass media, literature, temple art, religious texts, and rituals. Women and young girls should have access to Buddhist educational institutions and meditation practice, thus supporting them to take teaching roles. Women and girls should have their own temples where they feel safe, respected, and supported, and where spiritual assistance is provided to women who are experiencing suffering. Young girls should have more choices and be supported if they choose to live a monastic life, either for the short or long term. Buddhists should be actively involved in social work. Monks, nuns, laymen, and laywomen should live in harmonious, trusting, and respectful relationship with each other. Violence against women and other forms of violence in society should be reduced. Girls, boys, women, and men should have more choices, space, and freedom in choosing their life styles. Boys, men, and monks should not live in fear, hatred, or disconnection from themselves and others.

THE FOURTH NOBLE TRUTH: THE PATH AND THE WAY LEADING TO THE CESSATION OF WOMEN'S SUFFERING

The Fourth Noble Truth is generally explained through the Noble Eightfold Path, which is the vision and knowledge that leads to peace, insight, and enlightenment—a state of the end of suffering. The Buddha discovered this path through his practice and then taught it for forty-five years. This is the essence of his teaching and it is composed of eight categories: Right View, Right Intention, Right Speech, Right Action, Right Livelihood, Right Effort, Right Mindfulness, and Right Concentration. These eight categories are inter-connected, and each helps cultivate the others. The eight categories aim to promote and to perfect the three essentials of Buddhist training and practice (*sikkhā*): wisdom (*paññā*), ethical conduct (*sīla*), and mental discipline (*samādhi*).

Wisdom

The first two paths are wisdom. They consist of Right View and Right Intention.

❖ Right View
The Buddha taught that Right View means the acknowledgment of the Four Noble Truths (suffering, the root causes that lead to suffering, cessation of suffering, and the paths to the cessation of suffering). Based upon his wisdom, we can say that the suffering of women is not natural or normal and that it is not only the problem of women. Right View means to acknowledge and understand the root causes of women's suffering, to believe that the cessa-tion of that suffering is possible once the root causes are removed, and to achieve that state by following the right paths.

• *Right View of Karma*
Karma means action. The consequences of one action become a cause of further action. Our present is a result of our past, and it will determine our future. As Buddhists, we have traditionally believed in the past karma from previous lives that crosses through lifetimes. However, the Buddha himself did not want his followers to focus on the past but rather on the present where we can create the conditions to change the future.

There are beliefs that deeply influence many Buddhists but are not the Buddha's teaching. One particular non-Buddhist belief is the idea that happiness and unhappiness in this life are the result of actions in previous lives. This particular belief results in people not taking any action to change or improve their present life. Yet more importantly, for those who take advantage of others, this belief allows them to take no responsibility for their unwholesome deeds.

The right view and understanding of karma lead to wisdom and compassion, which guide people to take the right action. Because of the belief in cause and effect, it is so crucial that we make sure that in this present life we will not do any harm to ourselves and others. For a woman who has experienced violence committed by men, it is not due to her previous life karma but rather due to the acceptance and ignorance of the violence by women, men, the community, and society. In other words, it is because of the present karma practiced by people individually and collectively.

- *Right View of Interconnectedness*

In Buddhism we believe that nothing exists by itself and that there is a connection between all things. Women's problems are not only personal problems, no matter how the patriarchal culture often misleads us. The violence that individual women experience is a result of the structural violence of patriarchal society which has constructed the frame and conditions that allow the violence to take place. In order to remove the root causes of suffering, we need to work at the individual and structural levels. When an individual creates new karma, such as stopping violence against women, it affects the structural level. When structural change takes place, such as the promotion of women's ordination, individual women's lives improve.

- *Right View of Impermanence*

Patriarchy is socially constructed and, like everything else, it will cease once the conditions holding it up no longer exist. Impermanence helps us to be aware that as strongly and deeply rooted as patriarchy is, it does not escape the nature of impermanence. Oftentimes we feel that it has always been like this, and so it will never change, no matter how much and how long we try. As activists, we do get burned-out and feel despair when dealing with the problem of violence against women. Holding to the truth of impermanence helps us not to forget that there is an end to this suffering.

❖ Right Intention

The Buddha taught that Right Intention means to aspire not to harm one's self and others and to devise ways of stopping unwholesome deeds without ill intention. When thinking about the issue of violence against women, it is important to first look at our intention and what is in our minds. Right Intention comes from having the right view of the suffering that others or we are facing. Right Intention is about having clarity and pure aspiration in our mind before or while taking action. It helps to ask ourselves, "What is happening?; What causes this to happen?; What right actions can I take?; What are the aims of my actions?; Am I doing this for myself and my ego, because it disturbs me, or to relieve the suffering of others?" Clear thinking comes from the mind that is calm and awake. Without Right Intention we can make the situation worse. When we think with ill intention, we create the negative factors that cause the cycle of suffering to continue or to expand.

Ethical conduct

The next three paths consist of Right Speech, Right Action, and Right Livelihood. Right View and Right Intention comprise the basic wisdom that we use as a foundation and guidance for our ethical conduct. Right Speech, Right Action, and Right Livelihood are the skillful means that guide our action when we deal with the issue of violence against women. The reason we have to act with skillful means is that since we are all part of the male-dominated culture, we internalize it deeply. In patriarchal culture, we are trained to become a man and a woman. We are expected to think and act in the way that the culture expects us to—to the point that we often do it automatically without challenging or asking ourselves why.

If we are mindlessly acting without Right View and Right Intention, we will naturally accept, participate in, or ignore the system. For example, it is so common when we hear about a wife being beaten by a husband to think,

"Oh, this couple does that all the time"(accepting); or "She must have done something wrong to deserve that"(participating in); or "That's terrible! I wish that would not happen, but I cannot do anything to help" (ignoring). We need to deal with the issue with Right View and Right Intention so that our action is a clear and clean karma that will lead to reducing or ending the suffering.

❖ Right Speech

The Buddha taught that Right Speech means not saying things that are untrue, nonsense, impolite, and that cause disharmony and conflict. Speaking up about any form of violence against women is speaking the truth. Speaking this truth does not cause disharmony and conflict either in the family or society. Particularly in domestic violence, when a woman reaches out and asks for help, we need not traumatize her further by saying, "You must have done something wrong;" or "This is your karma." We have to challenge and educate the monks, men, and women when we hear them giving these messages to women.

We have to speak out about violence against women, because both the man and woman suffer physically, mentally, and spiritually. The woman suffers from the violence, but the man also suffers, because he lives in anger, hatred, and ignorance. Both of them lose the ability to purify their body, speech, and mind, which is the path to attain enlightenment.

❖ Right Action

The Buddha taught that Right Action is about not harming, not stealing, not being involved in sexual misconduct, not lying, and not using intoxicants. With this Right Action we will do whatever we can to stop violence against women and to help remove the root causes of violence that harm women. For example, as a Buddhist we will intervene when we encounter a man beating his partner, not only because we want to protect the woman from being harmed but also to stop the man from committing harmful action. If we stop his harmful action, he will not accumulate the bad karma that will cause suffering in his future.

The action we can take when we help women experiencing violence is to offer deep listening. If we do not have skills to help, we can ask others who are in this field to help. We should be mindful in our daily lives not to do anything that supports the continuation of violence against women. For example, when we see a company that uses women's bodies as sexual objects in their advertising, we can give that company feedback or boycott their product. These are some other forms of Right Action:

- Not consuming media or information that exploits women.
- Educating our children about the impact of mass media that depicts violence against women.
- Participating in creating new laws to protect women and laws that take action against men and institutions that commit violence against women.
- Creating structural transformation by demanding that religious institutions and state agencies grant women leading roles in religion.
- Participating in creating mechanisms that require monks and religious institutions to be held responsible for their actions of violating women's rights and dignity.
- Educating both bhikkhus and bhikkhunis, as well as novices, on gender issues and other relevant social issues.
- Reforming Buddhist education, training, and the process of ordination, particularly for monks, to help Buddhism become relevant to the modern world.

Mental Discipline

The next three paths are comprised of Right Effort, Right Mindfulness, and Right Concentration. Mental discipline is about training the mind rightly when we take action.

❖ Right Effort

It is crucial to concentrate our energy, effort, and action on removing the root causes of violence against women, while seeking to heal the symptoms. There is a story of a person trying to save a baby from drowning while floating down a river. Once that person saved one baby, more babies kept floating and kept that person busy and exhausted. Finally, the person stopped and reflected, "I better go upstream to see what is causing these babies to float in this river." This is the way to approach removing the root causes of suffering.

We need both individual and collective effort for the whole society to work to end the suffering of women because it is so deep-rooted in our society. Violence against women has a deep connection with other forms of violence, such as war, the way the state agencies use violence to deal with its citizens, and the way police use force to deal with drugs or crime issues. Human beings first learn to control and exploit each other from within their own family. The most common form of violence existing in every society is gender-based violence. When we accept, ignore, or feel powerless to deal with the violence in our family, then it is very easy for us to accept, ignore, or feel powerless to deal with other forms of violence in society.

❖ Right Mindfulness

Mindfulness helps us to be aware of our own minds, because it is the mind that guides our speech and action. This is particularly for those helpers, such as counselors, family members, friends, neighbors, medical people, religious leaders, healers, or concerned government officers, not to be trapped by our own internalized patriarchal belief systems. We have to be mindful and keep reminding ourselves not to replicate the dynamics of oppression when helping women. For example, patriarchal culture teaches us to deal with women or people with less power by using the "power-over" model, thinking that we know how to solve their problems, and thus telling them what to do about their life situation. Mindfulness helps the helpers to support these people in a power-sharing way.

One of the strategies I use is to find allies among men. Men need to learn to take responsibility to change this oppressive system that they are part of. Whenever I can, I co-facilitate the gender-based violence workshops with the monks or men who are supportive of our cause. Through working with some monks I have learned that there are some Buddhist teachings about family and relationships that clearly talk about how the husband should treat his spouse and the equality in their partnership. These are teachings I had never heard before in any preaching given by monks. Even my monk colleague said that because of my request he had to go through the text to look for them.

Mindfulness also helps create wisdom and inner peace, the core elements needed by helpers to work with women to end their suffering. The helpers work with the women to first use the Four Noble Truths to understand the suffering that they experience. Through understanding, compassion to oneself and others, calmness, and the ability to let go of past suffering, women can live in the present and have the wisdom to think about their future.

Working against a long and deep history of discrimination and oppression is very stressful and extremely difficult. Because of these challenges, we often get angry and feel hatred toward the people, group, or institutions that are involved in the oppression. Cultivating mindfulness practices will help us to not be overcome by the negative energy of bias, greed, anger, hatred, burn out, and hopelessness.

CONCLUSION: ACTION WITH UNDERSTANDING AND COMPASSION

There is a story of the Dalai Lama meeting with a friend, an elderly monk who had left Tibet after living twenty years in Chinese prisons and labor camps to join the Tibetan community living in exile in northern India. During those twenty years, the monk had faced immense suffering from brutality, isolation, and fear. When they met, the Dalai Lama asked him, "Were there ever times when your life was truly in danger?" The monk answered, "There were only a few occasions when I faced real danger, and those were the occasions when I was in danger of losing my compassion for the Chinese." The monk spoke about the heart of nonviolent action, which is the core teaching of the Buddhist path. He was in jail facing great physical suffering but his mind was peaceful and free. The Chinese authorities who tortured him were, in fact, themselves imprisoned in hatred, anger, and ignorance.

The challenge I continually face while working with religious groups in the region is resistance from both lay and ordained men because I am a woman and because the subject is women's issues. The resistance comes particularly from monks, who have many sources of power in society derived from gender, position, status, leadership, and the authority or sense of ownership of Buddhism. When their power is challenged by a lay woman in the role of a teacher, they are often uncomfortable and feel threatened.

In the early years of my work, I always felt angry, frustrated, hopeless, and isolated. Even today, in our region very few feminists are interested in Buddhism, both at an academic and grassroots level. It was not until I committed myself to Buddhist practice that I was able to deal with these emotional challenges more effectively. I have learned to understand the interconnectedness of wisdom and compassion that I need to have when facing any form of violence or resistance. The Buddha's teachings on impermanence, seeing things the way they are, and letting go help me deal with the isolation.

It is very common when facilitating workshops on gender, leadership, or feminist issues that I face resistance from monks and men. Their common behaviors are:

+ talking very long, oftentimes without much point
+ drawing conclusions
+ speaking for women
+ paraphrasing what a women has just clearly articulated
+ laughing or making jokes when women are speaking
+ showing signs of discomfort when asked to listen to a woman in pair work

They often refuse to participate in any experiential activity saying that it is for children or that it is not appropriate for them. However, then they do not hesitate to express their opinions when the group has finished an exercise and is reflecting on what they learned in a larger group.

Understanding the deep-rooted internalization of patriarchy in their thinking and behavior helped me understand why they act like this. What helps me to be calm, patient, and aware of what is going on in that moment is the understanding that they are victims of patriarchy. This understanding helps me to have compassion and lovingkindness toward their suffering and ignorance, the same way I have for my father.

Mindfulness practice helps me to have an awareness of my emotions that are arising within me and to be able to hold or be with them. When I am able to hold my own feelings, it helps me to hold the feelings of the other party with whom I am confronting. When I can hold myself that way I do not need to respond with anger and frustration, or by running away. I realize that it is not the person that is the problem I am working to change, but it is the deep-rooted patriarchal culture with which I am dealing. This understanding helps me not to take it personally. I understand that while I demand from men the understanding, compassion, and lovingkindness for myself and other women, the only way I will succeed is to give the same things that I demand from them. The transformation can only come from this understanding and compassion. It is only at a heart-level connection that I see no gender, no form, and no age. It is a connection as a human being who lives and suffers from the same culture.

Violence against women is not an independent action. An individual man, a group of men, or collective institutions acting against women are the result of the interconnectedness of various factors. It is an interacting of various elements, such as patriarchal culture, the lack of laws to protect women, economic issues, war, and conflict that cause women's suffering. Understanding the interconnectedness helps us see the problem within a bigger picture. When facing violence against women, this understanding helps us not to find fault with that particular perpetrator, either the individual, group, or institution. Particularly, when our action is driven by anger or hatred, we will lose sight of the big picture if we only focus our energy and emotions on fixing, changing, or getting rid of that particular actor alone. Through our understanding of interconnectedness, we will see that the perpetrator is also a victim of the system of violence.

Buddhism teaches that everyone and every sentient being has Buddha nature, which is an awakening nature and the potential to attain enlightenment. When we believe that the perpetrators also have these seeds of enlightenment and also want peace and happiness (but have ignorance or make mistakes just like us), we see no separation between us and them. We can have compassion and lovingkindness toward them the same way we have it toward ourselves when we are vulnerable. Further, we will do anything we can to help them realize their suffering and ignorance so that the seeds of awakening grow in them as well.

Wisdom guides us to know why there is a problem, and to know when and how to take what kind of action. Mindfulness, compassion, and lovingkindness guide the way we act. These elements also help us practice letting go when the action we take does not produce immediate results or meet our expectations, so that we will not lose our motivation, blame ourselves, or feel like giving up. Instead, we let go of our attachment to the outcome.

Although my work is fraught with difficulties and resistance from so many sectors of society, including some women themselves, it is also filled with sudden and heartwarming experiences with those whom I encounter. These experiences reinforce the sense of faith or confidence (*saddhā*) I have in my understanding of the Buddha's way and my application of it to the problems of gender. For example, a number of years ago I was doing a workshop on teaching dharma through experiential learning with some Theravada monks and nuns. One young monk who had attended a workshop of mine the previous year came to me and said:

> During that gender workshop last year, I was so angry to see you standing in front of the room above the monks and teaching us. Who were you to teach us? I was even angrier when you forced me to sit and to just listen to the nun talking. Today I want to apologize for thinking toward you in that way. The gender workshop did help me learn how to relate to women. Now I can talk to women without having fear.

One of the nuns who participated in the same workshop said to me during a social action trainers workshop that I co-facilitated a year and a half later, "Although we come from the same town, I did not talk to you during the whole workshop, because I thought that as a lay woman you had no right to teach us monks and nuns. When my eyes were opened later on I realized how ignorant I was not to see that you were trying to help us understand our own problems."

Such experiences have reinforced in me the belief that wisdom (*paññā*), ethical conduct (*sīla*), and mental discipline (*samādhi*) help us to effectively create an awakened society. The Noble Eightfold Path guides our body, speech, and mind—the very same elements that human beings use to cause any form of violence. Even if we feel that we have not yet arrived at the state of the end of suffering, when working and living our lives along this path we are already living an awakening experience. Awakening is about seeing and being.

CONCLUSION

THE KARMA OF THE RINGS:
A MYTH FOR MODERN BUDDHISM?

DAVID LOY

I sometimes feel appalled at the thought of the sum total of human misery all over the world at the present moment: the millions parted, fretting, wasting in unprofitable days—quite apart from torture, pain, death, bereavement, injustice. If anguish were visible, almost the whole of this benighted planet would be enveloped in a dense dark vapor, shrouded from the amazed vision of the heavens! And the products of it all will be mainly evil—historically considered. But the historic version is, of course, not the only one. All things and deeds have a value in themselves, apart from their "causes" and "effects." No man can estimate what is really happening at the moment sub specie aeternitas. All we do know, and that to a large extent by direct experience, is that evil labors with vast power and perpetual success—in vain: preparing always only the soil for unexpected good to sprout in. So it is in general, and so it is in our own lives. (*The Letters of J. R. R. Tolkien* 1981)

—J. R. R. Tolkien to his son Christopher, April 30, 1944

Throughout this volume, we have seen the importance of myth on the collective consciousness of Buddhists, specifically in the power of the *Jātaka* tales and the ethical meanings of their various episodes. In this essay, David Loy delves deeper into the power of myth and the meaning of stories for our lives, whether they are the more fantastical ones of the *Jātaka* and *The Lord of the Rings* or the more historical one of the Buddha himself. Whether they be fantasy or history, we need ethical stories to understand how to live our lives. Loy's essay shows us how to rediscover the perennial ethics of the Buddha in a more contemporary setting.

This essay is a condensed version of "The Dharma of Engagement," chapter 1 in David Loy and Linda Goodhew's book, *The Dharma of Dragons and Daemons: Buddhist Themes in Modern Fantasy* (Boston: Wisdom Publications, 2004). The author thanks his wife, Linda Goodhew, for her help in writing this chapter.

The Lord of the Rings as a modern Buddhist myth? That is not very plausible, on the face of it. As is well known, Middle-earth is derived largely from the Nordic and Germanic sagas that Tolkien knew so well. Although God is never mentioned, the tale also expresses some Christian influence, according to Tolkien's own admission (he was a devout Roman Catholic). There is no hint, either in the story or in its sources, of any Buddhist influences.

Moreover, Tolkien's fantasy world is built on a radical and quite un-Buddhist dualism between unredeemable evil (Sauron, Saruman) and uncompromising goodness (Gandalf, Frodo). The good as well as the bad use violence in pursuit of their goals, and we are entertained with plenty of it. Stupid and cruel as they may be, orcs remain sentient beings. From a Buddhist perspective, therefore, they must have the same buddha-nature as all other living beings, with the potential to "wake up" from their greed, ill will, and delusion. Bodhisattvas vow to "save" all sentient beings, in the sense of helping them to realize their true nature. In Middle-earth, though, no one has any interest in helping orcs awaken. The only good orc is a dead orc.

And yet . . . Tolkien's masterpiece achieves what he intended, which was to create a modern myth; and myths, as he also knew, have a way of growing beyond their creator's intentions. *The Lord of the Rings* is much more than an endearing fantasy about little hobbits, gruff dwarves, and light-footed elves. It has been repeatedly voted the novel of the century—according to some, it is the novel of the millennium!—because so many readers find it deeply moving as well. What is it about the tale that makes it so compelling, so *mythic*? One answer, for some of us at least, is that despite its European origins it resonates with Buddhist concerns and perspectives.

Evil, for example, is much more nuanced than it appears at first glance. "In my story I do not deal with Absolute Evil. I do not think there is such a thing, since that is Zero" (*The Letters of J. R. R. Tolkien* 1981, 243). As Gandalf reminds the Fellowship, "Nothing is evil in the beginning. Even Sauron was not so." Sauron too was corrupted, long ago, by his craving for the Ring. It is no coincidence that, as the foremost expression of evil, he is never seen (only his hand and "eye rimmed with fire"). Sauron is more effective as an abstract principle, so malignant and powerful that he could not be depicted as a believable person. The implication, in Buddhist terms, is that evil, too, has no self-being. Like everything else, it is a result of causes and conditions that we allow to infect and defile our minds.

There is also an essential, Buddhist-like thread of nonviolence that runs throughout the tale. Despite all the bloodshed, a repeated act of compassion—sparing Gollum's life—is crucial to the plot. Early in the story, when Frodo comments that it was a pity Bilbo did not stab Gollum when he had a chance, Gandalf contradicts him: "Pity? It was Pity that stayed his hand. Pity; and Mercy: not to strike without need. And he has been well rewarded, Frodo. Be sure that he took so little result from the evil, and escaped in the end, because he began his ownership of the Ring so. With Pity." It is important for Frodo's quest that he learns this lesson.

There is virtually no role for religion in Middle-earth, because "the religious element is absorbed into the story and the symbolism" (*The Letters of J. R. R. Tolkien* 1981, 172). Nevertheless, *The Lord of the Rings* can serve as a Buddhist fable because it is about a spiritual quest readily understandable in terms of the teachings of Buddhism. Despite Tolkien's demurral that it has "any meaning or 'message,'" his tale provides a myth about spiritual engagement for modern Buddhists. Frodo leaves home not to slay a dragon or win a chest full of precious jewels, but to *let go* of something, which is what one learns to do when following the Buddhist path. His renunciation of the Ring is not done to gain enlightenment, yet it nonetheless transforms him spiritually. The suffering he experiences on the way to Mount Doom deepens him, making him stronger and more compassionate.

From a socially engaged Buddhist perspective concerned to bring Buddhist teachings to bear on contemporary social issues, one of the striking aspects of the plot is that Frodo does not *want* to have the adventures he has. He embarks on the quest because it cannot be evaded. At the beginning Sam is excited about going to "see elves and all," but Frodo is more apprehensive, and for good reason. The Ring must be destroyed, and he is the best one to carry it. In some mysterious, inexplicable way the task has been appointed to him. There is nothing he hopes to gain from the journey. By the end, he and Sam expect to be destroyed themselves soon after the Ring is cast into the Chamber of Fire, and indeed they nearly are. Their total renunciation is a powerful metaphor for Buddhist practice. As practitioners, we are sometimes willing to give up everything for enlightenment—but that is the catch. It is the *self* that seeks to be enlightened, that still wants to be around to enjoy being enlightened. Self remains the problem. Frodo and Sam show us something deeper. They let go of all personal ambition, although not the ambition to do what is necessary to help others. In Buddhist terms, don't they become bodhisattvas?

Frodo's quest is not an attempt to transcend Middle-earth by realizing some higher reality or dimension. He is simply responding to its needs, which because of historical circumstances (the growing power of Sauron, now actively seeking the Ring) have become critical—as are the needs of our beleaguered earth today. The larger world has begun to impinge on his Shire (and ours). If Frodo were to decline the task and hide at home, he would not escape the dangers that threaten. The Dark Lord would soon discover him and his Ring, and the Shire along with the rest of Middle-earth would fall under his baneful control. When we consider the ecological and social crises that have begun to impinge on our own little worlds, is our situation any different?

So is Frodo's journey a spiritual quest or a struggle to help the world? In *The Lord of the Rings* these two are the same. Frodo realizes ("makes real") his own non-duality with the world by doing everything he can to help it. Middle-earth needs to be *saved*, not denied or escaped. The goal is not another world but another way of living in this one, even as nirvana is not another place but a liberated way of experiencing this one. In the process, Frodo learns that this world is very different from what he thought it was. And by doing what he can to transform it, Frodo transforms himself. That is how his selflessness is developed. Frodo does not change because he destroys the Ring. He changes because of his tireless efforts to destroy the Ring. His early adventures on the road to Rivendell challenge and toughen him, giving him the courage to be the Ringbearer. His own strength of heart and will grow from those encounters, teaching him initiative and perseverance, and eventually developing into his unassuming heroic stature.

THE POWER OF KARMA

Frodo's journey does more than illustrate the Buddhist path. It teaches us how karma works and even helps us to understand Buddhism today. Middle-earth is a morally balanced world. As Randel Helms has pointed out, the essential law of Tolkien's story is that good intentions lead to good results, while evil intentions end up being self-defeating (Helms 1974, ch.4–5). In Buddhist terms, we could say that Middle-earth is structured karmically: the way the main characters in Middle-earth act becomes the way Middle-earth responds to them. What they put out comes back to help or haunt them. This Buddhist-like principle of moral causation is one of the keys to the plot, recurring again and again.

It is easy enough to see how good intentions are rewarded, but the negative consequences of bad intentions are just as important to the happy ending. The best example is, of course, Gollum. He does not want to help Frodo and Sam. He wants to get his hands on the Ring. To do so, however, he must help them again and again. When they are lost, he leads them to Mordor. When they become stuck he shows them a mountain path that leads (through Shelob's tunnel) toward Mount Doom. At the end, when an exhausted Frodo can no longer resist the lure of the Ring, Gollum appears one last time to bite off Frodo's finger—and fall into the fiery pit, to be destroyed along with the Ring. Yet this can happen only because of the compassion toward Gollum repeatedly shown by Frodo and eventually by Sam too. King Theoden sums it up best in the inevitable aphorism: "Strange powers have our enemies, and strange weaknesses! But it has long been said: *oft evil will shall evil mar.*"

In Middle-earth this karmic law works as inexorably as gravity, but, as we know all too well, karma does not operate so neatly in our world—at least, not in the short run. Evil often seems to succeed; goodness has a harder time prevailing. "Here is perhaps the basic difference between the moral structures of Tolkien's world and our own. We know that intention has nothing to do with result" (Helms 1974, 75). According to Buddhism, however, intention has a lot to do with results in our world too, for intention is the heart of karma. But if, as religious scholars often point out, religious language should usually be taken metaphorically, Buddhist teachings about karma can be and perhaps should be understood less literally and mechanically than they usually are.

On our earth, as in Middle-earth, it is clear that karma does not mean all events are predestined to happen. Some inexplicable destiny has given Frodo responsibility for the Ring, as Gandalf and Elrond realize, yet what he does with it depends upon his own decisions. His success is not preordained. In both worlds, karma creates situations but does not determine how we respond to them.

There is, however, much more to say about what karma is and how it works. Karma and rebirth have become a problem for modern Buddhists that can no longer be evaded. To accept what the earliest Buddhist teachings say about them as literal truth—that karmic determinism is a "moral law" of the universe, with a precise calculus of cause and effect—leads to a severe case of cognitive dissonance for contemporary Buddhism. The physical causality that modern science has discovered about the world seems to allow no mechanism for karma or rebirth to operate. How should we as modern Buddhists respond to this situation?

In the *Kālāma Sutta*, sometimes called "The Buddhist Charter of Free Inquiry," the Buddha emphasized the importance of intelligent, probing doubt. We should not believe in something until we know its truth for ourselves. For us to believe in karmic rebirth in a literal way, simply because it is part of the Buddhist teaching (or part of the way that the Buddha's teaching has traditionally been understood), may thus be unfaithful to the best of the tradition. This is not to deny the *possibility* of a truth that we cannot confirm. The point is that our modern ways of knowing offer no support for those teachings, and given a healthy skepticism about the Iron Age belief systems of the Buddha's time, we should hesitate before making such a leap of faith. Maybe rebirth according to one's karma is literally true as an explanation of what happens after we physically die. However, it may not be true. Instead of tying our spiritual paths to belief in such a doctrine, isn't it wiser for us to be agnostic about it? Consider the way the *Kālāma Sutta* concludes. After emphasizing the importance of evaluating for oneself the spiritual claims of others, the Buddha finishes his talk by describing someone who has a truly purified mind.

> "Suppose there is a hereafter and there is a fruit, result, of deeds done well or ill. Then it is possible that at the dissolution of the body after death, I shall arise in the heavenly world, which is possessed of the state of bliss." This is the first solace found by him.

> "Suppose there is no hereafter and there is no fruit, no result, of deeds done well or ill. Yet in this world, here and now, free from hatred, free from malice, safe and sound, and happy, I keep myself." This is the second solace found by him.

> "Suppose evil (results) befall an evil-doer. I, however, think of doing evil to no one. Then, how can ill (results) affect me who do no evil deed?" This is the third solace found by him.

> "Suppose evil (results) do not befall an evil-doer. Then I see myself purified in any case." This is the fourth solace found by him. (*Kālāma Sutta* 1981, A.i.188)

These intriguing verses can be understood in different ways. The Buddha is speaking to non-Buddhists, so he does not presuppose a Buddhist worldview in describing the fruits of a purified mind. Yet there is another way to take this passage, which is more relevant for twenty-first-century Buddhists. Do our actions bear fruit in a hereafter? For the sake of argument, at least, the Buddha adopts an agnostic view in this sutta. Maybe they do, maybe they don't. In either case, a purified mind finds solace by cherishing good deeds and avoiding bad ones.

In this passage, as in many others, the Buddha's lack of dogmatism shines forth clearly. We can understand his tactful words as a skillful means for speaking with the Kalamas, who were weary of doctrinaire spiritual assertions. But we can also focus on the agnosticism about rebirth, which also implies a different understanding of karma and its consequences. If we are honest with ourselves, we really do not know what to think about karma and rebirth. Most of us would like to believe in the law of karma and literal rebirth, and we wonder if testimony about near-death experiences supports them. At the same time, they hardly seem compatible with what modern science has discovered about the physical world. So are they fact or myth? If I consider myself a Buddhist, do I have to believe in them? Here the Buddha speaks directly to our skeptical age: in the most important sense, it does not matter which is true, because if we know what is good for us we will endeavor to live the same way in either case.

Challenging a literal understanding is not to dismiss or disparage Buddhist teachings about karma and rebirth. Rather, it highlights the need for modern Buddhism to *interrogate* them. Given what is now known about human psychology, including the social construction of the self, how can karma and rebirth be understood today?

One of the most basic principles of Buddhism is interdependence, but we do not usually realize what that implies about the original teachings of the Buddha. Nothing has any "self-existence" because everything is part of everything else. Nothing is self-originated because everything arises according to causes and conditions. Yet Buddhism, as we know, originates in the experience of Shakyamuni, who became "the Buddha"—that is, "the awakened one"—upon his attainment of nirvana under the Bodhi tree. Different Buddhist scriptures describe that experience in different ways, but for all Buddhist traditions it is the source of Buddhism, which unlike Hinduism does not rely upon ancient revealed texts such as the Vedas.

As Buddhists we usually take the above for granted, yet there is a problem with it: it is a myth of self-origination. If the interdependence of everything is true, the truth of Buddhism could not have sprung up independently from all the other spiritual beliefs of the Buddha's time and place (Iron Age India) without any relationship to them. Instead, the teachings of Shakyamuni must be understood as a *response* to those other teachings, but a response that, inevitably, also *presupposed* many of the spiritual beliefs current in that cultural milieu— for example, popular notions of karma and rebirth, which were widespread at that time in India although not universally accepted. In some of the Pali suttas, the Buddha mentions remembering his past lifetimes. We should ourselves remember that the reality of past lives was generally accepted then, and that an ability to remember them was not unique to the Buddha or Buddhists.

Consider the following insightful comment that Erich Fromm made about another (although very different!) revolutionary, Sigmund Freud.

> The attempt to understand Freud's theoretical system, or that of any creative systematic thinker, cannot be successful unless we recognize that, and why, every system as it is developed and presented by its author is necessarily erroneous ... the creative thinker must think in the terms of the logic, the thought patterns, the expressible concepts of his culture. That means he has not yet the proper words to express the creative, the new, the liberating idea. He is forced to solve an insoluble problem: to express the new thought in concepts and words that do not yet exist in his language . . . . The consequence is that the new thought as he formulated it is a blend of what is truly new and the conventional thought which it transcends. The thinker, however, is not conscious of this contradiction. (Fromm 1982, 1, 3)

Fromm's point is that even the most revolutionary thinkers cannot stand on their own shoulders. They are dependent upon their context, whether intellectual or spiritual—which, to say it again, is precisely what Buddhist emphasis on impermanence and causal interdependence implies. Of course, there are many important differences between Freud and Shakyamuni, but the parallel is nevertheless very revealing: the Buddha, too, expressed his new, liberating insight in the only way he could, in the language that his culture could understand and that he himself was a product of. Inevitably, then, his way of expressing the dharma was a blend of the truly new (for example, *anattā, paṭicca samuppāda*) and the conventional religious thought of his time (karma and rebirth?) "which it transcends." The implication that there is always tension between what is new and what is conventional speaks directly to a possible inconsistency that has puzzled many Buddhists over the centuries: is *anattā* really compatible with the older, traditional beliefs in karma and rebirth?

During the time of Shakyamuni Buddha, karma and reincarnation were widely, although not universally, accepted religious principles. They were part of the cultural milieu within which he grew up. Earlier teachings such as the Vedas tended to understand them more mechanically and ritualistically. To perform a sacrifice in the proper fashion would invariably lead to the desired consequences. If those consequences were not forthcoming, then either there had been an error in procedure or the causal effects were delayed, perhaps until one's next lifetime. The Buddha's spiritual revolution transformed this ritualistic approach to controlling one's life into an ethical principle by focusing on our *motivations*. The *Dhammapada* begins by emphasizing this.

> Experiences are preceded by mind, led by mind, and produced by mind. If one speaks or acts with an impure mind, suffering follows even as the cart-wheel follows the hoof of the ox.

> Experiences are preceded by mind, led by mind, and produced by mind. If one speaks or acts with a pure mind, happiness follows like a shadow that never departs. (*The Dhammapada* 1993, Dh.1–2)

Here it may be helpful to distinguish a moral act into its three aspects: our *motivation* when we do something, the *moral rule* (for example, a Buddhist precept or Christian commandment, but this also includes ritualistic procedures) we are following, and the *results* that we seek. These aspects cannot be separated from each other, but we can emphasize one more than the others—in fact, that is what we usually do. (In modern moral theory, for example, utilitarian theories focus on consequences, deontological theories focus on moral principles such as the Golden Rule, and "virtue theories" focus on one's character and motivations.) In the Buddha's time, the Brahmanical understanding of karma emphasized the importance of following the detailed procedures (rules) regulating each ritual; naturally, however, the people who paid for the rituals were more interested in the outcome (results). Arguably, the situation in some Theravada countries is not much different today: monastics are preoccupied with following the complicated rules regulating their lives, while many lay people are eager to accumulate merit by giving gifts to them. Unfortunately, this arrangement loses the Buddha's great insight about the preeminent importance of our motivations. How should we today understand the originality of his approach?

The important point about karma is not whether it is a moral law involving some inevitable and precise calculus of cause and effect. More than a means to control what the world does to us, karma is better understood as the key to spiritual development: how our lives are transformed by our motivations. When we add the Buddhist teaching about non-self—the claim, consistent with modern psychology, that one's sense of self is a mental construct—we can say that karma is not something I *have*, it is what I *am*, and what I am changes according to my conscious choices. "I" (re)construct myself by what I intentionally do. My sense of self is a precipitate of my habitual ways of thinking, feeling, and acting. Just as my body is composed of the food I eat, so my character is composed of my conscious choices, constructed by my consistent, repeated motivations. People are "punished" or "rewarded" not for what they have done but for what they have become, and what we intentionally do is what makes us what we are. An anonymous verse expresses this well.

Sow a thought and reap a deed

Sow a deed and reap a habit

Sow a habit and reap a character

Sow a character and reap a destiny

Such an understanding of karma does not necessarily involve another life after we physically die. As the philosopher Spinoza expressed it, happiness is not the reward for virtue; happiness is virtue itself. To become a different kind of person is to experience the world in a different way. When your mind changes, the world changes. And when we respond differently to the world, the world responds differently to us. Since we are actually non-dual with the world—our sense of separation from it being a delusion—our ways of acting in it tend to involve reinforcing feedback systems that incorporate other people. People not only notice what we do, they notice why we do it. I may fool people sometimes, but over time my character becomes revealed through the intentions behind my deeds. The more I am motivated by greed, ill will, and delusion, the more I must manipulate the world to get what I want, and consequently the more alienated I feel and the more alienated others feel when they see they have been manipulated. This mutual distrust encourages both sides to manipulate more. In *The Lord of the Rings* Saruman and Wormtongue exemplify this cycle of negative feedback. On the other hand, the more my actions are motivated by generosity, lovingkindness, and the wisdom of non-duality, the more I can relax and open up to the world. The more I feel part of the world and at one with others, the less I am inclined to use others, and consequently the more inclined they will be to trust and open up to me. Frodo and Sam's encounter with Faramir is an example of such positive feedback.

Consistent with this view of karma, the traditional six realms of *saṃsāra* do not need to be distinct worlds or planes of existence through which we transmigrate after death, according to our karma. They can also be the different ways we experience this world, as our character, and therefore our attitude toward the world, change. For example, the hell realm becomes not so much a place I will be reborn into later, due to my hatred and evil deeds, as a way I experience this world when my mind is dominated by anger and hate.

THE KARMA OF POWER

What is the Ring? Its magnetic attraction is a profound symbol for the karma of power. We think we use the Ring, but when we use it, it is actually using us, *it changes us*—this is the essential karmic insight. Power corrupts, and the absolute power of the Ring corrupts absolutely. At the end even Frodo cannot resist it, as he stands exhausted before the Crack of Doom.

Power wants to be used, as Gandalf realizes, "A Ring of Power looks after itself, Frodo. *It* may slip off treacherously, but its keeper never abandons it." The Ring has a will of its own. It gets heavier. It wants Frodo to slip it on his finger. If he were to do this, though, it would corrupt him, as it corrupted Sauron and Gollum long ago. Gollum is Frodo's alter ego, a constant reminder to Frodo of what he could become.

Power is eager to test and display itself. What is the point of having an overwhelming military machine if you don't use it once in a while? When you create a new weapon (for example, a "smart" bomb), you want to see what it can do in a combat situation. The scientists who created the first nuclear bombs during the Second World War, all the while hoping these weapons would not be needed, learned about this the hard way. Once the bombs had been made, their own wishes were of no consequence. But is there something more to learn from the Ring of Power?

Buddhism has not had much to say about power. Traditional teachings warn more about sex and other physical cravings, which play almost no role in *The Lord of the Rings.* The absolute prohibition of sexual contact for monastics suggests that sexual desire is the archetypal craving that needs to be transcended in order to achieve the serenity of nirvana. Whether or not that was true in India twenty-five hundred years ago, our situation calls for a different focus. Today the primary challenge for socially engaged Buddhism is the individual and collective craving for power, which, Midas-like, destroys whatever it touches. Power and money may be quite valuable as *means* to some good end, but they turn destructive when they become *ends* in themselves. Sauron and Saruman, like Gollum, no longer have any goal but power itself—the power that is the Ring. With them Tolkien shows the suffering that results from a quest for power lacking a moral dimension.

In contrast, the strength that Gandalf, Aragorn, Frodo, and others demonstrate is shown not by accumulating or exercising power but in their willingness to give it up. Gandalf has no selfish craving for mastery. He wishes only to serve. "The rule of no realm is mine, neither of Gondor nor any other, great or small. But all worthy things that are in peril as the world now stands, those are my care. And for my part, I shall not wholly fail of my task, though Gondor should perish, if anything passes through this night that can still grow fair or bear fruit and flower again in days to come. For I also am a steward."

Gandalf gives us the definition and the model of a modern bodhisattva, the sort we need today. Are they so rare among us, or is it that the Saurons and Sarumans are so much more visible? And so much more powerful, in the conventional sense, because in our world it is not so much physical craving as lust for power that motivates the greed, ill will, and willful ignorance now endangering the earth. People have always craved power, but because of modern technologies there is now so much more power to crave and use; and because of modern institutions, such power tends to function in impersonal ways that assume a life of their own. Transnational corporations and stock markets institutionalize greed (never enough consumption or profit!) in a world where the centralized bureaucratic governments of nation-states unleash institutionalized ill will (horrific military aggression) in pursuit of their "national interests." Under the guise of globalization, ever more sophisticated technologies are deployed to extend the institutionalized delusion that dualizes us from the earth (by commodifying, exploiting, and laying waste to its furthest corners). Today these institutionalized versions of the three poisons are the Mordor that threatens our future. If Buddhist teachings cannot help us understand this, perhaps there is something wrong with our understanding of Buddhism.

Hobbiton expresses Tolkien's nostalgia for the vanishing rural England in the West Midlands of his youth, but we should not dismiss such homesickness with the reassuring Buddhist maxim that "everything passes away." Our collective attempt to dominate the earth technologically is related to the disappearance of the sacred in the modern world. If we can no longer rely on God to take care of us, we strive to secure ourselves by subduing nature until it meets all our needs and satisfies all our purposes—which will never happen, of course. Because our efforts to exploit the earth's resources are damaging it so much, the fatal irony is that our attempt to secure the conditions of our existence here may destroy us. Is there a clearer or more dangerous example of institutionalized delusion? We are one with the earth. When the biosphere becomes sick, we become sick. If the biosphere dies, we die. The technological Ring of Power is not the solution to our problems. It has become the problem itself.

Instead of seeking power, happiness for our heroes is connected with the ability to delight in the simple pleasures of everyday life: enjoying a glass and a song by a warm hearth in the company of others, for example. The fellowship of loving friends is contrasted with the greedy, private pseudo-happiness of those who seek only the Ring. Sauron, Saruman, Gollum: each tormented, solitary soul looks out only for itself, and knows nothing of the wide community of willing helpers that enables Frodo to complete his mission.

We need to recover such community and such an ecological sensibility if we are to make it through the dark times that threaten our world. We also need new types of bodhisattvas, inspired perhaps by the fresh models that Tolkien's myth provides for socially engaged Buddhism. As with Frodo on his improbable quest, it is easy to become discouraged. There is, however, something to remember at such times. Frodo's task was appointed to him in a mysterious way that he did not understand, because it cannot be understood. The implication is that the mission he and others undertook was successful in the end, because they were a part of something greater than themselves. For us, too, to be spiritual means opening up to a transformative power that works in us and through us when we do the best we can. Is that also true for the world that we are non-dual with? Who knows what is possible, or even what is actually happening today? Who, for example, anticipated the worldwide collapse of communism in 1989, or the sudden end of South African apartheid in 1994? The task of socially engaged bodhisattvas is not to unravel the mystery that is our world, but to do what we can to succor its sufferings in this time of crisis. Frodo and Sam discovered many unexpected helpers along their way, and so may we.

References

The Letters of J. R. R. Tolkien. 1981. Edited by Humphrey Carpenter. Boston: Houghton Mifflin.

The Dhammapada: The Sayings of the Buddha. 1993. Translated and edited by Thomas Byrom. Boulder, Colorado: Shambala.

Fromm, Eric. 1982. *The Greatness and Limitations of Freud's Thought.* London: Sphere Books.

Helms, Randel. 1974. *Tolkien's World.* London: Thames and Hudson.

The Kālāma Sutta: The Buddha's Charter of Free Inquiry. 1981. Translated by Soma Thera. Kandy, Sri Lanka: Buddhist Publication Society.

EPILOGUE

GIVING *DĀNA* THAT DOESN'T COST ANY MONEY AND LEADS TO NIRVANA

BUDDHADASA BHIKKHU

Thais usually interpret the benefit of giving to the Sangha (*dāna*) as a future reward, a better life in the future or rebirth in heaven. Such a belief is childish. One still remains stuck in the cycle of rebirth (*saṁsāra*). Giving can be looked at in two ways. In the first, one needs someone to receive the gift. In the other, there is no recipient. The former is bound to the cycle of rebirth; the latter is not. The first involves giving a material gift to someone, and giving forgiveness in return [a process fundamental to the merit making relationship of laity and monk]. The second is the giving of dharma. I'll call it the "giving of emptiness (*suññatā*)," which leads to release from rebirth. Another way of talking about this kind of giving is to say that it is to give nirvana as *dāna*.

Now some people say that I don't teach what the scriptures say, but just make things up. That's not the case. I give them different names and use different words. What giving nirvana as *dāna* refers to is producing or giving equanimity (*upekkhā*). For example, many people come to Wat Suan Mokkhabalarama. What they receive here is a coolness of heart, because they forget themselves and their selfish interests. This is not nirvana as an eternal condition, but it is a foretaste of what nirvana is like.

This article was translated by Donald K. Swearer and is taken from *Buddhism in Practice*, ed. Donald Lopez, 400–401 (Princeton: Princeton University Press, 1995), based on Buddhadāsa's essay, "Kan Hai Than Thi Mai Sia Ngoen Laeo Yang Dai Nipphan" ["Giving Dāna that Doesn't Cost Any Money and Leads to Nirvana"], 5–14 (Bangkok: Association for the Propagation of Buddhism, 1974). © 1995 Princeton University Press. Reprinted by permission of Princeton University Press.

The gift of emptiness means to give away oneself or to give up all selfish interests. This *dāna* does not need anyone to receive it, nor do we need
to feel that we give it. Indeed, if we really give this kind of *dāna*, there is
no self that gives it. If you ask what is given, the answer is—the self (Thai:
tua ku, that is, the gut sense of me/mine). What is given up is attachment
to the "I" notion of a self. What is left is freedom, consciousness composed
of awareness, wisdom, purity; freedom from the attachments of the five
aggregates, from grasping, and from suffering. To give with an expectation of a return is like investing with the expectation of a profit. For one to
"make merit" in the truest sense, one must give with a pure heart without
expectation of a return.

Actually, everything belongs to nature; it comes from nature; it returns
to nature. From this perspective we can see that nothing really "belongs" to
a particular individual. Only the foolish think that, "this is me" or "belongs
to me." The body and the mind that we think of as "belonging" to "us" we
must return to nature since in reality that is where they are.

The giving up of the self is nirvana. Another way of putting it is that nirvana
is freedom from the self, and all that attends to the self—from defilements,
suffering, rebirth, thirst, and grasping. This kind of giving is peace and equanimity. When our heart is at peace and we are freed from the bases of sense
obsession—that is nirvana. This is what I mean by "emptiness-giving" or
giving that leads to nirvana. We must give up nirvana in any sense that we
think nirvana is "ours." Likewise, a person who practices "emptiness-giving"
doesn't practice moral virtue (*sīla*), meditation (*samādhi*), or wisdom (*paññā*)
as something "other," something to be "got" or attained. S/he is [becomes]
morally virtuous, meditative, wise.

What is called merit (*puñña*) or merit making is for those caught up in
the world, because it tempts people to lose their way in the grasping of the
senses, to look for pleasure and enjoyment in this or that. Indeed, of all the
things that tempt people to be led astray and preoccupied, nothing exceeds
merit making. Nothing is so destructive of human freedom.

Ordinary folk think dualistically; they divide things into two sides: merit
and demerit, good and evil, hell and heaven, happiness and suffering, and

so on. They like one side and dislike the other. In conventional terms such distinctions are correct; however, such dualistic thinking is not correct for those who wish to eliminate suffering. In fact, what is called "merit" and "heaven" becomes another locus of attachment, thereby leading to more suffering. In order to transcend suffering, we must eliminate the source of attachment. The mind must be freed from the hope of both heaven and hell, merit and demerit, happiness and suffering. A person who has merit suffers. It is not the case that one who has merit eliminates suffering. To want anything is to suffer simply from having the desire itself. To escape suffering, hope for merit and heaven must be totally rooted out.

AUTHOR PROFILES

BUDDHADASA BHIKKHU was one of the most influential Buddhist monks and progressive teachers of the twentieth century. Born in 1906, he established a forest hermitage called Suan Mokkh in southern Thailand from where he developed his unique style of textual study harmonized with forest meditation practice. He was well known for his criticisms and subsequent innovations of Thai monastic orthodoxy as well as various orthodox Theravadin interpretations of the Buddha's discourses. He also was keenly aware of society outside and frequently made important commentaries on social issues. In this way, he became a central influence on leading progressive Buddhist monks and social leaders in Thailand for over forty years. He died in 1993.

MANGESH DAHIWALE is director of international relations at the Jambudvipa Trust in Pune, India. He has been involved in the development of their Nagarjuna Institute and Nagaloka Training Center in Nagpur that trains young Dalit Buddhists from all over India in Buddha Dharma and community organizing skills. He is also a member of the Trailokya Bauddha Mahashangha Sahayak Gana (TBMSG) founded by Ven. Sangharakshita to promote the advancement of Dalit Buddhists in India according to the vision of Dr. B. R. Ambedkar.

OUYPORN KHUANKAEW is director of the International Women's Partnership for Peace and Justice (IWP) based in Chiang Mai, Thailand. She is a Buddhist feminist trainer who has been working for peace and justice in South and Southeast Asia since 1995. From 1997 to 2001, she worked with the International Network of Engaged Buddhists (INEB) on the issue of empowerment and violence against women. In 2002, she co-founded IWP, a Buddhist spiritual feminist organization that continues her original work and expands it to include many issues including Buddhist and feminist counseling, nonviolence and conflict transformation, gender and sexuality, anti-oppression work, ally building between feminists from the global north and south, and mindfulness retreats for social activists. Aside from leading workshops, Ouyporn also writes and translates on the issues of women and Buddhism.

KHUENSAI JAIYEN is the director of the Shan Herald Agency for News (S.H.A.N.) based in Chiang Mai, Thailand. S.H.A.N. is an independent Shan media group that is not affiliated with any political or armed organization.

DAVID LOY is a professor, writer, and Zen teacher in the Sanbo Kyodan tradition of Japanese Zen Buddhism. He practiced Zen with Robert Aitken Roshi in Hawaii and then with Yamada Koun Roshi in Japan, where he completed formal *koan* training and became authorized as a teacher in the Sambo Kyodan lineage. His books include: *Lack and Transcendence: The Problem of Death and Life in Psychotherapy, Existentialism, and Buddhism; A Buddhist History of the West: Studies in Lack; The Great Awakening: A Buddhist Social Theory; Money, Sex, War, Karma: Notes for a Buddhist Revolution;* and most recently *The World Is Made of Stories.* He leads workshops and retreats nationally and internationally. www.davidloy.org

PRA PAISAN VISALO is the abbot of Wat Pa Sukato and director of the Buddhika Network for Buddhism and Society in Thailand. He is at once a leading public intellectual well versed in global and regional issues; a social activist having worked in a variety of NGOs for over thirty years; and an accomplished dharma practitioner and teacher who resides in his forest temple in northeast Thailand. He has worked extensively in the environmental movement, conflict resolution, and monastic reform within the Thai Sangha. More recently, he and his Buddhika Network for Buddhism and Society have been developing a network of religious and medical professionals working for more integrated spiritual and physical care for the dying.

SANTIKARO is a leading disciple and translator of the late Buddhadasa Bhikkhu. He served in the Peace Corps in Thailand for over four years, and then ordained as a bhikkhu in 1985. He became Buddhadasa's primary English translator and was abbot of Suan Atammayatarama, a training center for foreign monks next to Suan Mokkh. Among Santikaro's translations, *Mindfulness with Breathing* and *Heartwood of the Bodhi Tree* are prominent. In both Thailand and now in the United States where he resides, he has been active in inter-religious dialogue and socially engaged Buddhism. He is now building a dharma center in rural Wisconsin

NALIN SWARIS was born in Colombo, Sri Lanka, and was baptized into the Roman Catholic faith. He was ordained a Redemptorist Priest in 1962. After resigning from the ministry in 1969, he taught Social Philosophy and Methodology of Community Development for seventeen years at the Senior College for Social Work in De Horst, Dreibergen in the Netherlands. Before passing away suddenly in 2011, he had returned to his native Sri Lanka working as a freelance journalist and lecturer.

JONATHAN S. WATTS is a former staff and present executive board member of the International Network of Engaged Buddhist (INEB). He coordinates Think Sangha, a socially engaged Buddhist think tank. He presently resides in Kamakura, Japan, on the outskirts of Tokyo, where he has written and edited two books with the International Buddhist Exchange Center (IBEC), *Lotus in the Nuclear Sea: Fukushima and the Promise of Buddhism in the Nuclear Age* and *This Precious Life: Buddhist Tsunami Relief and Anti-Nuclear Activism in Post 3/11 Japan*, and also published *Buddhist Care for the Dying and Bereaved* with the Jodo Shu Research Institute (JSRI).

UPASEKA YASO is the Buddhist name of Yeshua Moser-Puangsuwan. Since refusing military conscription in 1971 during the close of the U.S. War on Indochina, he has maintained a vocation to promote pragmatic nonviolent alternatives to address human problems. He lived and worked in Thailand for fifteen years, during which he served as the Southeast Asia representative for the NGO Nonviolence International for more than a decade. He has been involved with the global movement to ban anti-personnel landmines since 1995, and in May 2005 became the International Campaign to Ban Landmines [ICBL] Global Thematic Editor. He currently works for Mines Action

Canada. He is author of numerous publications on nonviolent action, most recently *Speaking Truth to Power: Methods of Nonviolent Struggle in Burma*, and is frequently a guest lecturer at graduate programs in peace and conflict.

Min Zin is a regular contributor to The Foreign Policy's Transition Blog. He also serves as Burma's country analyst for several research foundations including Freedom House. He took part in Burma's democracy movement in 1988 as a high school student activist, and went into hiding in 1989 to avoid arrest by the junta. His underground activist-cum-writer life lasted for nine years until he fled to Thai-Burma border in August 1997. His writings appear in *The Foreign Policy*, *The New York Times*, *The Irrawaddy*, *The Bangkok Post*, *Far Eastern Economic Review*, *Wall Street Journal*, and other publications. He is a PhD candidate in Political Science Department at University of California, Berkeley.

INDEX

Abhidhamma, 25–26, 109
aggregates, five (*khandha*), 6, 246
ahiṃsā. *See* nonviolence
Aitareya Brāhmaṇa, 21
Ajivikas, 94, 102
Ajatasatru, King (Magadha), 93, 100, 177–78
All Ceylon Bhikkhu Congress, 117
Ambedkar, Bhimrao Ramji, 67–90, 129
  analysis of caste, 70–74
  civil rights movement, 76
  conversion, 77–78
  experiences of discrimination, 68–70
  on liberty, equality, and fraternity, 68, 71,
    74, 76, 81–82, 84, 87–88
  political views, 86–89
  vision of dharma and practice, 78–83
  vision of dharma and society, 83–86
Ananda, 77, 206
anattā. *See* not-self
Aṅguttara Nikāya. *See under* Pali Canon
anicca. *See* impermanance
Ariyaratne, A. T., 125–27
Arthaśāstra, 93–94, 101, 103, 107, 112, 122
ascetic, forest. See *samaṇa*
ascetic practice (*tapas*), 19
Ashoka, King, 91
  Brhadratha, King (grandson), 71–72
  Chandragupta, King (grandfather), 78, 93
  conquest and remorse, 102
  ecumenism, 71, 102, 116
  influence on Sri Lankan statecraft, 105–9,
    122, 126
  Mahinda (son), 105–6
  Mauryan empire, 71–72, 93
  relationship to monastic Sangha, 84,
    100–101

  rock edicts, 102, 104
  Schism Edict, 101 fn.2, 104
  statecraft, 101–2, 112
Ātman (self or soul), 19, 24–26, 28, 33, 94–95
Aung San, 161
Aung San, Suu Kyi, 164–65, 171, 172, 174
avijjā. *See* ignorance

Bandaranaike, S. W. R. D., 117–18
Bayinnaung, King, 161
Bhagavadgītā, 20, 21, 72
bhakti (theistic devotionalism), 20–22
bhāvanā. *See* meditation
birth (*jāti*), 5, 24–26, 46–55. *See also* species
bodhicitta (buddha mind), 138 fn.4
bodhisattva, 108–9, 122, 133, 136, 138, 240–41
Brāhmaṇa (texts), 17
Brahmanic rites and rituals, 17
  ancestor rites (*śraddhā*), 17, 20, 31
  ethics, 18, 51–52
  fire sacrifice (*agni*), 17, 102
  life cycle rites (*saṃskāra*), 17, 58
  sacrificial rites (*yaj-a*), 17–19, 31, 71, 94,
    102
Brahmanism, 17–19, 21–22, 25, 31–32, 50, 67,
  94, 123, 128, 141, 236
  causality and social system, 94–95
  conception of kingship as *devarāja* (god
    king), 103, 108–10, 121
  innate nature in, 47
  influence on Theravada, 17, 25, 141, 236
  repression of Buddhism, 70–74, 105
brahmavihāra (Four Divine Abidings), 135 fn.2
Brahmin (*brāhmaṇa*), 45–46, 51–52, 55, 71–72,
  97, 103–4
Brazier, David, 75

Buddhadasa Bhikkhu, ix, 25 fn.1, 28, 33 fn.2,
    33 fn.3, 99, 133 fn., 145
    three types of merit making, 145
Buddhaghosa
    Samantapāsādikā, 101 fn.2, 105
    Visuddhimagga, 25, 135
buddha nature, 222, 228
Buddhism
    bhikkhuni and social movements in
        Taiwan, 128
    capitalism and, 134
    decline and Muslim invasion, 73, 105
    definition of, 192
    democracy and, 67, 87, 93, 95, 162–64,
        191
    funeral Buddhism and Brahmansim in
        Japan, 128
    humanistic Buddhism, 68
    New Buddhism (*navayāna*), 68, 75–76
    nonviolence and, 192–96
    power and, 238–41
    sexism and, 200-224
    Third Buddhist Council, 100
    violence and revolution and, 177, 186–87,
        196–97
Buddhist Theosophical Society, 114
Burma, 15, 117, 201, 211
    civil society organizations in, 171
    democracy movement in, 162–64
    88 Generation Student Group, 164
    human rights in, 157, 175, 179–80
    samsāra discourse in, 158–61, 163
    Saffron Revolution, 164–65
    Shan State, 177, 179–81, 186–87, 204
    social passivity in, 173
Burmese Buddhism, 160, 179
    Christian influence on, 161
    community development and, 166, 172, 173
    cooptation by military, 179–81
    cooptation by monarchy, 168–69
    ethnic minorities and, 161
    htidaw (umbrella) hoisting ceremony,
        163, 169
    Marxist influence on, 117
    monastic Sangha, 161
    National Sangha Mahanayaka Council, 163
    political struggle and, 160–64

Saffron Revolution, 164–65
    samsāra discourse in, 158–61, 163
    Shwedagon Pagoda, 161, 166, 169, 180
    Young Men's Buddhist Association
        (YMBA) 161

Cambodia, 109, 201, 211
capitalism, 87, 119, 134, 140, 142–44, 170–71
caste and caste system, 21, 33, 35, 40–41, 45,
    51–52, 54, 67–74, 89, 94, 104, 109, 206
    "broken men", 72
    development in Sri Lanka, 109, 119
    struggle of untouchables/Dalits, 76
causality, 28–29, 237–38
cetanā. See intention; karma, as intentional
    action
Chandragupta, King (Maurya), 78, 93
classification of beings, 47–52, 57
classism, 27–28, 31–32, 40, 50, 144
Code of Manu (*Manu Smṛti*), 21, 54, 72
consciousness (*viññāna*), 30, 41, 80, 246
    ignorant, 24–27, 33, 98, 158
Coordinating Group for Religion in Society
    (CGRS), 146
craving (*taṇhā*), 5, 7, 24–27, 40–41, 64, 239–40
creationism and creator God, 23, 26, 28,
    30–31, 79, 94–95
Cūlavaṃsa, 108, 122
cultural violence, viii, 16, 179, 189–91, 208, 210
cyclic existence. See *samsāra*

Dalai Lama, 181, 220
dāna. See generosity
defilement (*kilesa*), 7, 9, 20, 33 fn.3,
democracy, 67, 87, 93, 95, 162–64, 191
dependent origination (*paticca-samuppāda*),
    5, 14, 16, 24–26, 30, 46, 56, 58, 60–61, 74,
    142, 158, 222, 234–35
Devanampiyatissa, King, 106
devarāja (god king), 103, 108–110, 121
    development in Southeast Asia and Sri
        Lanka, 108
dhamma dīkṣa (Buddhist initiation), 68,
    82–83, 85
Dhammananda (Chatsumarn Kabilsingh),
    206
Dhammapada. See under Pali Canon

dhammarāja (moral king or Buddhist monarch), 31, 100–101, 110
  development in Southeast Asia and Sri Lanka, 101
dhamma vijaya (conquest through morality), 106, 108, 112, 122
dharma, 67, 75, 78–80, 82–89, 91, 95, 98–99. 102–3, 106–7, 125–27, 141, 149, 165, 192–93, 223, 235, 245
Dharmaloka, Ven. Ratmalane Sri, 114
Dharmapala, Anagarika (Don David Hewaviratne), 114–16, 123, 125
dharma-mahāmātra (minister of morality), 102–4
Dharmasūtras, 21, 72
Diamond Sutra, 78
Dīgha Nikāya. See under Pali Canon
Dīpavaṃsa, 106–7
domestic violence, 196, 199–200, 207–8, 217
dullabhā (preciousness or scarcity), 174–75
  human rights and, 175
Dutthagamani, King, 106–7, 111, 121, 122

(Noble) Eightfold Path, 4, 42, 79, 80, 134, 192–94, 197, 202, 213–20, 224
emptiness (*suññatā*), 28–29, 142, 245–46
equanimity (*upekkhā*), viii, 15, 22, 35, 135, 181, 245
ethics and ethicization, 19–21, 30–31, 41–42, 64, 71, 81–82, 96, 164, 192, 194, 216–18, 227
  Brahmanic ethics, 18, 51–52
  civilizational ethics, 14, 91–93, 95, 102–8, 112, 116, 122, 125–26, 128
  Upanishadic ethics, 19–20, 25, 32
evil, 39, 228

feminism, 199–201, 209
field of merit (*puññakkheta*), 32, 34, 110, 115, 172
forest ascetics. See *samaṇa*
Four Divine Abidings. See *brahmavihāra*
Four Noble Truths, 185, 193, 201–2, 213, 220
fraternity. *See* liberty, equality, and fraternity
Friends of the Western Buddhist Order (FWBO), 85
French Revolution, 71, 87

Freud, Sigmund, 41, 235
Fromm, Erich, 235

Gambira, U, 165
Gandhi, 76–77, 126, 162, 194
Garudhamma (ten special rules for female monastics), 206–7
gender roles, 49, 209–10, 218
gender violence, 201–7, 211–15, 218–22
generosity (*dāna*), viii, 15, 32, 34, 84, 94, 110, 133–41, 145, 152, 162, 166–72, 237, 246
  as charity and aid, 148, 166–67, 172–73
  commodified, 141, 143, 151, 167
  as community development, 125, 147–48
  poverty and economic injustice and, 32–33, 125, 167–68, 170–71
  as forced labor, 169
  as "gift of labor" (*shramadāna*), 125
  rebirth and, 245
  as reciprocal exchange, 32, 94, 114–15, 123, 124, 129, 141, 146
  saṃsāra and, *159*
  superstition and, 168
  as *tan tod* in Thailand, 146
Gnanananda, Ven. Kiribathgoda, 121 fn.4
Gnanasiha, Ven. Henpitagedera, 126

Hindu texts
  Aitareya Brāhmaṇa, 21
  Bhagavadgītā, 20, 21, 72
  Code of Manu (*Manu Smṛti*), 21, 54, 72
  Dharmasūtras, 21, 72
  Ṛg Veda, 20, 72
  Upaniṣads, 18
Hinduization, 4, 42, 72, 108
Hpo Hlaing, U, 174
htidaw (umbrella) hoisting ceremony, 163, 169

idappaccayatā. See specific conditionality
ignorance (*avijjā*), 24, 74, 185, 204, 208, 217, 220, 223, 240
impermanence (*anicca*), 19, 25, 30, 55, 159, 184, 200, 215, 221, 235
India, 15, 67–89, 201, 206, 234
  absolute monarchies (Magadha, Kosala), 92–93, 100, 177
  civil rights movement, 76

early Aryan culture, 32–33
Kuru Pancala region (northwest), 17. 95
Majjhimadesa region (northeast), 18, 21, 63, 92
Mauryan empire, 20, 71–72, 93
political conflict, 92–93
saint-poets (Kabir, Nanadnar, Chokamela, and Tukaram), 74
socio-economic development in 6th cent. BC, 63, 71, 92–94, 98
Sunga Dynasty, 71–72, 103
tribal assembly republics (Licchavi, Shakya, Vajji), 31, 92–94, 100, 119, 126, 178
urban-based merchants (seṭṭhi), 94, 97
intention (cetanā), 7, 23–24, 79, 216, 231, 236, 237. See also karma, as intentional action

Jainism, 20, 22–23, 32, 94
Janatha Vimukti Peramuna (JVP) party, 119–20, 122, 126
Jātaka, 136, 142, 178, 185, 227 fn,
  Mahājanaka Jātaka, 142
  Mahosatha Jātaka, 182–83
  Vessantara Jātaka, 136–38
jāti. See birth; species
Jayatilake, D. B., 116
Jotika, Ven. Sao, 177 fn.
justice, 87
  economic injustice, vii, 16, 134, 145, 193, 211, 240
  personal suffering and social injustice, vii, 15, 39–41, 62, 64, 82, 145, 159–60, 205, 208
  restorative and retributive, 16, 22, 27, 39–40
  social, 82, 83, 134

karma
  as action or work, 10, 17, 19, 40, 55–57, 59–62, 214
  as activity (kiriyā), 7, 24, 59
  as ascetic action, 18–19
  collective or social, vii, 41–42, 57, 63
  as duty or role, 21
  as ethical action, 95, 215
  the end of, 3–5, 10, 79

as deterministic law or retribution, vii–viii, 15, 28, 40, 43, 61–62, 178, 208, 231–32, 237; past karmic determinism (pubbekaṭavāda), 13, 23, 29; theistic determinism (issarakaraṇavāda), 13, 23, 29
  as five natural laws, one of, 27, 79
  as intentional action, 7, 14–15, 20, 23–24, 26–27, 29–31, 35, 62, 79–80, 95, 110, 216, 231, 236, 237
  as material force, 20
  nirvana and, 8–9
  not-self (anattā) and, 8
  passivity and fatalism, vii–viii, 179, 181, 187, 202, 205, 207, 214–15, 217
  from past life, 202, 206, 214–15
  power and, 23, 238–41
  rebirth and, vii–viii, 3–5, 14, 19, 25–26, 28, 34, 39, 41–42, 58, 60, 142, 232–37
  result of (vipāka), viii, 6–7, 28, 157, 178, 233, 236
  Right View of, 214–15
  as ritual action, vii–viii, 17, 32, 79, 110, 236
  sexism and, 207
  social customs and, 27–28
  social injustice/justice and, vii, 15–16, 35, 39–40, 79, 145, 179, 207–8
  structural karma, 208, 231
  as unfathomable (acinteyya), 13, 29, 31
Khun, Luang Po, 143–44
kilesa. See defilement

Ladakh (India), 204
Law, Steven, 168
Ledi Sayadaw, 171
liberty, equality, and fraternity, 68, 71, 74, 76, 81–82, 84, 87–88
liṅga. See mark
Lokamitra, Dhammachari, 85
The Lord of the Rings, 227
lovingkindness (metta), 135 fn.1–2, 200
  political action and, 164–65

Mahabodhi Society, 123–24
Mahājanaka Jātaka, 142
Mahāvaṃsa, 106–7, 122
Mahayana Buddhism, 108–9, 122, 135, 179

bodhicitta, 138, fn.2
bodhisattva, 108–9, 122, 133, 240–41
    models of kingship, 108–9, 122
    perfections (*pāramī*), 78, 135
Mahosatha, 182–83
Mahosatha Jātaka, 182–83
Majjhima Nikāya. See under Pali Canon
mark (*liṅga*), 47–49
Marx, Karl, 43–44, 63
meditation (*bhāvanā*), 15, 24, 32, 33 fn.2, 34,
    73, 78, 99, 99 fn.1, 80, 110, 127, 134–35,
    141, 151, 158, 165, 200, 203–4, 212, 213,
    246; See also *samādhi*
    vocation of (*vipassanā dhura*), 98, 110, 120
merit and merit making (*puñña*), viii, 15,
    17, 19, 26, 32, 34, 95, 99, 110, 115, 121,
    129, 133–35, 140, 152, 162, 166, 237,
    246–47
    bun, 141–43
    as civic virtue, 152
    commodified, 140–44, 167
    community and, 145–46
    as compassionate social service, 150–51
    as doing "good", viii, 95, 115, 129, 133,
        140, 142
    economic injustice, 31, 145, 211
    field of merit (*puññakkheta*), 32, 34, 110,
        115, 172
    good, meritorious activity (*puññakiriya-
        vatthu*), 134–35, 141, 152, 149–50. See
        also *puññakiriyavatthu*
    local savings banks and, 148. See also *sat-
        cha sasom sap*
    monarchy, in relation to, 110
    proper intention, 150
    rebirth and, 135, 141, 144, 167, 202, 207
    as reciprocal exchange, 32, 94, 114–15,
        123, 124, 141, 149, 166
    saṃsāra and, 159
    three levels of, 149
    three types, according to Buddhadasa, 145
    as volunteerism, 150–52
metta. See lovingkindness
Mindon, King, 170
Moggalana, 186
monasteries
    as community centers, 140, 166, 180, 199

    as educational and economic centers, 98,
        103–4, 112, 123
monastic-lay relationship, 32, 83–86, 89, 95,
    104, 112, 115, 123, 128, 129, 139, 141,
    166, 172, 203
monks and monastic Sangha, 32, 68, 95. *See
    also* sangha
    caste and, 32
    corruption and decline of, 68, 73, 83–84,
        104, 113, 120, 123, 143, 205
    as counselors to women, 207, 211
    economic patronage and professional-
        ization of, 95, 97–98, 100, 109, 113, 120,
        168
    establishment of, 95
    gender and, 221, 223
    interpretation of texts by, 205–6
    meditation practice of, 212
    politicization of, 97, 100–101, 109, 116–19,
        125, 161–64, 169
    poor education of, 120–21, 129, 212, 218
    preceptor of (*upajjhāya*), 120, 212
    relationship to women, 32, 202
    revival and reform of, 129
    rural development and, 124–27
    secularization of, 120
    suffering of nuns and, 201, 203–4
    vinaya, 31, 100, 101 fn.2, 104, 109, 110, 115,
        120–22
    vocation of, 34, 83–85, 98–99, 115
    vocation of meditation (*vipassanā dhura*),
        98–99, 110, 116, 120, 123
    vocation as social service, 84, 115, 120, 124
    vocation of study (*gantha dhura*), 98–99,
        110, 116, 123
morality (*sīla*), 31, 82, 192. *See also* ethics;
    precepts; *sīla*

Nalanda University, 104–5
nāma
    as mental factors, 158
    as mind, 25–26
    as mind-body (*nāmarūpa*), 8
    as name, 50, 54
    as sense base, 25
    as subject, 24
Nargis Cyclone, 173

National Sangha Mahanayaka Council, 163
Network for Buddhism and Society, 149
nirvana, 8–9, 26–27, 33–34, 78–79, 98–99, 110,
    116, 121 fn.4, 129, 160, 230, 245–46
nonviolence (ahiṃsā), viii, 14, 20, 30, 106,
    126, 177–79, 181, 186, 190–96, 229
not-self (anattā), 6, 8–9, 25, 28–31, 41–42, 55,
    92, 94, 96, 142, 184, 234–35, 237
nuns' (bhikkhuni) ordination, 203, 206, 207,
    210–11, 215

Olcott, Henry Steel, 114, 118
Ottama, U, 162
offering robes to monks. See pa pa
overturning the bowl (pattam nikkujjana
    kamma) 162, 164

Pali Canon (Tipiṭaka)
    Aṅguttara Nikāya, 13, 22, 23, 29, 30, 58,
        134, 175
        Kālāma Sutta, 232–33
    Dhammapada, 25, 53, 64, 194, 236
    Dhammapada Aṭṭhakathā, 93, 178
    Dīgha Nikāya, 30, 134
        Aggañña Sutta, 53 fn.1, 110
        Brahmajāla Sutta, 97
        Cakkavatti Sutta, 31, 96, 110
        Kūṭadanta Sutta, 31
        Mahānidāna Sutta, 27
        Mahāparinibbāna Sutta, 31, 77, 93, 96,
            100, 174, 212
        Mahāsudassana Sutta, 60
        Sāmaññaphala Sutta, 93
        Siṅgālovāda Sutta, 31, 96, 171
    Dīgha Nikāya Aṭṭhakathā, 149
    Itivuttaka, 134
    Jātaka, 93, 100, 137, 178
        Mahājanaka Jātaka, 142
        Mahosatha Jātaka, 182–83
        Vessantara Jātaka, 136–38
    Majjhima Nikāya, 32, 57
        Ónāpānasati Sutta, 32
        Assalāyana Sutta, 49
        Madhupiṇḍika Sutta, 27
        Mūlapariyāya Sutta, 34
        Sallekha Sutta, 80
    Saṃyutta Nikāya, 15, 46, 81, 139

Ódittapariyāya Sutta, 78
    Chiggala Sutta, 178
    Sutta Nipāta, 4
        Mettā Sutta, 164, 186
        Vāseṭṭha Sutta, 46–59, 77
Palita, Ven. Horatapala, 120
Panito, Pra Subin, 148
Pannasekhara, Ven. Kalukondayave, 124
pa pa (offering robes to monks), 146–47
    books, 148
    as community development, 147–48
    corruption of, 147
    rice, 147
    seedlings, 148
Parakkamabahu, King 108
pāramī. See perfections
Pasenadi, King (Kosala), 177–78
Payutto, P. A. (Pra Dharmapitok), 27, 133 fn.,
    140, 142
perfections (pāramī), 78, 114, 133, 135, 138,
    166
precepts (sīla), 15, 31, 81–82, 99, 116, 120–21,
    124, 129, 134, 189, 195–96, 236–37
    political action and, 195
    five cardinal precepts (pañcasīla), 15, 30,
        82–83, 145, 157, 195–96
preciousness. See dullabhā
Premadasa, Ranasinghe, 121
puññakiriyavatthu (good, meritorious activ-
    ity), 134–35, 141, 152
    ten bases of, 149–50

Rahula, Ven. Walpola, 107, 117, 120, 122, 124
rebirth, 134–35
    generosity (dāna), 245
    karma, 3–5, 14, 28, 34, 39, 41–42, 58, 142,
        232, 234–36
    merit (puñña), 141, 144, 167, 202, 207
Ṛg Veda, 20, 72
ritualism, vii–viii, 7, 15, 17–23, 31–32, 35,
    51–53, 58, 67, 71, 79, 94–95, 102, 110–11,
    113–15, 124, 126, 128, 129, 134, 141–42,
    146, 150–51, 163, 236
rūpa
    as object, 25
    as human forms, 47, 50
    as life forms, 47

as matter, 158
as mind-body (*nāmarūpa*), 8
as sense forms, 25

Saffron Revolution, 164–65
samādhi, 121, 129, 187, 214, 224, 246
samaṇa (forest ascetic), 18, 31–32, 95–96
samsāra (cyclic existence), 9, 15–16, 19,
    39–41, 62, 110, 157–61, 163, 165, 175,
    177, 238, 245
    Burmese Buddhism and, 158–61
    fatalism and, 157
    investment in, 159
    political oppression and, 158–61, 163
    relationship to making merit (*puñña*),
        generosity (*dāna*), morality (*sīla*), 159
    as social discourse, 158–60, 163
sangha, 68, 83–84
    as authentic community, 96, 133, 139
    four assemblies, 13, 129, 139, 212
    as model society, 75, 83–84, 95–96, 139
Sangharakshita, 85–86
saṅkhāra, 24–26, 28–30, 59–63
    as the creation of culture, 60–61
Sarvodaya Shramadana Movement, 125–28
    as Buddhist revivalism, 126
    as Gandhianism, 126, 127
    impact in urban areas, 129
    as participatory development, 126
    peace activities of, 127
    relationship with monastic Sangha,
        126–27
    relationship with Tamils, 127
    relationship with western donors, 127
satcha sasom sap (savings with truthfulness),
    148
Senanayake, D. S., 116
Senanayake, F. R., 116
Seven Triplets, 185
sexism and patriarchy, 27–28, 31–32, 40, 50,
    74, 134, 142, 196, 201–24
Shan State (Burma), 177, 179–81, 186–87, 204
    "Burmanization", 179–81
    Gawnzoeng, General, 183, 186
    Shan United Revolutionary Army, 183
shramadāna (volunteer work camps), 125
Shwe Aung, U, 171

Shwedagon Pagoda, 161, 166, 169, 180
sīla, 15, 31, 81–82, 92, 99, 120–21, 124, 129,
    134, 135 fn.1, 136, 139, 159, 187, 214,
    224, 246
Siladitya, King Harsha, 105
Silaratana, Ven. Hendiyagala, 124, 125
Sitagu Sayadaw, Ashin Nyanissara, 173
social division of labor, 44, 51–54, 57
Solasapañhā (*Sixteen Questions*), 4
South Asia, 15, 201, 211
Southeast Asia, vii, 15, 107, 108, 111, 135,
    136, 139–40, 201, 204, 211
species (*jāti*), 47–52, 54–55. *See also* birth
species nature, 42–44, 46–50, 53, 55–56
specific conditionality (*idappaccayatā*), 4, 46
Sri Lanka, 40, 105–28
    British influence on, 112–13
    bureaucratic centralization in, 112–13, 121
    Christian influence on, 113, 119
    ethno-nationalism and, 113, 126
    Hindu influence on, 108–9
    as nation-state, 111–12, 122
    as pre-modern "galactic polity", 111–12
    Tamil people and, 106–7, 111, 126–27
Sri Lankan Buddhism, 41, 91
    All Ceylon Bhikkhu Congress, 117
    arrival from India, 100, 105
    Buddhist Theosophical Society, 114
    change under British, 113
    development of caste, 41, 109, 119
    educational movement and schools, 114,
        118, 125
    ethno-nationalism, 106–8, 116–17, 122
    Hindu influence on, 108–9
    Marxism influence on, 117, 119, 126
    politicization of monks, 116–19, 126
    rural development movement, 115,
        124–26
    Sarvodaya influence on, 126
    secular lifestyles, 120–21
    the secular state and, 116
    state religion, 106, 113, 118
    support from overseas, 120
    Vidyalanka monastic university, 114, 116,
        118–19, 124
    Vidyodaya monastic university, 114, 116,
        118–19, 123–24

Sri Lankan Pali chronicles, 101 fn.2, 105, 111
　Cūlavaṃsa, 108, 122
　Dīpavaṃsa, 106–7
　Mahāvaṃsa, 106–7, 122
structural violence, viii, 16, 35, 145, 179, 190–91,
　193, 195–96, 204–5, 208, 215, 240
suffering, cause of, 45, 75, 201–2, 214, 246–47
Sumangala, Ven. Hikkaduve Sri, 114, 123
Saṃyutta Nikāya. See under Pali Canon
suññatā. See emptiness
Sutta Nipāta. See under Pali Canon

taṇhā. See craving
Ten Rightnesses (sammatā), 4
Thailand, 15, 22, 109, 114, 128, 134, 140–52,
　171, 199, 201, 203–4, 206, 211
　Coordinating Group for Religion in Society
　　(CGRS), 146
　Network for Buddhism and Society, 149
　Pra Sekiyadhamma, 151
　Wat Pra Thammakai, 143–44
Thamanya Sayadaw, U Vinaya, 171, 172
theism, 28
theistic devotionalism. See bhakti
Theravada Buddhism, viii, 14, 17, 25, 100–
　101, 105, 133–35, 141, 157, 174, 179, 203,
　210, 236–37
　ordination of nuns, 210
Thittila, Ashin, 166
three trainings (sikkhā) or (sīla-samādhi-
　paññā), 121, 129, 187, 214, 224, 246
Tibetan Buddhism, 200–201, 203, 205, 210,
　211, 220
Tipiṭaka. See Pali Canon
Tolkien, J. R. R., 227
Trailokya Bauddha Mahasangha (TBM), 85
Triple Gem (Buddha, Dharma, and Sangha),
　171, 174, 184–85, 192

United States of America
　militarism, 189
Upaniṣads, 18, 99
Upanishadic ethics, 19–20, 22–23, 25, 32
upekkhā. See equanimity
untouchables. See caste

vassa (rainy season retreat), 150–51
Vāseṭṭha Sutta, 46–58
Vedas and Vedic culture, 17–19, 21, 31, 34,
　67, 74, 94–96, 108–9, 236
　Brāhmaṇa, 17, 21
　Purusha, 20
　Ṛg Veda, 20, 72
Vessantara Jātaka, 136–38
Vidudabha, King (Kosala), 93, 178
Vidyalanka monastic university, 114, 116,
　118–19, 124
Vidyodaya monastic university, 114, 116,
　118–19, 123–24
vinaya (monastic code), 31, 100, 101 fn.2, 104,
　109, 110, 115, 120–22
viññāna. See consciousness
Vinoba Bhave, 126
violence, viii, 27, 63, 68, 91, 120, 122, 150, 165,
　192, 195–96, 179, 182, 189–91, 213, 228
　cultural, viii, 16, 179, 189–91, 208, 210
　domestic, 196, 199–200, 207–8, 217
　gender, 201–7, 211–15, 218–22
　structural, viii, 16, 35, 145, 179, 190–91,
　　193, 195–96, 204–5, 208, 215, 240
　See also nonviolence (ahiṃsā)
vipassanā. See meditation
virtue. See sīla

Wat Pra Thammakai, 143–44
Weber, Max, 157
Wisara, U, 162
wisdom (paññā), 30, 78, 81–82, 121, 129, 134,
　135 fn.1, 138–39, 187, 193, 195, 201, 212,
　214–16, 220, 221, 223, 224, 246
　as jñāna, 19

Yewata, U, 162
Young Men's Buddhist Association (YMBA,
　Burma) 161